D1518448

Marx and Freud
Great Shakespeareans
Volume X

Great Shakespeareans
Each volume in the series provides a critical account and analysis of those figures who have had the greatest influence on the interpretation, understanding and cultural reception of Shakespeare, both nationally and around the world.

General Series Editors:
Peter Holland, University of Notre Dame, USA
Adrian Poole, Trinity College Cambridge, UK

Editorial Advisory Board:
David Bevington (University of Chicago, USA), Michael Cordner (University of York, UK), Michael Dobson (Shakespeare Institute, University of Birmingham, UK), Dominique Goy-Blanquet (University of Picardy, France), Barbara Hodgdon (University of Michigan, USA), Andreas Höfele (University of Munich, Germany), Tetsuo Kishi (Kyoto University, Japan), Russ McDonald (Goldsmith's College, University of London, UK), Ruth Morse (University of Paris 7, Denis Diderot, France), Michael Neill (University of Auckland, New Zealand), Stephen Orgel (Stanford University, USA), Carol Rutter (University of Warwick, UK), Ann Thompson (King's College, University of London, UK) and Paul Yachnin (McGill University, Canada).

Great Shakespeareans: Set I
Volume I: *Dryden, Pope, Johnson, Malone*, edited by Claude Rawson
Volume II: *Garrick, Kemble, Siddons, Kean*, edited by Peter Holland
Volume III: *Voltaire, Goethe, Schlegel, Coleridge*, edited by Roger Paulin
Volume IV: *Lamb, Hazlitt, Keats*, edited by Adrian Poole

Great Shakespeareans: Set II
Volume V: *Scott, Dickens, Eliot, Hardy*, edited by Adrian Poole
Volume VI: *Macready, Booth, Irving, Terry*, edited by Richard Schoch
Volume VII: *Jameson, Cowden Clarke, Kemble, Cushman*, edited by Gail Marshall
Volume VIII: *James, Melville, Emerson, Berryman*, edited by Peter Rawlings
Volume IX: *Bradley, Greg, Folger*, edited by Cary DiPietro

Great Shakespeareans: Set III
Volume X: *Marx and Freud*, Crystal Bartolovich, Jean E. Howard and David Hillman
Volume XI: *Berlioz, Verdi, Wagner, Britten*, edited by Daniel Albright
Volume XII: *Joyce, T. S. Eliot, Auden, Beckett*, edited by Adrian Poole
Volume XIII: *Empson, Wilson Knight, Barber, Kott*, edited by Hugh Grady

Great Shakespeareans: Set IV
Volume XIV: *Hugo, Pasternak, Brecht, Césaire*, edited by Ruth Morse
Volume XV: *Poel, Granville Barker, Guthrie, Wanamaker*, edited by Cary Mazer
Volume XVI: *Gielgud, Olivier, Ashcroft, Dench*, edited by Russell Jackson
Volume XVII: *Welles, Kozintsev, Kurosawa, Zeffirelli*, Mark Thornton Burnett, Kathy Howlett, Courtney Lehmann and Ramona Wray
Volume XVIII: *Hall, Brook, Ninagawa, Lepage*, edited by Peter Holland

Marx and Freud

Great Shakespeareans
Volume X

Crystal Bartolovich, Jean E. Howard and
David Hillman

continuum

Continuum International Publishing Group

The Tower Building	80 Maiden Lane
11 York Road	Suite 704
London SE1 7NX	New York NY 10038

www.continuumbooks.com

British Library Cataloguing-in-Publication Data
A catalogue record for this book is available from the British Library.

ISBN: HB: 978-1-4411-6664-7
     Set: 978-1-4411-6011-9

Library of Congress Cataloging-in-Publication Data
Marx and Freud / Crystal Bartolovich, Jean E. Howard and David Hillman.
p. cm. – (Great Shakespeareans v. 10)
Includes bibliographical references and index.
ISBN 978-1-4411-6664-7 (hardcover) – ISBN 978-1-4411-2801-0 (pdf)
1. Shakespeare, William, 1564-1616–Criticism and interpretation. 2. Marx, Karl, 1818-1883–Influence. 3. Freud, Sigmund, 1856-1939–Influence. I. Crystal Bartolovich. II. Jean E. Howard. III. David Hillman.

PR2976.M416 2012
822.3'3–dc23

2011046611

Typeset by Fakenham Prepress Solutions, Fakenham, Norfolk NR21 8NN
Printed and bound in Great Britain

Contents

Series Editors' Preface

What is a 'Great Shakespearean'? Who are the 'Great Shakespeareans'? This series is designed to explore those figures who have had the greatest influence on the interpretation, understanding and reception of Shakespeare, both nationally and internationally. Charting the effect of Shakespeare on cultures local, national and international is a never- ending task, as we continually modulate and understand differently the ways in which each culture is formed and altered. *Great Shakespeareans* uses as its focus individuals whose own cultural impact has been and continues to be powerful. One of its aims is to widen the sense of who constitute the most important figures in our understanding of Shakespeare's afterlives. The list is therefore not restricted to, say, actors and scholars, as if the performance of and commentary on Shakespeare's works were the only means by which his impact is remade or extended. There are actors aplenty (like Garrick, Irving and Olivier) and scholars too (Bradley, Greg and Empson) but our list deliberately includes as many novelists (Dickens, Melville, Joyce), poets (Keats, Eliot, Berryman), playwrights (Brecht, Beckett, Césaire) and composers (Berlioz, Verdi and Britten), as well as thinkers whose work seems impossible without Shakespeare and whose influence on our world has been profound, like Marx and Freud.

Deciding who to include has been less difficult than deciding who to exclude. We have a long list of individuals for whom we would wish to have found a place but whose inclusion would have meant someone else's exclusion. We took long and hard looks at the volumes as they were shaped by our own and our volume editors' perceptions. We have numerous regrets over some outstanding figures who ended up just outside this project. There will, no doubt, be argument on this score. Some may find our choices too Anglophone, insufficiently global. Others may complain of the lack of contemporary scholars and critics. But this is not a project designed to establish a new canon, nor are our volumes intended to be encyclopedic in scope. The series is not entitled 'The Greatest Shakespeareans' nor is it 'Some Great Shakespeareans', but it will, we hope, be seen as negotiating and occupying a space mid-way along the spectrum of inclusivity and arbitrariness.

Our contributors have been asked to describe the double impact of Shakespeare on their particular figure and of their figure on the understanding, interpretation and appreciation of Shakespeare, as well as providing a sketch of their subject's intellectual and professional biography and an account of the wider context within which her/his work might be understood. This 'context' will vary widely from case to case and, at times, a single 'Great Shakespearean' is asked to stand as a way of grasping a large domain. In the case of Britten, for example, he is the window through which other composers and works in the English musical tradition like Vaughan Williams, Walton and Tippett have a place. So, too, Dryden has been the means for considering the beginnings of critical analysis of the plays as well as of the ways in which Shakespeare's plays influenced Dryden's own practice.

To enable our contributors to achieve what we have asked of them, we have taken the unusual step of enabling them to write at length. Our volumes do not contain brief entries of the kind that a Shakespeare Encyclopedia would include nor the standard article length of academic journals and Shakespeare Companions. With no more than four Great Shakespeareans per volume – and as few as two in the case of volume 10 – our contributors have space to present their figures more substantially and, we trust, more engagingly. Each volume has a brief introduction by the volume editor and a section of further reading. We hope the volumes will appeal to those who already know the accomplishment of a particular Great Shakespearean and to those trying to find a way into seeing how Shakespeare has affected a particular poet as well as how that poet has changed forever our appreciation of Shakespeare. Above all, we hope *Great Shakespeareans* will help our readers to think afresh about what Shakespeare has meant to our cultures, and about how and why, in such differing ways across the globe and across the last four centuries and more, they have changed what his writing has meant.

Peter Holland and Adrian Poole

Notes on Contributors

Crystal Bartolovich is Associate Professor of English and Textual Studies at Syracuse University. She has published over 30 essays on topics ranging from early modern literature and culture to Marxist theory and the politics of globalization, in venues such as *Shakespeare Studies, Cultural Critique* and *New Formations*. With Neil Lazarus, she edited the collection of essays *Marxism, Modernity and Postcolonial Studies* (Cambridge University Press, 2002). She also edits the journal *Early Modern Culture*. Currently, she is working on two projects, one concerning the history and concept of the 'common', and the other examining the cost of the loss of so-called 'progress' narratives of modernity.

David Hillman is Senior Lecturer in English at the University of Cambridge, and a Fellow of King's College, Cambridge. He is the author of *Shakespeare's Entrails: Belief, Scepticism and the Interior of the Body* (Palgrave, 2007), and the editor (with Adam Phillips) of *The Book of Interruptions* (Peter Lang, 2007); (with Carla Mazzio) of *The Body in Parts: Fantasies of Corporeality in Early Modern Europe* (Routledge, 1997); and of Robert Weimann's *Authority and Representation in Early Modern Discourse: Reformation and Renaissance Fiction* (Johns Hopkins University Press, 1996).

Jean E. Howard is George Delacorte Professor in the Humanities at Columbia University. Her books include *Shakespeare's Art of Orchestration: Stage Technique and Audience Response* (University of Illinois Press, 1984); *The Stage and Social Struggle in Early Modern England* (Routledge, 1994); *Engendering a Nation: A Feminist Account of Shakespeare's English Histories*, with Phyllis Rackin (Routledge, 1997); and *Theater of a City: The Places of London Comedy 1598-1642* (University of Pennsylvania Press, 2007), which won the Barnard Hewitt Prize for outstanding work in theatre history. A co-editor of *The Norton Shakespeare*, she is working on a new book on early modern tragedy and one on the history play from Shakespeare to Caryl Churchill.

Adrian Poole is Professor of English at the University of Cambridge, and a Fellow of Trinity College, Cambridge. His monographs include *Shakespeare and the Victorians* (Arden, 2003) and *Tragedy: a Very Short Introduction* (Oxford University Press, 2005). He has co-edited with Gail Marshall *Victorian Shakespeare*, 2 vols (Palgrave Macmillan, 2003), and has written extensively on nineteenth-century novelists including Dickens, Eliot, Hardy, Stevenson and James. He is editor of the *Cambridge Companion to English Novelists* (2009) and one of the general editors of the *Complete Fiction of Henry James*, to be published by Cambridge University Press.

Note on References to Shakespeare

All references to Shakespeare are to *The Riverside Shakespeare*, gen. ed. G. Blakemore Evans, 2nd edn (Boston, MA: Houghton Mifflin, 1997).

Introduction

Adrian Poole

In 1936, a promising young writer and literary critic named Lionel
Trilling was teaching English at Columbia University. There was a move
in the Department to deny his reappointment and give him the boot. Not
because his PhD dissertation on Matthew Arnold was dragging its heels,
but because, so a senior colleague explained, 'as a Freudian, a Marxist,
and a Jew', it was thought that he would be 'more comfortable' elsewhere.[1]
Trilling argued his case and stayed on at Columbia to become, in the
decades after World War II, one of the leading figures in Anglo–American
literary and cultural criticism.

This volume has a special place in the series *Great Shakespeareans* in
so far as it focuses on only two figures rather than the usual groupings
of three or four. This is for the good reason that Karl Marx (1818–83)
and Sigmund Freud (1856–1939) left bodies of work that have – like
Shakespeare's – permeated to an unrivalled extent the ways we think
about many kinds of discourse and practice *other* than the ones they
explicitly addressed. These of course include the making of art, literature
and drama. From the early years of the twentieth century onwards, the
understanding and interpretation of Shakespeare have been coloured
and moulded by writers whose own thought has been indelibly influenced
by Marx and Freud. Many of them feature in the essays which follow or
receive consideration elsewhere in this series. Though all the figures who
have qualified for inclusion as Great Shakespeareans have left their mark
on the Shakespeare we know, the sheer reach of Marx and Freud over
the ways we think about Shakespeare is unequalled, not only for its direct,
but also its oblique and circuitous, impact. Other Great Shakespeareans
have generated epithets – Coleridgean, Dickensian, Empsonian – but
none with the imperial aspirations invested in the words 'Marxist' and
'Freudian'. Nor have any of the others found it necessary to assert their
independence from the legacy attributed to them, as both Marx and
Freud are said to have, declaring respectively, 'I am not a Marxist' and 'I
am not a Freudian'.[2]

The essays in this volume explore the many ways in which our Shakespeare has been shaped by Marxists and Freudians, but they also return with refreshing precision to what Marx and Freud themselves actually wrote about Shakespeare. In so doing, they reveal the often surprising and sometimes astonishing role played by Shakespeare in the very texture and structure of the later writers' work. As with many other Great Shakespeareans, perhaps above all those coming to maturity in the nineteenth century, Shakespeare's plays, characters and language provided Marx and Freud with a rich vocabulary for thinking and arguing. It is wonderfully illuminating to see the allusions to Shakespeare irrupting into their texts, often less well-known phrases and passages that testify to the intimacy with which they inhabit the mind of the writer, sometimes as if with a will of their own. Crystal Bartolovich describes Marx's method of citing Shakespeare as 'fragmentary and interruptive', a deliberate strategy to counter the ambitions of more appropriative 'holistic' readings, such as Goethe's of *Hamlet* in *Wilhelm Meister*. For Marx, Shakespeare is a critical ally in the task of disrupting the smooth surface of arguments and positions that seek to mask or deny contradiction. Freud was more tempted by the possibility of explanatory conquest, by readings that would unlock a play's inner secrets, but his ambitions are complicated and even thwarted by the mutinous independence of Shakespearean language and his own susceptibility to its wayward vitality.

David Hillman notes in passing that 'Freud shares with Marx a sense of the strength of the human will-to-ignorance – though for Marx this unconsciousness is of the social present rather than the individual past.' This will-to-ignorance consorts with the elevation of human reason that is often supposed to characterize 'modernity', and more specifically, the age of Enlightenment. One of the prime points of contact between Marx and Freud in their attraction to Shakespeare is his position in time, on the brink of a brave new world in which – for example – the word 'individual' finds its meaning drastically altered, no longer to connote the indivisibility of one member from a larger social body but precisely the opposite: the emergence of a new idea of the autonomous, rational, undivided, singular self. Shakespeare offered them a uniquely versatile resource for challenging, undoing and exposing its fallacies, and displaying instead the image of a self and body, whether social or psychic, as a polity radically at odds with itself. They do of course differ in the explanations they offer for the sources of this perpetual strife, and one would not wish to play down the hostilities subsequently waged between their adherents. But insofar as both Marx and Freud sought to liberate their readers from imprisoning delusion, Shakespeare was a crucial inspiration.

In his later years Lionel Trilling sought more comfort in Freud than in Marx (or in Jewishness). There is reason to believe that the title of one of Freud's works that meant most to him could be rendered in English more closely, if less grandly, as *The Discomfort in Culture* rather than as *Civilization and its Discontents.*[3] The departmental spokesman who recommended comfort 'elsewhere' might have been referred not only to Freud but to Shakespeare's Coriolanus, whose brave boast that 'There is a world elsewhere' proves to be unfounded. The elsewheres in Shakespeare, like all the others, strangers and aliens in his plays and poems, are paradoxically here, right now, part of this world. A world of 'discomfort', to put it mildly. Marx and Freud did not put it mildly, and to the enormous, complex, continuing enterprises conducted in their names, Shakespeare has made a vitally animating contribution.

Part I

Marx

Chapter 1

Marx's Shakespeare

Crystal Bartolovich

This particular volume of the Continuum series on the 'Great Shakespeareans' is notable in that – despite the apparent liability that neither Marx nor Freud is a 'Shakespearean' in the usual academic or theatrical senses – these two figures have been accorded more space than any of the others. Paradoxical as this state of affairs may at first seem, it is easy enough to explain. The privileged place of Marx and Freud in the series recognizes that they have not only produced work significantly inflected by a Shakespearean idiom, but also that their proper names are associated with projects – Psychoanalysis and Historical Materialism – each of which is, in its own right, a living practice. So while it is manifest that Shakespeare influenced their writing powerfully, Marx and Freud, more than any of the other figures in this series, are Shakespeare's equals in social impact. Rather than subordinating their projects to his, they enlisted Shakespeare as an ally in developing their own. The work of all three has, in turn, been used by many other thinkers, usually independently. Hence, an essay on Marx and Shakespeare, it seems to me, must recognize this equality – and the enduring life of both – in order to assess their combined power properly.[1]

My approach assumes, first, then, that Marx's Shakespeare has something to offer beyond what either Shakespeare or Marx offers alone. Further, I will underscore that the combination is potentially, at least, transformative and dynamic. In brief – to forecast a bit of my third section – Marx was particularly concerned – as any revolutionary would need to be – with how change occurs, yet he was fully aware that some human creations – such as Shakespeare's plays – endure despite monumental transformations in social relations, indeed in whole ways of life. Walter Benjamin would later refer to this phenomenon as 'afterlife', with the emphasis on 'life' – that is, not only do users change art over time (by translation, editing, remixing, etc.), but great works themselves actually change, since these works are inextricable from the networks of social relations in which they come to have meaning. To endure, then, is also to change. As Benjamin puts it: 'the concept of life is given its due only if everything that has a history of its own, and is not merely the setting for history, is credited with life .... And indeed, isn't the afterlife of works of art far easier to recognize than that of living creatures?'[2] Benjamin – knowing of course that *ars longa* is a classical trope, and that the 'so long lives this, and this gives life to thee' sentiments in poetry are ubiquitous – distinguishes his own position by insisting that his observation is 'un-metaphorical'; we might add that it is not therefore necessarily occult or theological. In the Marxian – materialist – way of understanding it that I will be elaborating here, art, like human life, has not only an 'individual' dimension, but also a 'social' one, which is collective and trans-generational, though currently – because the social conditions and relations that we inhabit are – conflicted. Marx taps into this living struggle; so, in turn, can we.

Indeed, Marx's relation to Shakespeare's afterlife, as we shall see, illuminates – and enacts – one of the most cited passages from his work, the suggestion that:

> In studying ... transformations [of society] it is always necessary to distinguish between the material transformation of the economic conditions of production ... and the ... ideological forms in which men become conscious of this conflict and fight it out. Just as one does not judge an individual by what he thinks about himself, so one cannot judge such a period of transformation by its consciousness, but, on the contrary, this consciousness must be explained from the contradictions of material life ...[3]

A great deal of ink has been expended attempting to interpret this passage in a way that releases it from the twin dilemmas of the 'base/superstructure' model and economic determinism. But as long as we take it to mean that it describes one way that ideological forms work, and that 'fight it out' implies multiple options at any given moment as well as a dialectical relation between conditions and consciousness, then the difficulties do not seem overwhelming. In any case, Marx's particular habits of literary quotation emphatically indicate that 'ideological forms' have multiple meanings, and that they do not have to be novelties in order to become sites in which 'men become conscious of ... conflict and fight it out.' Here, and elsewhere, in fact, he implies that a later age might actually be in a better position to assess and make use of 'ideological forms' than the age that first produces them, which certainly suggests that the conditions in which they are produced does not restrict their potential meanings with an iron fist. Furthermore, Marx's own citation practices indicate that art need not be overtly political to serve social functions. As a site of struggle, art is flexible, multiple, unpredictable; it exceeds – even resists – attempts to subordinate it completely to any one particular political exigency. This does not mean that art is politically useless, but, rather, variably useful. Marx's relation to Shakespeare, then, offers a means to ponder and intervene in issues crucial to our moment as well as earlier ones: what are the roles of art in society? How is it related to social change? How do art and criticism participate in education, and what sort of education best leads to reflective, vigorous and mutually enhancing social life?

Here I will concentrate on the space opened up by Marx's engagement with such questions, but also take them up for 'us' – readers in the twenty-first century, who inhabit Marx's 'afterlife' as well as Shakespeare's. In doing so, I will suggest that, in crucial respects, despite claims to the contrary in a post-1989 world, we have not yet moved 'beyond Marx' – which is not at all to say that Marx already has provided all the answers. Marx's own view of Shakespeare's work – indicated in his habit of frequent citation, as well as the way he used these citations – implied that his time had not moved 'beyond Shakespeare', though this did not mean that he assumed that the plays were timeless. With respect to Marx's own oeuvre, Jean-Paul Sartre cogently pointed out long ago that attempts to go 'beyond Marx' philosophically typically produce either an unacknowledged Marxism or pre-Marxist wine poured into post-Marxist bottles, but this does not mean that 'Marxism' is a reified artifact, handed down like a family heirloom to be preserved as is at all costs. To the contrary, Sartre insists: a 'living philosophy … adapts itself by means of thousands of new efforts … for the philosophy is one with the movement of society.'[4] Because we have not yet produced a world that even comes close to that posed as the fully human society by the *Communist Manifesto* – 'an association in which the free development of each is the condition for the free development of all' – we have not yet moved beyond the Marx who wrote those words.[5] And for Marx, Shakespeare had something to contribute to this aspiration, this struggle, but not in isolation, whether spatial (i.e. nationalist), temporal (i.e. relegated to a dead 'past' – even a golden one), cultural (i.e. segregated as high culture), or even – more controversially, perhaps – authorial (i.e. treated solely as the intentional 'genius' of reified artistic wholes).

For these reasons, as the second and third sections below will show, Marx uses Shakespeare citations critically – that is to say, as instruments of critique

– rather than authoritatively. Shakespearean characters and language are called in to help Marx cut through appearances, or mock pretension, and thus level the lofty via satirical or ironic deflation, rather than to gesture toward an ideal state of society, or illustrate a particular historical truth or tendency directly (the most important exception being Timon's tirades against money, which I shall examine in section 2). At the same time, however, Marx encouraged workers' groups to read Shakespeare – and cited the plays in his speeches and letters to them – as inspiration. Such pedagogical – as well as strategic – uses were both possible and necessary, because, for Marx, Shakespeare tapped his world materially – which is to say historically; for Marx, to 'Shakespearize' simply meant – as we shall see in the third section – to historicize: to offer a perspective on people – the history they make, as well as the conditions that are not of their choosing – in their particularity and generality, individuality and sociality.

At the same time, such manifest respect for Shakespearean depiction of human 'species being' (*Gattungswesen*, the concept that Marx used in preference to 'human nature') did not provoke Marx to read the plays as allegories of his own theories. Precisely because 'species being' is a materialist (historical) concept for Marx – not an idealist or 'natural' unchanging – one, insights about 'species being' that emerge at any given moment will necessarily have a shelf life.[6] This shelf life can be extended by new uses, however, which are an artwork's afterlife. It is worth underscoring this point, since Marxist Shakespeare criticism in the twentieth century almost inevitably reads the plays as allegories of materialist history or even of Marxism, having fitted itself to the professional demands of academic criticism, for which a 'reading' is now the commonly recognized unit of publication. To this extent, of course, Marxist Criticism is no different from any other 'reading'-based approach, all of which, in one way or another, subordinate the literary text to another code, through which the target text is 'read', however much it may also 'problematize', 'historicize' or otherwise meddle with the conventions of the practice. Hence, Kiernan Ryan observes in a recent number of *Shakespeare Survey* that 'for ... critics who might be characterized broadly as Marxist and humanist in orientation, *King Lear* is first and foremost a dramatic enactment of the transition from feudal to capitalist culture.'[7] One will hunt in vain, however, for a reference to *Lear* – or any other Shakespeare play – in the 'primitive accumulation' chapters of *Capital*. Indeed, the tragedies – so privileged in the history of Shakespeare criticism – are given relatively little attention as a group by Marx. The point here is threefold: first, that vast expanses of Marx's work are utterly devoid of any references to Shakespeare, even when he is developing the very concepts in which allegorizing via Shakespeare seems to come most readily to mind for critics today; second, that tragedy is not his preferred source material, despite the enduring preference for tragedy in literary criticism; and third, that Marx never produces 'readings' of Shakespeare's – or any other – literary texts per se. I should underscore that Marx's avoidance of readings reflects a clear choice on his part; extended readings of literature according to various codes were manifest in Marx's world. Not only does he not produce any, however, but he mocks – at great length – an attempt by a contemporary to generate a 'Hegelian' interpretation of a novel.[8]

It is crucial to recognize, then, that Marx's citation habits overwhelmingly tended toward, say, associating sanctimonious bourgeois economists with Dogberry or lying politicians with Falstaff, dialectically challenging the blind, pompous or misleading self-representations of historical individuals with carnivalesque ridicule. Thus, the comedies and the histories are the most frequently mined by him. These citations are rarely merely ornamental or incidental, however; as I will show, they are typically theoretically significant. Furthermore, such brief rather than extended deployment of Shakespeare and other literary texts assists Marx's formal (and political) investment in bringing multiple voices into explicit contention, as we shall see. Just the same, precisely because, for Marx, critique should always fit the historical situation, he does not propose or assume that strict emulation of his own – or any other past – practice will necessarily always produce emancipatory results. An antagonistic relation to an unjust status quo may require different strategies at different times and in different situations, as the Frankfurt School critics – especially Adorno and Benjamin – emphatically insisted.[9]

And, of course, talking about the world is never enough. 'Thesis 11' makes this clear: 'the point is to change it.'[10] But this injunction by no means renders the entire Marxist conversation superfluous – not least because liberatory social change is hard to bring about, and requires engagement on multiple fronts. Above all, it seems to demand persistence: the slow, often thankless, perhaps even wrong-headed in the details in any given moment, preparing of the way for revolutionary possibilities by collectivities and individuals, like Puck, who, after all the potion-wielding attempts to manage history in the forest, appears on stage performing a surprisingly ordinary 'huswifely' role, one that, as Wendy Wall reminds us, typically was 'too banal for representation': 'I am sent with broom before, to sweep the dust behind the door.'[11] Marxist critique is frequently just this sort of housekeeping – assuming, that is, that the dust is being swept out in the open from 'behind' rather than to 'behind' where it lies hidden. In any case, it seems likely that there will be no social transformation of any consequence without a lot of such sweeping out, a process whose ultimate benefits we, as individuals, may not live to see.

To be more concrete: the *Communist Manifesto*, as is often noted, was not yet the influential text in 1848 that it would become after Marx's death.[12] But it could not have had the afterlife it has had without Marx's persistence – and that of countless others – who refused to let it be swept behind the door of history. I underscore, then, that this afterlife is not only a temporal mediation, nor an individual one, but collectivist. The *Communist Manifesto* 'lives' at the intersection of the collective struggles that have animated it, the 'thousands of new efforts' to which Sartre refers. For Marx, Shakespeare's plays were enlisted to this cause. Re-constellated with Marx's prose, Shakespeare's poetry enables new connections and interventions. We owe a debt to the struggles that came before – Benjamin crucially reminds us – to redeem them by working persistently, broom (or pen, or placard, or weapon) in hand, to bring into being the just world toward which they moved.[13] When it comes, the redeemed world will be located at the intersection of the historical totality of all the efforts to achieve it. One way to explore this process at work, then, is to consider how Marx made what we might call common cause with Shakespeare, different as the poet and revolutionary might be when considered separately, to see what possibilities might arise for us to keep common cause with both.

I begin with a brief account of Shakespeare's place in the cultural milieu in which Marx grew up to get at why a German philosopher and revolutionary struggling to understand and explain how capitalism worked found it so useful to turn to an English dramatist – who wrote in the period before capitalism had fully taken hold – for support at key moments in his writing.

Travelling Shakespeare

Virtually every book and article on the topic of Marx and literature tells us that Marx identified Shakespeare as his 'favourite writer'; that his taste for Shakespeare was cultivated by his aristocratic future father-in-law, who enjoyed taking long walks with the young Marx to discuss literature; that he, his wife and children memorized long passages from the plays and entertained themselves by reciting them to each other. Out of intriguing biographical details such as these, a story of Marx's personal appreciation for Shakespeare can easily be constructed, and then used to account for the pervasiveness of citations of the plays in Marx's writing.[14]

These claims are all accurate and crucial, but I want to weave in another thread alongside them: a social one. The extremely enthusiastic adoption of Shakespeare's plays by German philologists, philosophers, translators, poets, teachers, directors, critics and readers from the late eighteenth century onward is well documented.[15] Shakespeare was used to celebrate modernity against the weight of classical tradition, individual 'genius' against deadening 'imitation' of that tradition, and the specificity of German literature against subordination to – French – Neoclassical 'rules'. 'German' Shakespeare is, then, I would suggest, a particularly striking example of poetic 'travel' in European letters – that is, 'travel' (as Edward Said has adopted it for 'theory') understood as movement *and* transformation.[16] This point is worth making because Said's crucial insight is that no matter how productive a particular theoretical concept or critical practice may be when it first emerges, if it is merely mindlessly and repetitively applied, without any adjustments for changed circumstances, it becomes an 'ideological trap'. Marx, as we shall see in section 3, makes a similar argument about 'history', with Shakespeare as his ally. J. H. Herder, among others, too, had a critique of the aesthetic status quo at this time, but his efforts, unlike Marx's, were directed to the agenda of freeing up space for the emergence of Germanic literary greatness by depicting the compulsion to imitate classical forms as anachronistic and, worse, just too fussily French. 'Shakespeare', thus, designated more than a literary proper name; it marked the site of a battleground.

Although Shakespeare's plays had first arrived in the Germanic countries the same way that they did in other parts of the continent – via travelling English players, often performing in popular venues from scripts that were much truncated and simplified to accommodate the language barrier – by the end of the eighteenth century, 'Shakespeare' had become a 'German' literary figure by name, and – coeval with the emergence of 'aesthetics' as a philosophical specialization – the embodiment of modern high culture.[17] The 1790s marked the peak of these trends with the appearance of Kant's *Critique of Judgment* (1790), Schiller's *Letters on the Aesthetic Education of Mankind* (1794), Goethe's *Wilhelm Meisters Lehrjahre* (1795–6) and the first of A. W. Schlegel's translations of Shakespeare's plays into German verse (1798). Shakespeare played an important role not only in the last, but the other three as well, perhaps most interestingly, as we shall see, in Goethe's novel, a 'Bildungsroman' [novel of development] in which a production of *Hamlet* – and numerous discussions about it – are bound up not only in the 'development' of the hero, but through him, of emergent 'German' artistic and national consciousness, and of the novel as a serious literary form.

From anonymous 'low' entertainment, Shakespeare is thus transformed into the embodiment of genius, modernity, high culture.

And, most important, German literary aspiration. Herder's principal move in his famous essay on Shakespeare, after all, was to repurpose elements of the 'moderns' side of French literary debates against – French – Neoclassical ascendancy in European taste formation. He thus emphatically distinguished the British dramatist from Sophocles (arguing that different times and conditions, of necessity, produce different literatures) while insisting that both are nonetheless 'brothers' – that is, equals – in the sense that what Sophocles was with respect to the ancients, Shakespeare is for moderns. Indeed, for Herder, Shakespeare's modernity actually intensifies his universality: 'Shakespeare speaks the language of all ages, peoples and races of men; he is the interpreter of nature in all her tongues .... And if Sophocles represents and teaches and moves and cultivates Greeks, then Shakespeare teaches, moves and cultivates northern men!'[18] In a gesture that was to become commonplace in Germanic criticism, Shakespeare is simultaneously described as 'universal' ('the interpreter of nature in all her tongues') and 'Northern [European]'. The subsumption of Shakespeare's 'England' into 'Northern [Europe]' finessed a proprietary claim by all 'Northern men', while asserting Nordic solidarity and superiority. It's Sophocles who, for Herder, is limited by the particularity of being an ancient Greek, tied to antiquity (and the Mediterranean), whereas Shakespeare's modernity, thanks to the miracle of ostensible historical progress, renders him more universal (in the dubious sense of northern Europe representing the pinnacle of human progress at the time). However, admiration for Shakespeare does not deter Herder from going on to make an explicit case for writers in 'our own degenerate land' to 'erect a monument' to Shakespeare in their own efforts, 'written in our own language'. In other words, Herder attempts to have his Shakespeare, Euro-centrism and German-ness too. The latter desire ends up being the most important, since Herder imagines with equanimity that the day will arrive when 'even [Shakespeare's] drama will become quite incapable of living performance', and German drama can step into the breach. In the meantime, German speakers would have to make do with Shakespeare and so numerous translations were produced, with a complete edition in verse appearing in 1833.[19] After these much-admired and influential 'Schlegel-Tieck' translations entered the German literary canon, one finds unapologetic proprietary references to '*unser Shakespeare*' [our Shakespeare], as well as assertions that Germans simply understood Shakespeare better than anyone else, even the English, and thus that the plays belonged to Germans by affiliation.

This cultural centralization of Shakespeare in Germanic countries is – significantly – largely a phenomenon of Marx's lifetime, which spans most of the nineteenth century (1818–83). Hence it is particularly crucial to recognize that Marx eschewed this Germanization of Shakespeare. For him, Shakespeare was neither English nor German, nor even particularly 'northern', but part of an emergent 'world literature' (*Weltliteratur*) that resisted such distinctions. To be sure, he borrowed the term from Goethe, but Marx's emphases are different. When Marx argues, with Engels, in the context of the *Manifesto*, that, because of the developments of modern industry according to the demands of capital, 'the intellectual creations of individual nations become common property', and that 'national one-sidedness and narrow mindedness become more and more impossible, [so that] from the numerous national and local literatures, there arises a world literature [*Weltliteratur*]', it would be a mistake to contain the radicalizing thrust of 'common property' (*Gemeiningut*) here within Goethe's vision of elite proprietorship of world culture.[20] Hence, Franco Moretti can argue, despite the imperializing baggage that World Literature has historically sometimes carried with it: 'I think it's time we returned to that old ambition of *Weltliteratur*' as long as we keep in mind that World Literature is not an 'object' but rather a 'problem'.[21] It was, of course, already a problem for Marx in the nineteenth century, since he deploys it less as a set of texts than as a concept through which to challenge 'one-sidedness' and 'narrow mindedness', refusing both the nationalist and elitist incorporation of Shakespeare (and other literary texts) so common in his time. In other words, Marx's dialectic of World Literature was more radical than Goethe's, since, for Marx, it asserts itself against regressive forces more generally, such that any boundary or hierarchy might become the object of its critique. Marx's use of Shakespeare indicates as much.

Above all, Marx's 'Shakespeare' is neither proprietary nor 'high cultural' in the sense of exclusionary elite possession of any kind: national, intellectual or even authorial (as I will discuss further in the next section). The first crucial lesson of Marx's Shakespeare, then, is that the revolutionary role of cultural forms cannot be considered in abstraction from history and concrete material struggles. In a Europe where Shakespeare was already being self-consciously deployed with nationalist and other exclusionary and hierarchizing agendas in mind – albeit via claims of his abstract 'universality' – Marx uses Shakespeare to challenge these agendas, but also to challenge existing social orders altogether – goals which require different tactics in different situations, as we shall see in the ensuing two sections.

The Proletariat's *Lehrjahre*

I have already noted above that Goethe's *Wilhelm Meisters Lehrjahre*
[Apprenticeship] was one of the principal texts through which the
introduction – and appropriation – of 'Shakespeare' was enacted in
German-speaking Europe. Indeed, Stephen Greenblatt avers that it's
'probably the most influential of all readings of *Hamlet*' – anywhere.[22]
This novel's pivotal role in Shakespeare's subsequent reception is reason
enough for Shakespeareans to pay attention to it, but I want particularly to
underscore that, as Greenblatt says, it offers a 'reading' of *Hamlet* – quite
literally. And that this reading – not only its content but its form (i.e. how it
is unfolded in the novel) – is bound up in the young hero's 'development'
[*Bildung*], which, too, has implications for Shakespeare's interpretation.
Briefly: the eponymous middle-class son of a prosperous businessman
resists his father's vocational pressure to work for him by taking up with a
troupe of actors in fulfillment of a childhood fascination with theatre. At
first, his connections are merely social, but slowly he becomes more and
more formally entangled with them as an investor, writer, manager and
actor, until he, ultimately, assumes the leading role of *Hamlet*. Wilhelm
then shares his interpretation of that play at length in conversations with
others after he first reads it, and then, later, prepares for the performance
– including cutting, tweaking and rewriting the script to get it into a form
that everyone in the company can agree is playable – and, finally, as they
enact the drama onstage.

What is at the heart of this reading? "The time is out of joint; O cursed
spite! That ever I was born to set it right.' 'In these words', Wilhelm
explains, 'lies the key to Hamlet's whole behaviour; and it is clear to
me what Shakespeare set out to portray: a heavy deed placed on a soul
which is not adequate to cope with it.'[23] Hegel and many others would go
on to track the journey of this 'soul' for their own purposes, but for the
moment I am more interested in emphasizing how Wilhelm comes to this
conclusion. Goethe makes it clear that this reading was the effect of an
arduous process of forcing the parts of the play to form a coherent whole
in Wilhelm's mind:

> I learnt the part [of Hamlet] and tried it out, feeling that I was becoming
> more and more identified with my hero. But the further I progressed in
> this, the more difficult it became for me to perceive the structure of the
> whole, and finally I found it almost impossible to acquire an overview. So
> I went right through the play from beginning to end without skipping,

and found that several things didn't fit together in my mind. At times the characters seemed to contradict each other, at times their speeches, and I well-nigh despaired of finding the right tone in which to act out the role as a whole with all its different nuances and deviations. I battled my way through that thicket for a long time without seeing a way out, until I finally found one particular path ....[24]

Wilhelm's reading produces its Idealist content only by smoothing out contradictions, removing elements that don't 'fit', and reworking other parts, until the play moves down 'one particular path' without 'deviations'. Meanwhile, his life, too, is being subjected to a similar process, its 'one particular path' scripted for him by the Society of the Tower, a secret society that has been guiding his itinerary, even as he thought he was making his own way. With Wilhelm's avid acceptance of the Society's script, Goethe was trying to solve the riddle of how to have (ostensibly) free 'individuals' and stable 'societies' at the same time. To negotiate this thorny predicament, the early theorists of '*Bildung*' propose that what each individual desires above all is integration with the status quo; he simply has to 'learn' that this is so, that 'it is advantageous for him to lose himself in a larger whole.'[25] The integrative 'development' of individuals in the Bildungsroman in this way was inextricable from the development of both modernity and the Nation-State. As Joseph Slaughter has summed this perspective: 'the plot and form of the classical Bildungsroman bridges the transition from ritual, feudal, agricultural and cyclical time to modern, secular, historical time, when evolution itself becomes the dominant hermeneutic for plotting human social events.'[26] And the principal agenda of this enterprise was to constrain history in such a way as to avoid one event in particular: revolution. It was as part of this project that *Hamlet* – and his 'Consciousness' – became the origin of the modern for Hegel.

Jean Hyppolite has even, intriguingly, suggested that Hegel's *Phenomenology* itself has a Bildungsroman structure (though – for Hegel – it is a 'science' in content). In Hyppolite's influential reading, the *Phenomenology* 'is the novel of philosophic formation; it follows the development of consciousness, which, renouncing its first beliefs, reaches through its experiences the properly philosophical point of view, that of absolute knowledge.'[27] Along the way, the 'individual I' and the 'human I' become one, which is the work of '*Bildung*'.[28] Specifically, the *Phenomenology's* 'task is to lead individual consciousness to become aware of the spirit of its times, to become aware of its own substance, its inorganic nature, and simultaneously to rise thereby to an absolute knowledge which claims to transcend all temporal development, to surmount time itself.'[29] According to Hyppolite, in describing this itinerary of Consciousness, Hegel set himself the same task that Shakespeare had in *Hamlet* – and Goethe had in *Wilhelm Meisters Lehrjahre.*[30]

Marx's views of both the novel and Shakespeare – it should come as no surprise – are quite different. Early on, in the *Holy Family*, Marx offers at length his views of the relation of literary culture and politics, one of the few times that he does so. In an extended critique of a laudatory review of Eugène Sue's best-seller *Mystères de Paris* that had appeared in a Young Hegelian journal, Marx argues that the method of the critics in that venue amounted to nothing more than the projection of Idealist allegories on the text, no matter what the books they read actually said. Marx's lengthy listing of the abuses performed on Sue's novel by 'caricatures' of Idealism is both amusing and revealing. Homing in first on the reviewer's apparent inability to read the words actually on the page in front of him, so rapt is he with Hegelianisms, Marx then moves on to his much more serious charge: that the same techniques that blind the Young Hegelians to what novels say also make it impossible for them to correctly assess the under-lying historical tendencies that show why bourgeois readers would rush to buy them. Above all, he objects that 'Absolute Criticism has learnt from Hegel's *Phänomenologie* … the art of converting real objective chains that exist outside me into merely ideal, merely subjective chains, existing merely in me and thus of converting all external sensuously perceptible struggles into pure struggles of thought.'[31] The reviewer of Sue's novel frankly admires its aristocratic hero, with his self-aggrandizing charitable schemes (which, Marx shows, are impossible to realize, as presented) and his self-righteous meting out of punishments and rewards – an attitude, Marx argues, that betrays a bourgeois contempt for the 'mass' of people, even as it offers titillating forays into the teeming alleys and brothels of Paris in which Sue's novel moves. Thus, in the end, the Young Hegelians' approach leads not only to error, but also to genuine ideological threat, reinforcing the very status quo it claims to subject to 'criticism'. Marx therefore thought it necessary to educate his readers in an alternative reading practice to the 'Hegelian' one (the subtitle of *The Holy Family* is 'a critique of critical criticism'). As is well known, Marx also described his task in *Capital* as being 'exactly opposite' to Hegel's dialectical method, which he took to be encased in a 'mystical shell' that had to be cracked open with the hammer of materialism to extract its 'rational kernel'.[32] Typically, this claim is understood in terms of content. In the argument that follows, I will also consider its implications for the form of Marx's magnum opus, *Capital*,

which, I show, has as its goal the pedagogic exposure of material contradiction in the social order. This means that it does not unfold as Goethe's
novel does – or, rather, it does not unfold as Hegel's *Phenomenology*, read
as a Bildungsroman, does. To the contrary, in *Capital*, Marx produces an
unBildungsroman – one in which Shakespeare has a very different role to
play than he does for Hegel (or Goethe).

The 'classic Bildungroman' – European novels in the tradition of
Goethe's *Wilhelm Meisters Lehrjarhe* – had as their ostensible goal advocacy of
human development, but such novels attempt to accommodate readers to
capitalism by guiding them to 'interiorization of contradiction', as Franco
Moretti has brilliantly argued.[33] Written at a time when the influence of
these novels was especially profound, *Capital* situates social contradictions
neither in individuals, nor in readings which discover contradictions only
in order to excise them (as Wilhelm does when he reads *Hamlet*), but
instead in the social order viewed as a totality. In this way, Marx reposi-
tions the 'struggles in thought' of the Young Hegelians back into concrete
struggles in the world – a corrective, as we shall see, he did not think
Shakespeare's plays required.

For both Goethe and Marx, Shakespeare had an important role to
play in their respective, opposed, projects, which indicates, once again,
how important 'ideological forms' have themselves been as sites of social
struggle. A 'reading' of *Hamlet* of the kind that Goethe offers via Wilhelm
is something that Marx does not provide in *Capital*, or anywhere else.
Instead, he typically cites Shakespeare in a way that we might describe as
fragmentary and interruptive, rather than a holistic, as if Shakespeare's
plays were – for Marx's purposes – so many arsenals of slings and arrows
with which to attack outrageous fortune. This interruptive strategy is, as we
shall see, one of the distinguishing features of what I will call Marx's collectivist writing practice, so very different in effect from that of Goethe in the
Lehrjahre, or of Hegel in the *Phenomenology*. And the difference stems from
their opposed goals, an emphasis on education for primarily individual
versus primarily social development, with the latter being Goethe's preoccupation. In the *Manifesto*, Marx and Engels emphasize, Communists resist
any 'culture' [they use *Bildung* here] that is 'for the enormous majority,
a mere training to act as a machine', and any 'education' that has as its
principal goal the transformation of children 'into simple articles of
commerce and instruments of labor.'[34] Thus, though Marx never wrote
a tract specifically devoted to the question of education, his theoretical
writing, especially *Capital*, casts itself in an educative role – or, more specifically, serves an 'unlearning' function – for the worker, who is challenged

by it to resist reduction to a 'machine' and relegation to the status of an 'article of commerce', not by exhortation, but by confrontation with explanations of how capitalism works as an engine of exploitation, so that he will be provoked to transform this dubious world. In the *Holy Family*, Marx explains to the Young Hegelians and whomever else will listen: 'if man is shaped by his environment, his environment must be made human.'[35] The hero of such a process cannot be 'Consciousness', but actual men, in struggle to make their environment humane.

Both the Bildungsroman and Marx, in other words are concerned with the individual and the social, but their emphases are opposed.[36] As the novel increasingly takes on as one of its vocations the insertion of the individual subject into the widening sphere of capitalist modernity – that is, subordinating the individual to the social – Marx resists both the subordination of individuals and the atomizing 'individualism' that belonged to this process – though not, I would suggest, without having learned a trick or two along the way from his second favourite author after Shakespeare: Goethe. Given what I've argued so far, this may come as a surprising revelation, but need not be if we recall that the value of literature does not rely on authorial intentionality for Marx. All great art exceeds the artist by folding into its fabric more social and historical content than its individual creators could possibly be aware of. Goethe's struggles in his writing to make sense of the world in which he found himself are no exception. Moretti proposes that the dilemmas with which the writers of early capitalism such as Goethe were confronted included, most pressingly: freedom versus happiness, mobility versus identity and metamorphosis versus security. 'Youth' was deployed as a figure through which to negotiate these crises; it offers a social orientation toward the future for which modernity believed itself the agent, while simultaneously illustrating the perils (to the status quo) of uncontrolled choice and change. In other words, the crisis of the modern state threatened by 'revolution' is displaced on to a crisis of 'Youth' aspiring to 'maturity'. In Goethe's case, the Bildungsroman – unlike *Faust* – 'resolves' the 'problem' of 'youth' by the 'compromise' of individuals acceding to 'agreement, homogeneity, consensus', ostensibly without giving up 'individuality', but, demonstrably, subordinating themselves to social norms, and situating any leftover tensions in themselves. Moretti puts it this way: 'When we remember that the Bildungsroman – the symbolic form that more than any other has portrayed and promoted modern socialization – is also the most contradictory of modern symbolic forms, we realize that in our world socialization itself consists first of all in the interiorization of contradiction.'[37] It is not insignificant, then, that

Marx – though, too, invested in a 'future' orientation for society – shows a clear citational preference for *Faust* when he draws on the great German writer, as he often does. But more important, whereas Goethe tracks the progress of Youth to Maturity, and Hegel from individual Consciousness to 'Absolute Consciousness', Marx guides workers to become a revolutionary 'Proletariat'. Where Hegel and Goethe seek to bypass revolution, Marx seeks to provoke it. *Capital* thus draws on, but takes the dialectically opposite path to, the Bildungsroman, systematically forcing contradictions into the open, and insisting that they be dealt with socially – and overcome structurally – rather than being internalized by individuals.

As part of this project, what is striking about the references to Shakespeare in *Capital* when we examine them as a series (though I am not suggesting that Marx inserted them into the text self-consciously as such) are the insights that they provide concerning the technique and trajectory of volume 1 of *Capital* as a whole, and its reliance not only on literary citation, but also on the capacity of literature to interrupt and denaturalize embedded social norms. With pointed references to *Henry IV*, *Much Ado About Nothing*, *A Midsummer Night's Dream*, *Timon of Athens*, *As You Like It* and *The Merchant of Venice*, Marx conjures up Shakespeare to punctuate key points, challenging the reader by defying her expectations, including the sanctity of literary texts as aesthetic wholes, since he often cites Shakespeare in ways that wrench the meanings of phrases and characters in ironic or novel directions, situating them in a larger chorus of other voices. Indeed, Marx cites many hundreds of reports, articles, books and records in *Capital* I, the range of which can be breathtaking for readers – nowadays in particular: the excellent 'Index of Quoted and Mentioned Literature' in the Marx-Engels Collected Works edition of *Capital* I, extends for 35 pages of entries, many with multiple citations (the commonly available English editions have much less inclusive indexes – misleadingly so for any study of Marx's citation practices). I particularly want to emphasize the 'collectivist' character of this citation density. Almost always, Marx deploys quotation dialectically, as a challenge to other writers – and to readers. This is why the reading of *Hamlet* as an untroubled coherent 'whole' that Goethe's Wilhelm unfolds in his Bildungsroman is something we find nowhere in Marx's work, which demonstrates, emphatically, that contradictory totality and coherent whole are not the same. This said, let us now enter *Capital*, and see where its Shakespeare allusions take us.

Challenging the commodity

The earliest citations of Shakespeare in *Capital* are not only jocular but also
directed to commodities – or, rather, via ironic pathetic fallacy, directed to
the people who have naturalized a capitalist view of the world, in which
commodities have taken on the heroic (among other) roles properly
belonging to people. This is theoretically significant. Because *Capital*
begins in the sphere of circulation, where mystification prevails, Marx uses
hyperbole to expose its absurdities, bringing us into close encounters with
the 'wooden brains' of tables and other objects in a world where buyers and
sellers have become mere 'guardians' of these remarkable beings, that, in
market societies, seem to take on a life of their own in direct proportion
to their sapping of life from producers. Later we will discover that Capital
– via the Capitalist – is the 'Vampire' – but early on, Marx takes the 'real
abstraction' – the effects of appearances in the marketplace – seriously,
because he assumes his readers do. He then translates the seemingly
'natural' behaviour of commodities into the 'historical' behaviour of
people. Shakespeare is enlisted to help him with this task, and, then again,
at each ensuing step in the process of our education.

First, Falstaff's quip about Mistress Quickly ('a man knows not where
to have her') is utilized to figure the bewildering status of the commodity
as it appears in the capitalist marketplace: 'the objectivity of commodities
as values differs from Dame Quickly in the sense that "a man knows not
where to have it"' (138). The entire exchange in *1 Henry IV* alluded to here
is significant for Marx's purposes. To set the scene: the Prince has previously emptied Falstaff's pockets while he was sleeping in Quickly's tavern.
He discovers nothing of value there ('tavern-reckonings, memorandums
of bawdy-houses, and one poor penny-worth of sugar-candy'). Later,
when Falstaff awakes, he accuses Quickly of harbouring pickpockets, a
charge that instigates a heated quarrel between them. In the midst of this
dispute, the Prince arrives and assumes the sovereign role of judgement.
The ensuing exchange sets up two parallel contrasts: Quickly as 'honest'
person versus 'thing' or 'stewed prune' [prostitute or bawd – brothels were
called 'stews'], and the contents of Falstaff's pockets being valuable versus
being negligible. In settling the latter – by offering an account of his earlier
inventory – the Prince also undertakes to settle the former: being 'honest',
Quickly is not a 'thing' (3.3.52–169). Let us now see how this comic drama
of (mis)recognition works with Marx's discussion of the commodity form.

In the chapter on 'The Commodity', Marx, too, sets up a series of
contrasts. He summarizes his argument just before the reference to Dame

Quickly as follows: 'Commodities come into the world in the form of use-values of material goods, such as iron, linen, corn, etc. This is their plain, homely, natural form. However, they are only commodities because they have a dual nature, because they are at the same time objects of utility and bearers of value.' (138) Then, he comes to Shakespeare's hostess: 'the objectivity of commodities as values differs from Dame Quickly in the sense that "a man knows not where to have it". Not an atom of matter enters into the objectivity of commodities as values; in this it is the direct opposite of the coarsely sensuous objectivity of commodities as physical objects [i.e. use values].' The resulting 'mystery' leads him to propose that there must be a third, 'purely social', ingredient at work: labour, which lies 'hidden' in the commodity, which seems to possess 'value' as its own 'socio-natural' property, displacing the direct 'social relation of the producers' via their labour into 'a social relation between objects' – a condition that he calls 'fetishism'.

The fetishized commodity 'differs from' Dame Quickly, then, because, unlike the Prince, Marx cannot sort the commodity definitively into one category or the other: it is irreducibly both a value and a use-value as a commodity: dual and contradictory in its being. In the Henriad, Mistress Quickly appears variously as the 'honest' innkeeper and the person who is also a marketable object, a woman who sells herself: a prostitute. In the scene to which Marx alludes, however, the Prince uses his authority to recognize Dame Quickly as soon as he sees her as the wife of an 'honest man', a characterization immediately contradicted by Falstaff's assertion that the tavern has 'turned bawdy-house [brothel]', a charge that he amplifies in the insults he hurls at Quickly, such as 'stewed prune' and 'thing'. She adds to the confusion herself when she replies naively to Falstaff's sexual innuendos ('a man knows not where to have her') with unintended salaciousness ('thou or any man knows where to have me!'). The Prince, however, cuts through Falstaff's bluster and Quickly's confusion alike, declaring her an 'honest woman' and Falstaff a 'whoreson, impudent, embossed [swollen, foaming at the mouth] rascal', putting each character in his or her ostensibly proper place, by his princely authority. The contradiction of the capitalist commodity form cannot be sorted out in this way, however – which does not stop mainstream political economists and other apologists for capitalism from trying to assert this sort of princely decisionism. Marx insists, however, that such decisionism must be unveiled for what it is: an idealist smoothing over of contradiction in thought, or argument, when the contradictions of capitalism can only be undone by changing the material conditions of production.

Thus, a typical target for Marx in *Capital* is the organic intellectuals of capitalism, whose studied blindness to contradiction (Gayatri
Spivak helpfully describes such generalized obtuseness as 'sanctioned
ignorance'), are only excelled by their spectacular feats of illogic in
defending the excesses and injustices of capitalist relations.[38] So, while
Marx ushers in Dame Quickly to assist him in confronting the reader with
the irreducible (in thought) dilemma of the commodity form, he deploys
the muddled constable ('write me down an ass!') from *Much Ado About
Nothing* – after he has carefully worked through the ways that commodities
simply refuse to settle into formal stability – in order to figure the idiocy
of mainstream political economists, who uncritically attribute human
qualities to commodities, thereby perpetuating misunderstanding rather
than elucidating the workings of capitalism.[39]

Specifically, at the end of the chapter on commodities Marx sardonically
observes: 'who would not call to mind at this point the advice given by
the good Dogberry to the night-watchman Seacoal? 'To be a well-favoured
[attractive] man is the gift of fortune; but reading and writing comes by
nature' (177).[40] In *Much Ado*, the constable Dogberry makes this comment
while choosing men for the Watch in his usual malapropism-saturated
manner, and thus attributes Seacole's educational attainments to 'nature'
rather than 'nurture'. Marx's point is that the very bourgeois audiences
who might laugh in superiority at the bumbling of the constable are just
as prone to the error he makes themselves. Indeed, the question under-
writing Dogberry's observation is one that is inextricable from theorization
of the commodity form: what comes from nature, and what from nurture
[production]? With his detailed command of Shakespeare, Marx probably
has in mind here something along the lines of one of Rosalind's challenges
to Celia in *As You Like It*, which deploys a similar vocabulary. Celia observes,
'those [women] she [Fortune] makes honest she makes very ill-favouredly',
to which Rosalind retorts: 'now thou goest from Fortune's office to
Nature's: Fortune reigns in gifts of the world, not in the lineaments of
Nature' (1.2.37–42). Like Celia, Dogberry – and his political economist
kindred – mistake the social 'world' and its historical forces, such as human
production, for 'Nature'. This, for Marx, is fetishism – which he takes
as his mission to challenge. Where capitalist ideology would have us see
only 'nature', he re-inserts human 'history' – and underscores that history
under conditions of capitalism delivers only contradictions, however hard
mainstream political economy may try to smooth them out.

Shakespeare's plays, Marx implies, are far more attuned to the distinction
between 'nature' and 'history' than political economists. Marx, thus,

observes: 'if commodities could speak, they would say this: our use-value may interest men, but it does not belong to us as objects. What does belong to us as objects, however, is our value. Our own intercourse as commodities proves it. We relate to each other merely as exchange values.' With derision, Marx then quotes passages from mainstream political economists who write, as if, he says, 'commodities [were] speak[ing] through their mouth[s].' His point, of course, is that commodities do not speak, but that nonetheless they are rendered talkative by the human qualities falsely attributed to them, as bourgeois economists, remarkably, transform themselves into ventriloquists' dummies of their own projections. In the course of displacing a capacity for human cognition and (un)reason on to the commodity, and offering up of their persons to its transcription, mainstream economists, Marx proposes, not only invert human/object relations, but get the relation of value and use-value backwards at the same time: 'So far no chemist has ever discovered exchange-value either in a pearl or a diamond. The economists who have discovered this chemical substance, and who lay special claim to critical acumen, nevertheless find that the use-value of material objects belongs to them independently of their material qualities, while their value, on the other hand, forms part of them as objects.' Once again, History and Nature find themselves mystifyingly trading places, given the exigencies of capitalism.

In a stunningly apt redeployment and elaboration of Marx's use of Dogberry, Slavoj Žižek has pointed out recently that capitalism still has the same trick of manipulating 'nature' and 'culture' up its sleeve, though it keeps changing the terms with the times: 'to be a computer expert or a successful manager is a gift of nature today,' he observes, 'but lovely lips or eyes are a fact of culture.'[41] Legitimate conflict, Žižek argues, has been almost entirely displaced onto the domain of 'culture' (ethnicity, say, or religion) that is understood as 'personal' idiosyncrasy writ large, while the 'administration' of capital continues all the while, as if by nature, unchangeable. Žižek repeats Marx's move here for a similar purpose: to surprise his reader into recognition of the outrageous inversions of nature and culture that characterize late capitalism. Dogberry's obvious mistaking thus makes its way into three successive texts, each of which attempts to sharpen our own sense of how easy – and how problematic – it is to muddle the world human beings make with a 'nature' that they supposedly cannot change.

Challenging money

OK, the reader of *Capital* may now concede, it is a little silly to anthropomorphize commodities, but what about Money and the Market? Don't they perform amazing feats all on their own? After all, I just read on 'Citywire' that 'the financial sector record[ed] some heroic gains over the course of the day.'[42] Marx anticipates these very sorts of questions, and addresses them next, once again with some assistance from Shakespeare. Further elaborating the theme of fetishism in the chapter on money, Marx satirically applies Lysander's lament in the first scene of *Midsummer Night's Dream* – that 'the course of true love never did run smooth' – not to refer to human lovers, but to figure the relation of commodities to money. In this way, he exposes the perversity of a social order in which not only are things routinely assumed to have taken on the most important human functions, such as love, but also in which economic 'decisions' are ceded to the marketplace, which controls human lives just as tyrannically as do Egeus and Theseus in Shakespeare's play:

> The price of the commodity ... is merely the money name of the quantity of social labour objectified in it. But now the old-established conditions of production in [for example] weaving are thrown back into the melting-pot, without the permission of, and behind the back of, our weaver. What was yesterday undoubtedly labor time socially necessary to the production of a yard of linen ceases to be so today, a fact which the owner of the money is only too eager to prove from the prices quoted by our friend's competitors .... We see then that commodities are in love with money, but that 'the course of true love never did run smooth' ... (202).

Oversupply makes the price of linen drop, because, if there is more linen than men (who can pay) care to use, more labour was expended in the producing of linen than was socially necessary. The market cares for no man or woman, any more than the elders in the play care for the wishes of Lysander and Helena. Markets leave people, and even their objects, effectively unloved, because they are simultaneously irrational and indifferent – again, like Egeus – and rely on the very contradictions they are meant to resolve. In other words, though inhuman, the market is accorded a sovereign power that, if exercised in the political realm, would be denounced as tyrannical. Yet, every day the market is ceded – indeed, praised for assuming – this authority.

More specifically, the indifference of money is absolute precisely because money is not human, yet it is accorded absolute power, as if it were sovereign: 'Just as in money every qualitative difference between commodities is extinguished, so too for its part, as a radical leveler, it extinguishes all distinctions' (229). Marx glosses this observation in a footnote with a speech from *Timon of Athens*, to which he returns several times in his work. In Shakespeare's play, once wealthy Timon is impoverished by profligate generosity, and abandoned by men he once considered his friends. Digging in the ground for roots to salve his hunger pangs, he comes upon a chest of gold and expresses his disgust, thus:

> Gold? Yellow, glittering, precious gold?
> … Thus much of this, will make
> Black white, foul fair, wrong right,
> Base noble, old young, coward, valiant.
> … what this, you gods? Why this
> Will lug your priests and servants from your sides,
> Pluck stout men's pillows from below their heads.
> This yellow slave
> Will knit and break religions, bless th' accurs'd,
> Make the hoar leprosy ador'd, place thieves,
> And give them title, knee, and approbation
> With senators on the bench. This is it,
> That makes the wappen'd widow wed again;
> … Come, damn'd earth,
> Thou common whore of mankind … (4.3.26–43).

Timon here observes that money is a sort of social prosthesis that can be made to stand in for any desirable human attribute, while its lack is interpreted as a personal failing – which is indeed the argument that Marx is making himself at this point in *Capital*: actual human qualities are rendered irrelevant by money, which displaces them. Above all, though, what I want to note about this passage is how unusual it is in Marxian citation of Shakespeare, which virtually never quotes the plays in support of any direct insight about economic processes, thereby rendering literature a mere source akin to, say, the slew of inspectors' reports Marx cites, or the work of other political economists, who accidentally or actually reveal the workings of capitalism. This unusualness does not derive from *Timon* being accorded special attention because it was Marx's 'favourite play' – a frequent claim for which there is no evidence.[43] It is more likely that Marx did not typically cite Shakespeare 'authoritatively' in this way because capitalism did not exist as a fully developed mode of production when Shakespeare was writing. However, Marx can cite Timon as a sort of expert witness on money, because the money form precedes capitalism.

The location of Marx's most extensive commentary on *Timon* is relevant as well: 'The Economic and Philosophical Manuscripts' are a collection of notes never intended for publication (375–9). What these notebooks reveal in the case of the *Timon* passage is a rare instance of Marx 'thinking with Shakespeare', drawing him into a direct exchange concerning economic concepts, rather than, as usual, drawing the poet's capacity for depicting the world complexly to his own strategic rhetorical and conceptual purposes.[44] What Marx recognizes and particularly admires in Shakespeare's speech on money is its ability to figure money's contradictory aspects so aptly and powerfully, a strategy with which he makes common cause, and will later conceptualize. He sums: 'Shakespeare brings out two properties of money in particular: (1) it is the visible divinity, the transformation of all human and natural qualities into their opposites, the universal confusion and inversion of things; it brings together impossibilities; (2) it is the universal whore, the universal pimp of men and peoples.' Marx then elaborates: 'the divine power of money lies in its nature as the estranged and alienating species-essence of man which alienates itself by selling itself' (377). That is, we confront ourselves – our own productive and creative power – in money, but do not recognize it as such. Money denatures individual qualities by providing a substitute for them: 'He who can buy courage [a bodyguard or a weapon, for example] is brave, even if he is a coward … ; it is the power which brings together impossibilities and forces contradiction to embrace' (379). Perhaps even more interesting, Marx muses in relation to Shakespeare's passage that (lack of) money has the ability to transform need into effective non-need, since the only need recognized in a market society is the one you can pay for: 'if I have no money for travel, I have no need, i.e. no real and self-realizing need, to travel …. Money, which is the external, universal means and power … to turn imagination into reality … similarly turns real human and natural powers into purely abstract representations, and therefore imperfections and tormenting phantasms' (378). To wish to travel, without means, is merely torment, experienced as an 'imperfection' – that is to say, a contradiction internalized.

We have seen this proposition that Marx teases out of Timon's speech before. Moretti's analysis of the early Bildungsroman emphasized its ability to address social contradictions by encouraging their subjective internalization. The gap between desire and 'reality' is decided in favour of the latter – understood as the status quo – without the slightest indication that the world should change to free individuals from oppression. 'Maturity', is defined, in these terms, as the itinerary of subjective accommodation to a world in which commodities and the market are ceded 'human' qualities and yet perpetrate inhumanities. Marx's *Capital* fights this accommodation at every turn. Beginning with the commodity form, Marx debunks its seemingly unassailable given-ness ('a commodity appears at first sight an extremely obvious trivial thing') by indicating its strangeness, its contradictions, which capital cannot address as such. Built on a sandy foundation of contradiction, capital's structure cannot but be precarious, Marx goes on to propose, even though it appears – and this appearance is a real abstraction, with undeniably powerful effects – to be unassailably firm and eternal. Thus, by charting capitalism's contradictions at every turn, *Capital* maps the world as if it had not yet been seen by his readers, seeking to transfer the denigration and doubt – or complacency and self-importance – that capital tries to instill in its subjects, from individual internalization back to the social sphere where they belong, so that men can become conscious of these contradictions and fight them out: it is an unBildungsroman.

The necessity of continued challenge to a world in which the flaws of capitalism become internalized by its subjects is illustrated by Sharon O'Dair's recent reading of *Timon*. O'Dair seeks to bring a pro-Market populism to bear against an 'anti-capitalist' romanticizing of Feudalism, which she associates with Marxism. Citing Marx's response to Timon's money speech, O'Dair claims: 'Marx would like us to agree that what happens to Timon is predictive or symbolic of what will happen to society under the influence of money and capital. But making this argumentative leap depends partly upon an idealization of what Timon was, of his liberality and generosity; it depends upon an idealization of the old order of feudalism, of economic irrationality, and of stratification by status.'[45] Since Marx always dismisses romantic views of Feudalism as 'reaction', whether he finds them among disgruntled elites or utopian socialists, this is a very odd claim.[46] His 'anti-capitalism' is everywhere oriented toward the future, not the past, as I will show in the next section. O'Dair does not recognize this, however, because she is interested in the present alone; she advocates the capitalist status quo because 'markets, [have] allowed the vulgar a voice in the determination of value', and thus she insists that '[a]nticapitalism among writers and academics is clearly bound up with antipopulism, with a need to keep the masses at bay and to delegitimate their voices, their judgments.'[47] To the contrary, Marxists, especially those working in a Gramscian tradition, have specifically and persistently attacked such intellectual elitism, but, for them, advocating greater access to consumer goods for the working class, does not mean admiring the 'voice' the market supposedly 'allows' them.[48] Marxism instead points out not only that the working class has had to struggle for every gain – and is now losing ground – but, more important, that markets restrict 'voices' more than they 'allow' them. We can 'choose' between Cheetos and Fritos, to be sure, but meanwhile the most important decisions are made elsewhere. Should the millions spent on advertising to get kids to eat Cheetos perhaps be devoted to making sure all people have enough decent food to eat?

Marx deploys Timon to critique such limits to our collective voices – including the limits imposed by the view that social 'inequality is … in the nature of things' – and that some 'status' hierarchy is a 'given' in all societies – as O'Dair claims.[49] From a Marxian perspective, this is a confusion of 'nature' and 'history', which, as we have seen, Marx was especially keen to dispel. All 'status' institutions are necessarily parasitic on the means of production; therefore, as *Capital* puts it, refuting a nineteenth-century argument concerning the primacy of 'status', similar to O'Dair's: 'the Middle Ages could not live on Catholicism, nor the ancient world on politics' (176). Marx foregrounds this irreducible materialist lesson, via *Timon*. No man lives on status, but, ultimately, only by his relation to the means of production. Furthermore, this claim implies that when the means of production are 'common property', then status would be more likely to be equal as well. Marx goes on to make this point next in *Capital*.

Challenging the working class

Since the main goal of *Capital* is to inform concrete social struggle, it should come as no surprise that – while the 'commodity' takes centre stage at the start of the book – by its end, the appearance of the commodity is ruptured, and the 'working class' becomes the main focus – specifically, 'the influence of the growth of capital on the fate of the working class' (762). The itinerary of the book's logic moves us from an emphasis on the commodity and money which is displaced by one on labour; then a focus on individual labour is displaced by social labour; and, finally, the worker is depicted in collective form: workers. In this way, the book educates the reader for conscious participation in a heroic, revolutionary Proletariat, negating the Bildungsroman's internalizing, atomizing thrust. *Capital* is, then, an intervention in 'development' – not social development at the cost of individuals, but rather the development of the Proletariat whose struggle will end class society and institute one in which, as the *Manifesto* puts it, 'the free development of each is the condition for the free development of all.' This social emphasis, in other words, affirms individuals far more than any novel that has as its mission accommodating subjects to the demands of Capitalism, which merely atomizes human beings from each other. Capitalism might seem in this way to affirm individuals, but actually denatures them, by desocializing them, even as it subordinates individuals to social norms. Alienation, then, is alienation from the self as well as others. Shakespeare proves particularly valuable to Marx in making these points.

An allusion to *As You Like It*, for example, appears at the close of Marx's carnivalesque treatment of one of his mainstream-economist targets. Marx presents the Capitalist's case against the ten-hour day agitation in story-telling language drenched with irony: 'One fine morning, in the year 1836, Nassau W. Senior, who may be called the Clauren of the English economists, a man famed both for his economic science and his beautiful style, was summoned from Oxford to Manchester, to learn in the latter place the political economy that he taught in the former' (333). Heinrich Clauren, the pen name of a prolific, best-selling sentimental novelist in Berlin at the time, is conjured up here to mock the dubious taste of the European middle classes in their literary and economics reading alike. Both, Marx pointedly suggests here, are equally obfuscating rather than revealing, equally sycophantic rather than rigorous, and equally questionable in style. To demonstrate these qualities, Marx quotes at length from Senior's pamphlet *Letters on the Factory Act, as it Affects the Cotton Manufacture*. In it, Senior claims to offer an 'analysis' (Marx adds a taunting '!' – in parenthesis – after the word) of the legislation to limit the working day to ten hours, warning that, if it passes, cotton mills will have to close down, since their entire profit derives from production after the tenth hour. As might be expected, Marx mocks this piece of putative logic relentlessly.

To do so, he develops the story-telling form of the section's first line by unfolding a fantasy in which Senior ventriloquizes Marx's own 'analysis', translating Senior's mainstream economics into Marx's own idiom, before an imaginary auditory of Manchester manufacturers. Marx seems to find writing this scene to be a delicious exercise, and has Senior address the manufacturers with patronizing little flourishes, such as 'We now come to the ticklish point, so watch out! The last working hour but one is, like the first, an ordinary working hour, neither more, nor less' (335). Most important for our current discussion, however, we find the following passage, at the tail end of which is an adaptation of a line from *As You Like It*:

> ... the heart of man is a wonderful thing, especially when it is carried in his wallet—[but] you take too pessimistic a view when you fear that a reduction of the hours of labour from 11½ to 10 will sweep away the whole of your net profit ... [T]his fateful 'last hour' about which you have invented more stories than the millenarians about the Day of Judgment, is 'all bosh.' If it goes, it will not cost your 'pure profit', nor will it cost the boys and girls you employ their 'pure minds.' Whenever your last hour strikes in earnest, think of the Oxford professor. And now, gentlemen farewell, and may we meet again in a better world, but not before' (338).

The allusion to Shakespeare, unmarked in any way, perhaps adds a private joke to the scene for Marx, since readers whose taste drew them to the likes of Clauren and Senior might not have sufficient familiarity with the plays to get the reference, but the work the citation performs for the knowing is complex and fascinating.

As You Like It is a comedy that begins with a world turned upside down from the point of view of its final scene, where a 'better world' seems on the cusp of appearing; in the terms of C. L. Barber's well-known interpretation – or one along the lines of Harry Berger on 'green worlds' – it is one of Shakespeare's 'festive comedies', in which the norms of the dominant social order are inverted in a green world that, ultimately, makes possible a transformation of the dominant society, righting wrongs and sorting various displaced persons into their ostensibly proper places in a lavish dispensing of poetic justice.[50] To be sure, reams of feminist and queer commentary have rightly called into question the extent to which we can – or Shakespeare did – accept heterosexual marriage as a 'happy ending', but that these plays stage contrasts between relatively worse and better worlds diegetically seems beyond dispute. In *As You Like It*, an alternative social order is consti-tuted in the forest of Arden, and its reintegration with its outside is announced by a messenger at the end of the play, who explains that, due to a sudden (offstage) conversion of the villainous usurping Duke Frederick by an 'old religious man', the forest exiles are now welcome in the social order that they had fled or been banished from previously (5.4.160). All of this is significant to Marx's use of the play, which turns on a seemingly trivial line, and indicates, once again, how his deep knowledge of the plays permitted him to draw on them in surprising and resonant ways.

Indeed, many Shakespeare scholars might puzzle a bit over where exactly 'farewell, and may we meet again in a better world, but not before' hails from. Still, it is a quite perfect allusion for Marx's purposes. It comes from the mouth of a very minor character in *As You Like* – Le Beau, a courtier to the villainous Duke – but one who fits nicely into the Nassau Senior role that Marx is presenting at this moment in his text, since Senior, too, is a very minor character as far as Marx is concerned, but one who, as courtiers often are, is positioned to have greater influence than his talent warrants. But this is not the only way that the reference is working. In the play, Le Beau turns up – despite his connection to the Court – to warn Orlando that the Duke is out to get him, and that he should flee:

> Good sir, I do in friendship counsel you
> To leave this place. Albeit you have deserv'd
> High commendation, true applause, and love,
> Yet such is now the Duke's condition
> That he misconsters all that you have done.
> The Duke is humorous—what he is indeed
> More suits you to conceive than I to speak of (1.2.261–7).

Then, just before Le Beau departs, he adds 'Sir, fare you well: / Hereafter, in a better world than this, / I shall desire more love and knowledge of you' (1.2.283–5).

Since Marx is imagining Senior, against the professor's recent activity as an ideologue for Capital, speaking instead on behalf of the wronged workers, it is quite delightful that he would think of Le Beau, speaking outside of his expected social role to protect Orlando. The line itself, furthermore, calls attention to Le Beau's recognition that a 'better world' is not only desirable but possible, while Marx's addition of 'but not before' is of course fitting in the specific situation that he is depicting, in which Senior is addressing the capitalists rather than the wronged party.

Form, too, is significant. The power of the section of *Capital* in which this particular Shakespeare allusion appears derives from its massing of citations – an overlay of voices – in which the situation of the workers is movingly described by various commissioners and report writers, for whom Marx has sincere respect. The chapters of Part III of *Capital* (especially 'The Working Day') offer the most explicit illustration of what I have described briefly above as Marx's collectivist writing practice, through which we are encouraged to understand the social totality as a site of struggle. Whereas Hegel's *Phenomenology* is resolutely monologic – one scholar has aptly described it as a 'narrated monologue' – Marx's *Capital* is insistently dialogic: it calls attention to heteroglossia in a way that Hegel's great book does not.[51] For Mikhail Bakhtin, we should recall, all language is necessarily 'heteroglossic' – that is, being social, it necessarily contains multiple voices inflected by different interests and points of view – but normative 'correct' or 'official' language seeks to adjudicate among the voices, to render it 'monologic' in the interest of elite hegemony.[52] Written texts, thus – with a variety of implications – can be situated on a continuum from more to less heteroglossic in effect. Marx's *Capital*, I am suggesting, belongs on the far left of this continuum. Indeed, what makes the many inspectors' reports Marx cites in the 'Working Day' chapter particularly effective, is that they often contain interviews with the workers themselves, giving their voices (albeit heavily mediated) a place in Marx's text too. By constellating the apologists for capital with alternative perspectives – literary, historical, journalistic and so on – Marx illustrates a social totality riven by contradictions, and draws otherwise atomized positions into explicit struggle.

From the reports issued by various commissions in England, Marx cites passages such as: 'Children of nine or ten years are dragged from their squalid beds at two, three, or four o'clock in the morning and compelled to work for a bare subsistence until ten, eleven or twelve at night, their limbs wearing away, their frames dwindling, their faces whitening, and their humanity absolutely sinking into a stone-like torpor, utterly horrible to contemplate' (353). And the workers themselves are called to the bar in a trial of the crimes of capital: 'J. Murray, 12 years of age, says: "I turn jigger and run moulds. I come at 6. Sometimes I come at 4. I worked all night last night, till 6 o'clock this morning. I have not been in bed since the night before last. There were eight or nine other boys working last night. All but one have come this morning. I get 3 shillings and sixpence. I do not get any more for working at night. I worked two nights last week" ...' (354). Marx comments on this grim testimony in appropriately Gothic terms: 'Capital is dead labour which, vampire like, lives only by sucking living labour' (342). Then, to decisively knock the final nails in the coffin of Capital's case, Marx marshals the self-incriminating defences of capitalists themselves – their outrageous claims that if the mills don't work long hours, the workers, children included, will simply fill their time with idleness, vice and crime – and that factory profits will dry up. These counter-voices brought together do battle most effectively, with 'J. Murray' and his fellows emerging the clear victors. For this reason, as much as I admire David Harvey's work, I cannot agree with his speculation that Marx's habit of citation and commentary can be attributed to the fact that 'he didn't have a photocopying machine'.[53] Hegel didn't have a photocopying machine either, and yet the *Phenomenology* looks nothing like *Capital.* Both Hegel and Marx work dialectically, but in vastly different ways, which are an effect of a methodological choice in each case. Marx's materialist dialectic, and his investment in the formation of collectivity in the world, not in the Mind, inspires his display of many voices in contention. Indeed, Marx's book, unsurprisingly, with its many voices, sometimes looks a lot more like a play – a Shakespearean play, with a large and diverse cast.

It is virtually impossible to imagine Hegel being 'dramatic' in this way – pausing the itinerary of the unfolding of Consciousness to propose something like, 'Let us listen … to the polemic between Postlethwayt … and MacGreger …', as Marx does, frequently, in *Capital* while unfolding the itinerary of the 'Proletariat', coming to consciousness of its rightful heroic place, so that it can act in the world (385–6). At the same time, the 'listening' to which *Capital* enjoins us, is very different from the kind that we find in the classical Bildungsroman, where, as Moretti argues, learning to have a proper conversation, and above all, to listen, is the mark of an assimilating socialization, of dismissing ones 'critical individual autonomy' as 'prejudice' (as in *Pride and Prejudice*).[54] Conversely, Marx seeks to provoke, not suspend, critical individual autonomy. And since Shakespeare's drama works very differently from the novel, Marx can draw effectively on the plays to make this point as well, soliciting from us, perhaps, something like Brechtian intellectual engagement.

For example, as Marx shifts his emphasis to the workers, he cites *The Merchant of Venice* twice, in opposed ways. Shylock is initially ushered in ('Ay, his breast, / So says the bond') as a prefiguration of capitalist mill owners' 'lynx-eyed' recognition that while they were not permitted by the Act of 1844 to force children to work for more than five hours before midday without allowing them a 30-minute break, there was no such provision for other times of day (399–400). Children as young as eight were thus simply being shifted to the afternoon, and then directed to labour from 2 until 8:30 without any break at all, manifestly against the spirit of the law. Marx inserts, in response: 'Ay, his breast ….' Following this appearance in his most bloodthirsty guise, however, Shylock later reappears, in a lovely dialectical twist, to speak for the workers. Because capitalism wrenches everything to its own advantage, without respect for any human consideration, it demands absolute flexibility from workers, but offers no guarantees for their welfare. Their skills and tools can be wrenched from them, or rendered superfluous, without any warning or compensation. Hence Marx can imagine the workers, with the dispossessed Shylock of the play, saying: 'you take my life / when you do take the means whereby I live' (618). By drawing attention to a moment in which Shylock seems to be most in power, and then a second, where he seems least so, Marx reminds readers that no participant in capitalism is safe, no matter how ruthless or cunning, much less industrious or earnest. He also, however, shows us the way that *The Merchant of Venice* itself is inhabited by contradiction, doubleness and complexity that makes it endlessly useful for reading the social order against the grain of how its apologists would like it to be read. Through such examples, Marx anticipates that the Proletariat will learn how to properly negotiate contradiction: to challenge the social structures that produce it rather than assuming that the problem lies always within themselves.

****

Summing up our journey through *Capital*, I want to underscore an important aspect of Marx's technique, both in the trajectory of the book as a whole, and in its individual parts, where we have watched him put Shakespeare to use: he is a materialist dialectical thinker. What does this mean, exactly? 'My dialectical method, is', he tells us, 'in its foundations, not only different from the Hegelian, but exactly opposite to it.' (102) He explains further that, 'for Hegel, the process of thinking, which he even transforms into an independent subject, under the name of "the Idea", is the creator of the real world, and the real world is only the external appearance of the idea.' For Marx, instead, 'the ideal is nothing but the material world reflected in the mind of man, and translated into forms of thought.' This reversal of emphasis has its implications for style as well as substance. Marx is sensitive above all to contradiction in concrete social relations: commodities and use-values are utterly at odds; capitalists claim certain values, but act in contrary ways; bourgeois historians and apologists for capitalism tell certain stories, but 'actual history' tells another; they treat appearances as reality and people as things. Only transforming the mode of production can address the contradictions materially as such. Nevertheless, *Capital* teaches us how to see contradictions, so that we can resist being accommodated to capitalism by the numerous attempts of bourgeois apologists to 'resolve' contradictions ideologically. As part of his campaign to combat these widespread efforts to smooth over the irreducible contradictions of capitalism, Marx draws Shakespeare into *Capital* in an antagonistic, ironic way, using fragments from the plays to mock or give the lie to prized mainstream assumptions that attempt to suture the contradictions of the status quo.

Such deployments of Shakespeare are not merely 'decorative' or rhetorical, but methodologically – practically – significant: Marx cannot – and emphasizes that he cannot – resolve social contradictions in his book; they are material, an effect of capitalist social relations. Shakespeare fits into this project particularly usefully from Marx's point of view because the playwright, being already widely recognized as 'universal' – in a narrow European, bourgeois sense – Marx can deploy him to recode universalism against the elitism, and nationalist prejudices, with which the concept was typically – albeit paradoxically – bound up. Deploying the plays in a carnivalesque manner to castigate follies that are not yet seen widely as such, Marx both taps the power of, and adopts as his own, Shakespeare's 'universal' status, which he assumes extends to the working class – less as the heirs of the 'groundlings' of Shakespeare's own time, than as the potential Proletariat of his own. In this, at least, the historical record seems to confirm him, since Andrew Murphy, without any particularly Marxist agenda, observes in *Shakespeare for the People* that by the mid-nineteenth century, with the rise in education levels and the decrease in price of editions of Shakespeare as well as the formation of reading circles and Shakespeare clubs – over and above the already robust presence of Shakespeare on the stage – 'the working class really had taken possession of Shakespeare.'[55] Murphy's emphasis on agency is crucial. Marx's writing and engagement with the working men's associations not only assume it, but encouraged it. Marx's citation habits in *Capital* imply that the universal class should be brought into such affiliation with great poets, whose work, albeit not immediately directed to the class struggle, still had a role in it, through proper use.

Always Shakespearise!

'Historical Materialism' often gets a bum rap. Its critics use the same adjectives (linear, teleological, crude, etc.) to dismiss it again and again, rarely referencing the many theoretical developments in Marxism since the nineteenth century.[56] Typically, they not only fail to take account of these ongoing efforts, but, ironically, disregard what is perhaps the most important point of any materialist dialectical approach, Marx's above all:

since history is a process directed toward liberation, repetition is a trap.[57] History is always a site of struggle, to be sure, but not always the same struggle; so, if the purpose of radical theory is to enable concrete liberatory action under specific historical conditions, then its concepts, arguments and tactics cannot be static. I have already noted above Edward Said's trenchant reminder that, for theory, even 'a breakthrough can become a trap if it is used uncritically, repetitively, limitlessly.'[58] My burden in what follows will be to show that Said's observation is still relevant today as a warning to scholars and theorists. It would not, however, have been news to Marx, who keenly recognized that repetition is a pitfall for history as a well as theory – not least because people already embedded in hierarchical societies had a troubling penchant for repeating variations on them. Thus, while Marx's theoretical works, such as *Capital*, as we have seen, devote themselves to unfolding concepts necessary to a critical understanding of capitalism, the 'historical' works, such as *Eighteenth Brumaire*, show that these concepts – such as 'class' – when brought to bear on the complexity of events, will necessarily be challenged by them. This challenge is not a rebuff to theory, but to reification. On the one hand, then, in *Capital* we are provoked to unlearn our tendency to mistake historical conditions for 'nature', by confronting capital with concepts that expose its historicity. In *Eighteenth Brumaire*, on the other hand, we learn to situate ourselves in history even as it is unfolding, letting concepts and ourselves be productively unsettled by events rather than simplistically reifying them into allegories in a pat, mechanical, repetitive way. Marx's deep suspicion of reification impacts on his view of Shakespeare as much as anything else, of course; but, far more interestingly, Shakespeare was bound up in Marx's attempt to formulate a critical, flexible and nuanced understanding of history in the first place.

Indeed, my playful reference to Fredric Jameson's 'Always Historicize!' in the title to this section is there because, as we shall see, for Marx, to 'Shakespearise' is to historicize in a particular way.[59] Drama for Marx provides a particularly instructive metaphor for the movement of history in several senses. For one thing, comedy often looks for much of its length as if a tragedy is unfolding – and vice versa. More important, in live drama, the cast can at any time go off script – improvise or ad lib – a characteristic of performance that Marx considered a crucial possibility for history. In history, sticking to the script that elite interests attempt to impose always impedes forward movement, and ensures that the world never advances beyond inequality and injustice. In this negative sense, history has always been 'teleological' – that is, prevented from any 'end' other than repeated forms of oppression. Marx insists that this particular script must be rewritten by means of the liberatory collective performance he called revolution. Because Marx's understanding of how literature works is, in fact, inextricable from his theorization of history as an effect of struggle toward revolution, whose terms and demands cannot be predicted fully in advance, he appreciates the subtlety and nuance – as well as the contradictoriness and range – of Shakespeare's drama.

We know that this is the case because he said so in his response to Ferdinand Lassalle's play chronicling the early sixteenth-century 'Knight's revolt' in Germany, which Marx judged to be too politically crude, and thus he encouraged his friend to 'Shakespearise more' to improve it.[60] As he dispenses this advice, Marx elaborates his views of literature in ways that lay to rest some typical misapprehensions of communism as demanding the subordination of history to abstract teleology, the individual to the general and literature to propaganda. To 'Shakespearise', it turns out, is Marx's term for avoiding these problems, which are all too evident in Lassalle's play.

In a letter to Lassalle, Marx first somewhat perfunctorily applauds *Franz von Sickingen's* 'composition and action' and claims that the play 'excited' him, but the bulk of the response is given over to stringent critique. He faults the clumsiness of the verse (although he also observes that mere 'formal polish' is not preferable), but above all he finds the characterization askew, both in terms of focus, and, especially, in terms of what he calls 'abstraction' – which is to say, he claims that Lassalle makes the characters mere 'mouthpieces for the spirit of the times', a technique he associates with Schiller, as opposed to Shakespeare, whose plays he finds far superior. What he misses in *Sickingen* in particular are the telling details that permit what is 'characteristic in the characters' to emerge – that is, what distinguishes them. For example, he complains that 'Hutten [Sickingen's main ally] is, to far too great a degree, merely a representative of "enthusiasm", which is boring. Wasn't he also witty, an infernal wit, and hence hasn't he been done a grave injustice?' In other words, actual history is an effect of relations among individuals in all their idiosyncrasy and contradictions, not of allegorical figures representing abstract social forces. To be true to both art and history, then, Lassalle must, as Marx put it, 'Shakespearise more'. Marx emphatically asserts that successful art cannot empty out history and its actors into dull one-sided abstractions, mere 'representatives' of political positions, however admirable those positions may be. Indeed, he identified the latter tendency in Lassalle as playwright to be his 'principal failing'.

Marx does not suggest, however, that a progressive play about Sickingen should not (or cannot) be written, nor that a tragedy with Sickingen as hero is impossible. To the contrary, he insists that a play on this topic, even a tragedy, can be artistically powerful and politically instructive for the nineteenth century, but that an artist is obliged to both assess the historical situation correctly, and deal with it poetically. The passage is worth quoting at length:

> Sickingen and Hutten were bound to go under because they imagined themselves to be revolutionaries ... and, just like the *cultivated* Polish aristocracy of 1830, turned themselves on the one hand into the organs of modern ideas while on the other actually representing a reactionary class interest. The aristocratic representatives of revolution—behind whose catch-words of unity and liberty there still lingers the dream of the imperial past and of club-law—ought not in that case to monopolise the interest as you make them do; rather the representatives of the peasants (of these in particular) and of the revolutionary elements in the towns should provide an altogether significant and dynamic background. This would have enabled you to give expression in far greater measure precisely to the most modern ideas in their most unsophisticated form; whereas, in fact now, the dominant idea, apart from *religious* freedom, is civic *unity*.

Because of Lassalle's emphases, Marx goes on to complain, the 'Lutheran-Knightly opposition' falsely appears to be 'superior' to the 'plebian-Munzerian', while anachronistic concerns, such as nationalism ('civic unity') are given disproportionate weight. These comments are not only interesting for what they reveal about Marx's understanding of history, but also the relation of Shakespeare's drama to it, since, according to Marx, Shakespeare does not make the mistakes that Lassalle does.

Specifically, Lassalle's play is too narrow – it tries too hard to limit history to specific didactic lessons in a way that Shakespeare's plays do not. We need to be clear here, however; it is not that past events have nothing to teach later times. Marx and Engels both thought that they did, and were, in fact, especially interested in the Peasants' Revolt in relation to the events of 1848. As Engels put it in the *Peasant War in Germany*:

> In 1848 as well [as in the Peasant War], the interests of the opposition classes conflicted and each class acted on its own ....The mass of the nation—petty burghers, their associates (artisans) and peasants—was

left in the lurch by its as yet natural ally, the bourgeoisie, because it was too revolutionary, and partly by the proletariat because it was not sufficiently advanced. Divided against itself the mass achieved nothing, and opposed fellow opponents on the Right and Left. As to provincial narrow-mindedness, it could hardly have been greater among the peasants in 1525 than it was among the classes participating in the movement of 1848.[61]

In both moments, an opportunity for liberatory forward movement is lost, leaving almost everyone worse off. The pedagogic purpose of Engels's analysis is clear: to link the failure (or success) of forging class alliances to revolutionary outcomes. One can now see why the massacre of the Paris workers and the triumph of Louis Napoleon in the mid-nineteenth century would so readily bring to mind the sixteenth-century routs of the peasants to Marx and Engels, and why they would so urgently insist on Lassalle getting the historical analysis right: the Peasants' Revolt was not part of the dead past to them; it was an incomplete project, a tragic failure that demands eventual redress by a comic ending. Emphatically choosing the knights over the peasants as his heroic agents of liberation, Lassalle allies with a dead past, Marx suggests. Shakespeare's plays, for Marx, never make this error, precisely because the central action is cross-hatched with a rich and elaborate 'significant and dynamic background' in which manifold historical forces and interests emerge.

The solution, though, according to Marx, would not be for Lassalle to depict Sickingen as joining forces with the towns and the peasants (since he did not), but rather to depict him as confronting the contradictory historical situation in which he found himself as fully as possible, and have him speak appropriately to that situation, rather than as a modern liberal holding forth about 'rights' and so forth in a presentist, politically-correct way. This does not at all mean it would be necessary to represent Sickingen as anti-heroic, nor the peasants as heroic, but rather that one must make the characters true to themselves as social individuals and thus to the specificity of the historical situation they inhabit. Indeed, it should now be manifest that Marx did not approve of the crude yoking of art to 'politics', much less encourage it – the later deformations of Socialist Realism notwithstanding. Marx appreciated and judged drama not according to its declaration of any explicit political agenda, but rather its degree of aesthetic sophistication, concreteness and nuance – criteria that put Shakespeare at the pinnacle from his point of view.

Above all, for Marx, Shakespearean characters refuse reduction to allegories of political positions, while Lassalle's do not. Lassalle's treatment of character thus offends Marx's aesthetic sensibilities, but also, more important, his political ones. In fact, the relationship between the 'social' and the 'individual' implied by Marx's understanding of 'character' soundly refutes later critics of Marxism who have argued that it requires a subordination of the 'individual' to 'the social'. In the *Economic and Political Manuscripts*, we find this unequivocal assertion: 'my own existence is social activity' such that 'it is above all necessary to avoid once more establishing "society" as an abstraction over against the individual. The individual is social being. His vital expression – even when it does not appear in the direct form of communal expression, conceived in association with other men – is therefore an expression and a confirmation of social life' (350). Unlike the individual for Hobbes or Freud, then, for Marx the 'individual' and the 'social' are not 'naturally' at odds with each other. There is no 'asocial' form of the individual. For Marx, there are only better and worse forms of sociality, without which individuality has no meaning: we are, even as most ourselves, social creatures, through and through. The struggle of Communism, thus, is toward 'the true resolution of the conflict between … individual and species' – a conflict which derives from a contradictory social order, not inherently conflicted individuals (348). If individuals were no longer forced to be crudely underdeveloped by the pressures of the market (Marcuse will later famously refer to this as being 'one dimensional'), nor rendered 'stupid' – as Marx puts it – by private property, we would at last be free to develop ourselves fully – collectively and individually at the same time (351). Of course we cannot fully imagine this free 'individual' outside the just social conditions and relations that would give rise to and support it, but literature can help challenge the status quo enough to open an ideological fissure through which we might squeeze toward that better world via concrete struggles. Given his understanding of the (social) 'individual', it is not surprising that, for Marx, a highly particularized character in literature not only affirms the 'individual', but points to truths about the social order and history that individuals – collectively – inhabit. The plays of Shakespeare were considered noteworthy in presenting just such 'characters', according to Marx (as well as many of his contemporaries), and for this reason he draws on them himself, copiously, to develop points he is trying to make, but it must be underscored that his reasons for doing so are as much political as aesthetic.

The truth-value of Shakespeare's plays is further enhanced, in Marx's view, by the particular historical moment in which they emerge: a moment of flux in which capitalism was in the process of formation, but had not yet triumphed, and thus, a time in which ideas which would later become dominant were emergent in 'unsophisticated forms'. Perhaps no aspect of Marx's work has aroused more comment (positive and negative) in Shakespeare studies than claims such as this, which appear to situate the 'origin' of capital in the sixteenth century, making it supposedly roughly coeval with the emergence of the First Folio. However, the way that Marx tells the story of primitive accumulation is actually more complicated, as Richard Halpern has shown. Marx is more concerned, for one thing, with the non-synchronous than he is typically given credit for – and he did not assume either that Shakespeare was his contemporary, nor that he belonged to a dead past. In the 'Introduction' (1857) to the *Grundrisse* (the preparatory notebooks for *Capital*) Marx provides a tantalizing, albeit brief, reflection on this 'uneven development of material production relative to e.g. artistic development'.[62] Although this 'e.g.' is often not mentioned in discussions of this famous passage, it insists that art is not the only aspect of social life Marx recognizes can be out of synch with 'material production'. Indeed, Marx's implication is that the list might be quite extensive; even in the fragmentary state of the *Grundrisse*, it includes warfare, education and historiography as well as law, and suggests that 'international relations' and 'means of communication' can impact on this uneven development.[63] In literature, Shakespeare and Greek drama are Marx's specific examples of 'uneven-ness' – that is, bodies of work which preserve their appeal and significance beyond the time and place in which they are first written. In part, this endurance is an effect of the complexity and artistry of the works themselves, but, in addition, as Marx's comments to Lassalle emphasize, events and art of earlier times can shed light on later ones, even though they are not identical to, nor fully coeval with, them. Indeed, that they can do so distinguishes for Marx an incomplete project from the dead past – a distinction that I will develop in the rest of this chapter. In terms of an 'incomplete project', as we shall see, to 'Shakespearise' is to be open to the future by refusing to be overly bound to the ideological scripts of either the present or the past.

'Well worked, old mole!': reading history for the drama

'History', for Marx, is what people make. As the famous passage in the *Eighteenth Brumaire* puts it: 'Men make their own history, but not … under circumstances they themselves have chosen' (146).[64] History is, thus, distinct from – though inextricably bound up with – 'Nature' which is its limit.[65] Because we make the social world that we inhabit – albeit, not under conditions of our own choosing – mistaking history for nature is among the more serious theoretical errors. Above all it is dangerous because it can lead to a fatalism, an association of unchanging natural cycles with human history, and thus to sentiments such as: 'the poor will always be with us', 'there is nothing new under the sun', or 'dust thou art, and unto dust shalt thou return.' These Biblical variations on the cycle theme, alongside their Greco-Roman counterparts – especially Fortune's wheel – permeate Judeo-Christian culture generally, continuously reappearing in new guises. Marx persistently urged a break with such cyclical thinking – which he saw as fully ideological. The opening lines of the *Eighteenth Brumaire* remind us of this unfortunate repetition compulsion: 'Hegel remarks somewhere that all the great events and characters of world history occur twice. He forgot to add: the first time as tragedy, the second as farce.' Marx goes on to argue that the only way to effect a release from such cycles is revolutionary rupture. Intriguingly, however, one of his most influential and resonant images for this break – the old mole – involves what at first glance, at least, appears to be a repetition or return of its own. We shall have to look more closely at this seeming paradox.

Marx's 'old mole' was itself so far from being 'new', in fact, that it was borrowed at least twice: from Shakespeare, via Hegel.[66] It would subsequently go on to burrow its way through various red newspapers and speeches, and creep its way into the erudite precincts of French theory as well as British and American Shakespeare Criticism. So powerful and influential, indeed, has its afterlife been, that Michael Hardt and Antonio Negri (repeating a similar pronouncement by Deleuze) recently felt compelled to declare it dead to make way for a different figuration of revolution.[67] Derrida, too, downplays the mole – which he only brings up once, in order to dismiss it – captivated as he is by the ghost as a figure of Communism to come in *Specters of Marx* – a mistaken emphasis, as I will show.[68] In any case, the mole's death is a rumour that has been highly exaggerated. Since my purpose in this section is to highlight Marx's insistence on the importance of being able to distinguish between the dead past and incomplete projects, the debate over the mole's vitality is theoretically significant. As any gardener (or visit to an online gardening forum) will tell you, keeping moles permanently at bay is not so easy. That is one of the natural history lessons, no doubt, on which the enduring power of the old mole depends.

Nevertheless, we must keep reminding ourselves that we are not dealing here with any ordinary garden mole. The 'old mole' is not natural, but rather a poetic figure for movement – of a ghost (Shakespeare), Consciousness (Hegel) and History (Marx). But in Marx's case, it should be underscored, the mole is also a mark of (not solution to) a particular problem: how to point toward something that does not yet exist? The *Eighteenth Brumaire*, where the mole rears his nose for the first time in Marx's work, emerges out of the revolutionary disappointments of 1848. Considerable organized insurrectionary activity – especially, but not only – in France, seemed at first to be directed toward continuing the most liberatory aspects of the 1789 Revolution. But the 1848 revolution – as has always been the case with revolutions so far – transformed into reaction, and succeeded only in repeating the bloody and regressive aftermath of 1789 as farce. Many commentators have noted that such drama references – beginning with the first lines of the *Eighteenth Brumaire* – are invoked many times in the ensuing discussion, and are not casual. Unlike farcical 1848, earlier revolutions (English, French) had been tragedy in more than a metaphorical sense for Marx: not only did they fail to achieve their full liberatory potential, but they were acted according to a script borrowed from the past – classical or Old Testament – and with the principal players wearing masks appropriated from those (dead) earlier scenes. Marx muses: 'in these [earlier] revolutions … the resurrection of the dead served to exalt the new struggles, rather than to parody the old' (parody being the effect of the aftermath of 1848). A little later, he adds: 'earlier revolutions have needed world-historical reminiscences to deaden their awareness of their own content. In order to arrive at its own content the revolution of the nineteenth century must let the dead bury their dead. Previously, the phrase transcended the content; here the content transcends the phrase' (149). 'Here' is precisely where we have not yet arrived, however: even now we still inhabit the land of the dead from Marx's point of view. We must learn, thus, to understand the 'old mole' as a 'phrase' – a figure for Revolution in search of its 'content' – a script that has not yet been written. The mole is 'old', then, not because it belongs to any particular 'content' from the past, but because the struggle against the deadening scripts of oppression is old. When revolution finally ruptures with these cycles of oppression, the world will be new. This 'new' world is the mole's desti-nation despite its great age – a goal that will render prior history universally visible as the 'nightmare' that it is, but consign that nightmare entirely to the dead past, while the revolution completes, at last, the numerous incomplete projects (slave revolt, food riots, strikes – rebellions of all kinds against oppression) which have been preparing its way – attempts at liberation that have been hitherto truncated or suppressed (146).

Hamlet as a site from which to draw this resonant 'old mole' is multiply significant. First of all, it is a tragedy – the genre, for Marx, of all pre-revolu-tionary history (with the occasional variant of the decay into 'farce', as with Napoleon III) – in which time is characterized by repeated cycles of oppression. Second, the ghost that Hamlet calls 'old mole' ('Well said, old mole, canst work in the earth so fast?' 1.5.162–3) is itself a 'repetition', a walking simile of the former King's self, emptied out and strangely changed: the dead past walking ('the same figure like the King that's dead', 1.1.41). As such, it is one of numerous *memento mori* in the play – reminders not only of death, but of the levelling of death, as Hamlet illustrates when he first proposes to call the ghost 'Hamlet, King, father, Royal Dane' but shortly after 'boy', 'old mole', 'fellow' and 'pioneer' (all in the space of Act 1, scene 5) – which, as many critics have noted, denotes a vast comedown for the 'perturbed spirit'. For Marx, however, that death levels individuals in this way is much less significant than that the dead past has been levelling collective history, flattening it out into a continuous repetition of horrors. The dead past, in this sense, does not mean unimportant, or lacking in effects – in the play, Old Hamlet's past wars still have effects in Elsinore's present, as Fortinbras's plans for war to avenge the loss of his father, and his father's losses, indicate; and even the ghost gives, rather than submits to, commands. 'Dead', instead, designates that the past belongs to repetition: the same old scripts of inequality, injustice, war, oppression and revenge that elites keep writing to everyone else's cost. As Raymond Williams once put it – concerning actual, not dramatic, history: 'very few titles to property could bear humane investigation, in the long process of conquest, theft, political intrigue, courtiership, extortion and the power of money', and so, he advises, 'if we have humanity to spare, it is better directed to the unregarded men who were making and working the land … under the old owners and the new.'[69] The aspirations and struggles of such 'unregarded' people belong to an incomplete project of human liberation, against the weight of the dead past. Marx, thus, was invested in teasing out the historical traces of 'unregarded men' – in part through Shakespeare's attention to them (which adds a third significance to the 'old mole' being drawn from *Hamlet*, as we shall see).

We do, after all, meet an 'unregarded m[a]n … working the land' in that play's graveyard scene. To understand what Marx would have appreciated about this 'Clown', 'Sexton' or 'Delver', as he is variously described, we need not assume, as some critics have, that Shakespeare's characterization of the gravedigger and other 'peasants' is sympathetic.[70] For Marx, what matters is that such characters are there at all, in a tragedy, inserting comedy into its fabric. The gravedigger also, however, significantly, introduces the trace of collective resistance from below, via the language of a folk saying that emerged in England at least as far back as the English Peasants' Revolt

(1381): 'when Adam delved and Eve span, who was then the gentleman?'[71] 'Delve' is an Old English word, largely now replaced by 'dig', though dialectically still common, as it was in Shakespeare's day, according to *OED*. It is nonetheless very rare in Shakespeare's canon; there are only four uses of the word in any form in his extant work: one in the sonnets and three in the plays – two of which are in *Hamlet*. The rarity of use puts added onus on the word, and the context in the gravedigging scene associates it very strongly with social levelling from below. Not only is the Sexton addressed as 'Goodman Delver', but he asserts that 'there is no ancient gentlemen but gardeners, ditchers and grave-makers – they hold up Adam's profession' (5.1.29–31). To his interlocutor's expression of doubt, he insists that Adam was indeed a gentleman, since he was 'the first that ever bore arms' – which he clarifies – again, in his response to his companion's doubt – with a punning literalization of 'arms', thus universalizing them (at least among men – Eve is conspicuously absent from his observations at this point): 'could he dig without arms?' What fascinates about this scene is that while Hamlet's later mournful meditation on death as a leveller focuses on its capacity to level socially downward – to decay lords, lawyers, landlords and even conquerors into mere dust to be thrown around by a 'mad knave' and 'ass' like the gravedigger, who sings at his work, indecorously, from Hamlet's point of view – the gravedigger himself imagines a levelling up – that all men, having arms (which he is using at that very moment for the exact activity he is describing), should be accorded equal respect. And the play associates these opposed views with the comic (equality) and the tragic (inequality), respectively – a generic association that will not be without significance to Marx's borrowed mole – a digger, too.

For dig the clown does, throughout the first half of the scene, right before our eyes. And sings. And jokes. Perhaps in this way performing 'more' – as Hamlet worries in his advice to the players – 'than is set down for him' (3.2.39). Clowns are notorious script extenders and rewriters – improvisational experts. They do not simply 'repeat' but add, extemporize and steal scenes, pushing the script beyond its limits.[72] It is no wonder, then, that Marx would find revolutionary potential in the comic mode – especially since the clown is so attuned to something that Hamlet is not: to inequality as unnatural. For the clown, a historical memory of revolt and struggle is as keenly adduced as the 'natural' cycles – arguably calling attention to the un-naturalness of human history all the more. In the central action of the play, the designated 'un-natural' content of human history is 'murther'; not only is it called 'un-natural', but it interrupts the 'natural' cycles of life and death visibly by leading to the appearance of the perturbed spirit (1.5.25).

Ghosts, after all, are conspicuously unnatural: they belong to neither history nor nature. As Hamlet's father's spirit notes, his 'days of nature' are in the past (1.5.12). Thus, the characters in *Hamlet* habitually refer to the ghost as 'it' to distinguish it from the former monarch. This ghost, then, is not only a *memento mori*, but an emblem of interruption of natural cycles by terrible crimes, which keep the dead, unnaturally, 'perturbed'.

But there are, the clown reminds us, crimes against collectivities – and history – as well as individuals and 'nature'. To his fellow clown's observation that Ophelia's burial in consecrated ground was only brought to pass because she was a gentlewoman, the Sexton remarks: 'and the more pity that great folk should have count'nance in this world to drown or hang themselves, more than their even-Christen' (5.1.25–9). Death may be a 'leveller' then, but burial apparently is not always so. In a more coherent form, this fantasy of earthly 'even'-ness had in fact been the theme of John Ball's infamous sermon on Adam, from which the 'delving' proverb came into the written tradition in England: 'if it had pleased God to create serfs, surely in the inception of the world He would have appointed who should be a serf and who should be a lord.'[73] By the mid-seventeenth century, the Digger leader Gerrard Winstanley would put this assertion in the strongest possible terms, arguing that inequality among men was itself the Fall, the original sin, not a punishment for it.[74] In this tradition, all human history is unnatural, not only because it is not in accordance with Nature, since men were not created 'naturally' unequal (Eve tends to remain a lacuna in these speculations), but also because inequality is man's doing, not God's, and therefore is fully historical. The 'digger' scene in *Hamlet*, too, brings this theme of unnatural inequality strongly to the fore, however muddled the clown's musings may be. On the face of it, of course, these repeated demands for equality in human history may themselves look like just one more cycle, one more thing that is not new under the sun – much as Marx's recycling of the mole might appear. But to understand either in this way would be to obscure their aspiration to unsettle cycles. In the *Eighteenth Brumaire*, Marx, as we have seen, makes a distinction between 'phrase' and 'content'. Demands for equality are indeed 'repeated' again and again historically – but only as phrases. The 'content' of history keeps remaining the same: one form of inequality replacing another. 'Revolution' in Marx's sense is the moment when the 'content transcends the phrase' at last, and reveals the earlier struggles to have been incomplete projects, preparing the way for ultimate accomplishment of liberation (the burrowing mole being this aspiration incarnate).

The mole thus has affinities with Doomsday, the sign under which *Hamlet*, too, figures a break with inequality, poverty and other human miseries, and, above all, death. Just as he brings the historical memory of peasant revolt into the graveyard scene, the clown also alludes to Doomsday: the end of cycles of flesh to dust. He banters with his companion over a riddle: 'What is he that builds stronger than either the mason, the shipwright, or the carpenter?' (5.1.41–2). The answer: 'A Gravemaker. The houses he makes last until doomsday' (5.1.58–9). In the biblical book of Revelation, the day of judgement (doomsday) is the time when the dead will all be sorted into new permanent accommodation, either in the New Jerusalem or the burning lake of fire, since all 'the former things are passed away' (Rev. 21.4). Apocalypse thus undoes the Genesis of Creation, Fall, and Curse ('dust thou art ...') by ending for good the cycles that Genesis sets in motion; the last book of the Bible undoes the first. For Marx, the possibility of short-circuiting these supposedly natural cycles is, however, the work of history not a Divine plan: a rewriting of the script of Apocalypse, such that people – rather than God – make the redeemed world.

This secularizing gesture is at the heart of what it means to transform 'revolution' from repetition to rupture. 'Let the dead bury their dead!' says Marx, in his own rejection of supposedly 'natural' cycles imposing themselves on human history. In both Matthew (8:22) and Luke (9:60), we have versions of Christ using these words to chide a potential (anonymous) apostle, who asks to bury his father before joining Christ's ministry. The injunction to 'let the dead bury their dead' is there an instantiation of rupture, of rewriting the social script, so that one breaks with all old relations completely to become new. Alain Badiou has thus argued that the Christian break with the past (in his case, via St. Paul) – when secularized – can serve as an ur-metaphor for revolutionary rupture as such.[75] Here Marx anticipates him with a similar gesture. By citing scripture to his own purposes – against scripture – Marx rescripts agency as the collective struggles of people. His project in the *Eighteenth Brumaire*, where he meditates not only on burial, but also on the very much alive old mole, is a historical analysis of current events – that is, a situating of them, pedagogically, in a broader and longer historicity by teasing out the underlying situation that informs contradictory or seemingly random, inexplicable or unconnected appearances. One tendency he uncovers is the unfortunate proclivity of revolutionary activity to be deferred, deflected, deterred or even reversed by competing interests – thus, seemingly buried. Above all, though, he seeks to recover 1848 as part of an ongoing incomplete project – to distinguish its liberatory elements from the dead weight of repetition by diagnosing the balance between these two opposed forces.

As I have already observed, 1848 had been a time of frenetic direct organizational and insurrectional activity in which Marx himself had participated: this was the moment out of which the *Communist Manifesto*, with its arresting opening reference to the 'spectre haunting Europe' had emerged. From the far side of 1851, however, with revolutionary activity largely suppressed, the spectre didn't look so terrifying. New times call for a new metaphor, and a new mode of action – one more cautious and patient: 'the Revolution is thorough', Marx insists.[76] It is still ongoing, but in repressive times, it moves underground (not in the sense of secret societies – though there were those – but in the sense of being less visible). The crucial point Marx conveys to readers in this image, then, is that the struggle for human equality and freedom – a struggle bathed in the blood of not only the Paris Proletariat, but also countless others, stretching back into distant ages – does not belong to the dead past: it is simply incomplete. For this reason, the ultimate figure of Revolution for Marx is not the ghost – a visitor from the land of the dead – but the mole – who still, albeit subterraneanly, humbly, lives and works its way through the land of the living.

In more hopeful days, when they wrote the *Manifesto*, Marx and Engels had announced that the Bourgeoisie would produce their own 'gravediggers' [*Totengräber*] in the Proletariat.[77] In the *Eighteenth Brumaire*, the gravedigger is reimagined as a mole, who will eventually emerge from having been buried. The mole, which had been no more than a 'phrase' in *Hamlet*, an appellation or jocular epithet thrown out by the prince alongside several others, all of which refer only catachrestically to the ghost, is later singled out by Marx for transfiguration: '... the revolution is thorough. It is still on its journey through purgatory. It goes about its business methodically. By 2 December 1851 it had completed one half of its preparatory work; it is now completing the other half .... And when it has completed this ... Europe will leap from its seat and exultantly exclaim: 'Well worked old mole!' (236–7). The reason for the shift from 'said' in *Hamlet* to 'worked' in Marx is obvious enough: in a book that continually draws distinctions between saying and doing, phrase and accomplishment, doing is all.[78] Similarly, the shift from a ghost called a 'mole' (phrase) to a mole figuring revolution by working toward it (content), is therefore crucial – and allies the mole with the gravedigger far more than the ghost. In the play, the ghost comes from the dead past, but the gravedigger, with his Apocalyptic and revolutionary references, weaves in the possibility of historical short-circuiting, the end of cycles of death and oppression.[79] And, like the mole, the clown is both a 'digger' and a 'worker', but certainly not a ghost. In fact, since there is no exit noted for the gravedigger in any early edition, he may be digging still – like the mole. For Marx, in any case, the appearance of characters like the gravedigger in Shakespeare's plays opened them to the future, not because such characters piously intoned politically correct points of view, but because the 'unregarded men' who form the 'significant and dynamic background' to the main action, carry with them the traces of other histories, other possibilities, which are mostly consigned to work underground, or otherwise out of view: incomplete projects. The ghost conversely is a spectre of repetition, not only in repeating the 'King', but also generically: he wanders in from revenge tragedy, already mouldily unfashionable when Shakespeare wrote *Hamlet*: the dead past.

The *Eighteenth Brumaire* takes as its project an assessment of the skewing of revolutionary energy by the dead past, such that history does not necessarily move – as Hegel asserts that Spirit does in the *History of Philosophy* – 'ever forward'.[80] Revolution, for Marx, since it is a human and earthly process, has no existence beyond what men make in their collective history. Marx's mole, then, is very different from Hegel's, because 'revolution' is not an abstraction that exists apart from the living human beings, whose struggle it is. The Ideal's progress, via Consciousness, is assured. Materialist History's is not. Real human beings, inhabiting specific social structures, do not all have the same interests, and therefore not only act at cross-purposes to each other, but also, often, in misrecognition of their own actions: hence, they 'timidly conjure up spirits of the past' when they are confronted with the possibility of creating 'something which does not yet exist'; furthermore, inhibiting groups disguise the crude and 'limited content of their struggles' in heroic language and imagery, while the groups with genuine revolutionary potential encounter 'repeated interruptions of their own course', and thus they must 'return to what has apparently already been accomplished in order to begin the task again' (150). In this way, Marx makes a distinction between the groups who take repetition as their strategy, or even their goal, and those whose movements are impeded by repetition – the first use the dead past as a crutch or smokescreen, while the latter use the 'repeated' challenges to their forward movement as a chance to hone their skills for future struggle ('they constantly engage in self-criticism'). When Marx likens revolution to the 'old mole', he does so in the context of a process that is anything but straightforward or certain, and which depends upon worker revolt on its own, unprecedented terms – not spectral repetition – to succeed.

For this reason, Marx has none of the triumphal certitude of Hegel; his use of *Hamlet* in the *Eighteenth Brumaire* is closer to the tragic outrage of its fifth act than to the subversive irreverence of its first, from which the 'old mole' comes. Marx finds himself in Horatio's position of storyteller at a time of 'plots and errors' (5.2.394). His contempt for the antics of the bumbling Napoleon III is manifest, but he nonetheless recognizes that the suffering, especially the 'blood of the Paris proletariat' that flowed in its streets, is no farce. The revolution, forced to 'the underworld of history', burrows through miseries Marx meticulously documents as costs too high, better averted (241). He is not, then, providing a road map for revolution as a repetition of the past, nor is he making any promises concerning the future, even in his bitter image of a Europe one day rising up to acknowledge the forces that its elites have so effectively buried, mole-like – for the moment. The revolution's underground course will, of necessity, as in the past, be irregular and unpredictable – and it will get nowhere at all if men don't struggle to 'make history' along just lines. Rather than a map, then, *Eighteenth Brumaire* offers a cautionary tale of a dead end – which Marx recodes as an incomplete project, awaiting a redeeming comic ending, presaged by the gravedigger's memory of revolts past and Apocalypse to come. In the meantime, repetition, according to Marx, is our tragedy.

It is not, however, an inevitable script. As tragic as human history has been heretofore, Marx insists the last act is yet to come. History, for Marx, we must recall, is like Shakespearean drama, in which comedy and tragedy, clowns and kings, intermingle, and the final act might go either way. Thus a brief speech Marx delivered at the anniversary of the *People's Paper* has a much more hopeful tone than the *Eighteenth Brumaire*. It opens with a reflection on the 'so-called revolutions of 1848' and concedes that it merely produced 'small cracks and fissures in the dry crust of European society'; but, Marx adds, when one looked 'beneath the apparently solid surface' one discovered 'oceans of liquid matter, only needing expansion to rend into fragments continents of hard rock'.[81] He uses this volcanic image to arouse and encourage the workers, pointing out that not only below the surface, but everywhere, the pressure for change is palpable: 'the atmosphere in which we live weighs upon everyone with a 20,000 lb force.' This force is a sort of materialist irony – the trope dialectic enacts – since every claim and act of capitalism is accompanied by its opposite: 'In our days, everything seems pregnant with its contrary: Machinery, gifted with the wonderful power of shortening and fructifying human labour, we behold starving and overworking it; The newfangled sources of wealth, by some strange weird spell, are turned into sources of want; The victories of art seem bought by the loss of character.' After elaborating the contradictions of the moment a little further, Marx concludes with a reprise of the 'mole' metaphor from the *Eighteenth Brumaire*, but transforms it too: 'In the signs that bewilder the middle class, the aristocracy and the poor prophets of regression, we do recognise our brave friend, Robin Goodfellow, the old mole that can work in the earth so fast, that worthy pioneer – the Revolution.' The tone here is as confident and encouraging as the *Eighteenth Brumaire*'s was exasperated. It is also, pointedly, written in the present rather than the future tense. Since conditions for Revolution had not improved by 1856 when Marx made this speech, the genre and context instead must account for the difference. Not all comedy, apparently, is the farce in which Napoleon III had been playing a leading role; to the contrary, the deployment of Robin Goodfellow in such obviously positive terms here, as the mole's alter ego, engages comedy as an ambassador of hope not derision: working-class dreams – midsummer or otherwise – have a material basis and can be realized, if the tricksters and the gravediggers would combine their forces.

The movement from tragedy to comedy is also crucial. I noted above that Marx's citations of Shakespeare do not typically come from the tragedies – a norm for which the 'old mole' is a conspicuous exception. What we find in Marx's use of the mole, though, is an emphasis on its burrowing away from the tragedy in which it finds itself toward comedy. When Marx explicitly combines the mole with a clown in the *People's Paper* speech, he underscores that history is a script that we not only must be open to, but must work to transform. Puck, we should recall, is a fairy and a prankster, but also a worker: 'Those that Hobgoblin call you, and sweet Puck, / You do their work, and they shall have good luck' (2.1.40–1). He even makes the play's final speech, broom in hand, as if he were not only a fairy-clown, but a stagekeeper, the playhouse employee who swept the stage. His appearance in Marx's speech is added evidence for the association of Marx's mole with the gravedigger (another worker-clown) in *Hamlet* – as I have argued for above – rather than the ghost. A clown-mole also takes the emphasis from tragedy and the threat of repetition, and allies the figure emphatically with comedy and rupture. Clowns rescript and steal the show, just as the workers are enjoined to do. The cycle of oppression can be broken at last, if we keep brooms at the ready to sweep a comedy from the relentless jaws of the tragedy of our own, not Nature's, making.

Back to the land?

To 'Shakespearise', we have learned, is to be open to the full range of social forces and relations rather than being bound to any particular narrow ideological script, past or present. All great art, for Marx, is inhabited by possibilities for a liberated future denied by these ideological scripts, although often the alternatives can only be found at the margins, or in the 'background', of drama or other such works. As we have seen, this prompts him to deploy Shakespeare quotations very differently from the way a scholar producing a 'reading' would be likely to do. In any case, no matter what he is interpreting, his method is exactly the opposite of Wilhelm's in Goethe's novel, as I showed earlier, since Marx seeks to expose contradictions rather than to explain them away. And, yet, his command of Shakespeare and his respect for the perspectives his plays open up could hardly be greater. Keeping this in mind, I have been trying to show that though he may not look like much of a 'Shakespearean' in practice, especially when compared to scholars or directors, he is a very Great Shakespearean indeed, when considered from the point of view of his own project, which so frequently required him, in effect, to 'Shakespearise'.

The 'Shakespearise' advice he gives to Lassalle illustrates Marx's investment in art's relation to history understood as 1) a site of struggle, 2) an effect of human making (albeit not under conditions of our own choosing) and 3) therefore ultimately capable of putting an end to the unnatural (i.e. historical) 'cycles' of oppression that have characterized human existence hitherto. Such a break with the past would require a new kind of 'revolution' – rupture rather than repetition – and a rescripting of history in terms of comedy rather than tragedy (or farce). This view casts the past as a site of both dead and living forces – constraints and incomplete projects en route to liberation – whose effects on any given situation are not entirely predictable in advance. It also implies 'teleology' in the weak sense of people working collectively toward a goal, rather than the strong sense of History or God having a goal in mind. This emancipatory goal had not been achieved when Marx was writing, and, obviously, still has not. To the contrary, explicit and implicit cycles thematize everyday life to a remarkable degree, as fashion, politics, popular culture and even postmodern theory empty out the past into one long smorgasbord of citable moments, which keep us firmly embedded in the status quo, while the 'new' is declared again and again. In the face of this repetition, radical theory in the early years of the new millennium has seen a highly visible return to questions of Marxism and rupture in figures such as Alain Badiou and Slavoj Žižek. In Shakespeare Studies, however, explicit Marxism remains quite marginalized. Nevertheless, arguably, in it, as in 'English' more generally, the imprint of Marx – and Freud – is so deep and pervasive that it affects reading practices and habits of historicizing, even when the

theoretical roots are no longer recognized, keeping Marx, however unconsciously, a site of struggle in our field.[82]

So when Marx is adduced – consciously and carefully – in Shakespeare
Studies, one is compelled to take notice. In a brilliant reading of *Hamlet*,
Margreta de Grazia has argued recently that Marx's account of primitive
accumulation and Hegel's *Philosophy of History*, with their emphasis on 'land
that is left behind', have so deeply permeated modern thought that it inflects
Hamlet in a way that goes against the grain – or rather ground – of the play.[83]
This is so much the case, she implies, that even many critics who are not affil-
iated with Marxism (indeed, who may actively eschew it) have internalized
its (and Hegel's) periodizing imperatives, with the result that: 'the critical
tradition that has identified *Hamlet* with the onset of the modern period has
ignored the centrality of land.' She proceeds to show – as part of her larger
project to reinterpret *Hamlet* as concerned above all with succession and
patrimony rather than with consciousness and subjectivity – that the play is
utterly obsessed with land, a preoccupation that she meticulously charts in
her fascinating explorations of conquest, the Doomsday book, Goodman
Delver and even the topography of Tudor graveyards.

The play's refusal to leave land behind manifests itself for her not least in
Hamlet's association of the ghost with a mole – a moment in the play, as we
have seen, that Marx borrowed from Shakespeare (and Hegel) for his own,
quite different purposes. In de Grazia's reading, the polyvocal resonances
of 'mole' link human flesh (mole on the skin) and earth (mould – a variant
spelling of mole, from the Old English *mouldwarpe*), and draw the image
sharply in the direction of a recursive world history, at odds with what
she views as the modern (Hegel–Marx) 'linear' one.[84] She thus associates
Hamlet's mole with 'revolution' in what she takes to be its unmodern sense
of repetition, in contrast with

> Hegel's idealist and Marx's materialist accounts, [in which] the tunneling
> of the mole represents the long hard forward movement of history
> toward an emancipatory end, particularly as it accelerates into the last
> stretch of the modern age. Both metanarratives mark the start of that
> latest stretch with a rupture from land: the former with the Reformation
> and the renunciation of the Holy Land and the latter with primitive
> accumulation and the expropriation of a population from the land. In
> this tradition, *Hamlet* has served to accommodate a parallel trajectory,
> dramatizing the struggle of consciousness, through halting advances, to
> attain self-determination, and its tragic failure to do so. In that modern
> context, land has no place: the mole is in flight from the mold ... [85]

Against this 'tradition', she argues that perhaps we should not be so hasty in abandoning attachment to land – at least when we are reading *Hamlet*, which she argues presents us with a mole that is bound up with 'the biblical narrative in which man's life is rounded with dust'.

These are not, however, elements of the play that Marx himself would have found irrelevant, it seems to me, though his emphases are different. In fact, as any reader of de Grazia's book and this chapter would realize, our readings overlap as much as they diverge. This is because Marx's attention to what Williams called 'unregarded men' leads him to notice that many details of history are lost or obscured, and thus must be dredged up by radical historians. In this sense, Marx, as de Grazia, fervently insisted that in order to make the 'modern', much had to be forgotten – and he agrees that land is central to the story. Where they differ is on what primitive accumulation means. For Marx, it points to the origins of capitalism, not 'modernity' per se, which, arguably, Marx would insist we do not yet inhabit, given that Capitalist 'modernity' exhibits a dismaying proclivity for repetition; Adorno and Horkheimer made this argument explicitly in *Dialectic of Enlightenment*. In any case, Marx's (and Marxist) periodization puts primary emphasis on the mode of production, not 'modernity'. Furthermore, whatever scholars working in the 'tradition' of associating Hamlet with the 'modern' may be guilty of, Marx is so far from advocating any sort of sanctioned ignorance about historical struggle over land, that he makes exposing the negative effects of such repression his central point in the primitive accumulation chapters of *Capital*, at which door de Grazia lays partial responsibility for the 'modern' attitude she finds suspect. It may well be, then, that a 'forgetting' of Marx as much as of 'land' is at fault in producing the 'modern' blind spot she describes.

For Marx, the '*Ursprung*' [origin] of capital covers over a 'secret' just as the commodity form does – in fact, the two secrets are related, and equally damaging. In the case of primitive accumulation, he gets at the 'secret' by way of a challenge to the Judeo–Christian 'nursery tale' which serves as its cover:

> Long, long ago there were two sorts of people; one, the diligent and above all frugal elite; the other, lazy rascals, spending their substance, and more, in riotous living .... Thus it came to pass that the former sort accumulated wealth, and the latter sort finally had nothing to sell except their own skins. And from this original sin dates the poverty of the great majority who, despite all their labour, have up to now nothing to sell but themselves, and the wealth of the few that increases constantly, although

they have long ceased to work. Such insipid childishness is every day preached to us in the defense of property (873–4).

The problem, of course, is not with story-telling per se (even though Marx is a materialist), but that the story pushes from view the 'conquest, enslavement, robbery, murder, in short, force' that was, and is, required to establish and maintain capitalism, and thus impedes revolutionary resistance (874).

And it is a repeated violence. Primitive accumulation was only very partially completed in its 'pure form' as Marx describes it in the final chapters of *Capital*. When he was writing, in fact, the vast majority of persons on the planet – including in Europe – would still have been both rural and involved in agriculture in some way. The global population was not even half urban until 2009.[86] Primitive accumulation is, then, as Richard Halpern has argued, necessarily a theoretical explanation, not a historicist one, and, as much recent Marxist theory has emphasized, it is also an ongoing project, a site of continuous, vicious repetition wherever capital establishes itself, or re-establishes itself after a period of neglect.[87] The theory of primitive accumulation, in fact, seeks to explain the origin of capital, beginning not with historical conditions as *Eighteenth Brumaire* does, but from a logical and conceptual proposition: to be forced to sell their labour, workers must have no other choice – there must be no other recourse to the 'means of production' than via the capitalist owner of them. It suggests how a particular set of social relations would most likely emerge – especially one between buyers and sellers of labour power – to replace earlier more explicit forms of oppression, in which elites either owned the labourer outright (slavery) or used repressive apparatuses to regulate (or exclude) him as a serf or guild-member (Feudalism): 'the process ... which creates the capital-relation can be nothing other than the process which divorces the worker from the ownership of the conditions of his own labor' (874). Land, of course, is the fundamental means of production, so it figures prominently in the account of the historical unfolding of primitive accumulation in England that Marx then goes on to narrate, but it is a struggle over land as a means of production he describes, not a leaving of it behind. Thus, Marx's mole's journey through, and ultimate explosive emergence from, the soil figures a goal of rupture with this set of oppressive social relations set in motion by dispossession of the peasantry from land, not a rupture with land itself. With industrialization, the productivity of land may increase such that fewer people are required to work it, but land cannot be 'left behind' completely. Indeed, the bulk of

persons actually working the soil – as farm labourers, gravediggers, miners
and so on – were in the main the very same persons that had been working
it before their dispossession. Their relationship to it and each other, as
well as to elites, changes, but only to repeat the old script of inequality and
oppression in a new form. So there is change, yes – but also repetition – far,
far too much repetition, from Marx's point of view.

The *Eighteenth Brumaire* is intent on diagnosing the failure of revolution
as rupture, and, in the end, it too brings us to land and repetition. Its
final chapter, where the old mole appears, is particularly preoccupied with
land, since in it, Marx finally offers the historical punchline to the grim
joke that was the rise to power of Napoleon III: the peasants. Napoleon
III was able to circumnavigate various elites and consolidate his autocratic
rule by winning the support of the peasantry – the vast majority of the
population in France at the time. He accomplished this remarkable feat,
Marx argues, despite the fact that the interests of the peasants as a group
were actually not well served by his mediocre rule, because their isolation
on smallholdings at an extremely low level of development limited them
intellectually, politically, socially and economically. The poverty of French
peasants was so dire because – even though the first Napoleon had won
their support by his land redistribution schemes that made peasant 'private
property' the norm in the French countryside – the place of the feudal
landlords in sloughing off a surplus from agricultural labour was quickly
taken up by the banks, who reduced the rural population to a primitive,
animalistic existence as an effect of grinding indebtedness:

> the peasant's small holding is now only a pretext that allows the
> capitalist to draw profits, interest and rent from the soil, while leaving
> the tiller himself to work out how to extract the wage for his labor. The
> mortgage debt burdening the soil of France imposes on the French
> peasantry an interest payment equal to the annual interest on the entire
> British national debt. Owing to this enslavement by capital ... small
> peasant property has transformed the mass of the French nation into
> Troglodytes. Sixteen million peasants (including women and children)
> live in hovels [*Höhlen*], many of which have only one opening ... (242).

Whereas once he had been bound to the soil as a serf, the post-Napoleonic
peasant is now bound to the soil as a debtor, a position all the more galling
because it is overlaid with the ideology that he is a 'free' proprietor of
the soil. The serf was made 'free', Marx emphasizes, to be reduced to
endebted servitude to capital and a continuing primitive existence – not

only working the soil, but actually inhabiting it. '*Höhle*', it should be underscored, is not really the German word for 'hovel' (which would be '*Hütte*', a humble manmade shelter) but rather for 'cave', 'hole' or 'burrow', which picks up directly on Marx's 'Troglodyte' image. 'Burrow' seems an especially good fit here, in fact, since it better puts us in mind not only of Troglodytes, but also of moles – as it should, since such associations have a long history.

Already in Shakespeare's time the 'poorer sort' might be associated with moles, either because they worked underground (as, for example, miners) or because they were forced to live in 'burrows':

> The Towne of Nottingham is seated on a Hill, which Hill is almost of one stony Rocke, or a soft kinde of penetrable sandy stone; it hath very faire buildings, many large streetes, and a spacious Market place: a great number of the inhabitants (especially the poorer sort) doe dwell in vaults, holes, or caves, which are cut and digged out of, (or within) the Rocke: so that if a man be destitute of a house, it is but to goe to Nottingham, and with a Mattock, a Shovell, a Crow of Iron, a Chizell, and Mallet, and such instruments, he may play the Mole, the Cunny, or the Pioner, and worke himselfe a Hole, or a Burrow for him and his family: Where, over their heads the grasse and pasture growes, and beasts do feed; faire Orchards and gardens are their coverings, and Cowes are milkt upon the tops of their houses.[88]

That a 'great number' of people would have lived thus, in a city where there were 'very faire buildings, [and] many large streetes' in the early seventeenth century when *Hamlet* was first being performed, gives an added poignancy to the Sexton's 'gravedigger' riddle, since the houses of these living peasants are virtually indistinguishable from those of the dead. It inflects, too, potential peasant revolt, which can even more strongly evoke the Apocalypse: the living rising up from their grave-like dwellings in anticipation of the dead doing so.[89] In Marx, this anticipatory Apocalypse is secularized: when Marx witnessed the mol(e)lification of the peasantry of his own time, reduced to living in 'vaults, holes or caves', he links them to potential revolution, alongside the proletariat, with no divine intervention or inspiration required. What would be required, however, is exposure of the ideology that blamed the poor for their plight, or associated it with an ineradicable 'nature', rather than showing it to be an effect of social structures that can be transformed by organized resistance.

Marx would not have been surprised or embarrassed, then, to be confronted with a *Hamlet* whose central action concerns elite struggles over land, or Hamlet's dispossession, or one in which the 'old mole' and 'revolution' are tamed into cycles expressed in Biblical themes of flesh and grass. Everything in his writing suggests that he would have expected this. Nor would these themes have undermined his appreciation of the play. However, given his interest in the peasant revolt, and peasants as a force that can be ruptural or regressive, I suggest that this interest, too, decisively inflected the mole Marx extracted from the play. *Hamlet* has both regressive and progressive potential woven into it: the traces of history that have left their mark. Some strands in the play – at any given moment – belong to the dead past, repetition, conservatism; others belong to its emancipatory aspirations, its 'future' – incomplete liberatory projects. Marx would have us be open to the latter, while recognizing the former. *Hamlet*, then, could not be situated at the origin of the 'modern' for Marx in any simple sense, and yet a gesture toward a (post-Capitalist) modernity worth having is bound up in its fabric. Marx always read Shakespeare in this way as an ally, foregrounding with him incomplete struggles for liberation, and furthering them – a project which is not literary criticism in the typical sense of the term, to be sure, but it is nonetheless a use of Shakespeare that he – and we – cannot live without.

****

In the mid-1960s, even before the dashed hopes of 1968, Michel Foucault infamously asserted that 'Marxism exists in nineteenth century thought like a fish in water; that is, unable to breathe anywhere else.'[90] There are countless ways to consign Marx to the land of the dead, and to continue to 'speak with the dead' – as manifestly many still do, in the case of both Marx and Shakespeare.[91] As I write these words in 2011, however, Marxism is still breathing away in millennial waters, not only in radical theory, but in the popular imagination of peasant insurgencies and urban uprisings alike around the globe. I am invested in this living Marx, not a dead one, just as he was invested in a living Shakespeare, not a dead one. Shakespeare's scripts were cross-hatched for Marx with a rich 'background' that gave the numerous forces and voices of history play: the clowns as well as the heroes – and ghosts. This formal attribute opened his texts to alternative futures that Shakespeare himself could barely have imagined, if at all. It was these alternative possibilities, however – the heteroglossic struggles in the text – that drew Marx to Shakespeare again and again. This is not a Shakespearean's Shakespeare, perhaps, but it is a vital one. Along these lines, my chapter has argued for a Marxism understood as an 'incomplete project' – part of the 'Long Revolution' as Raymond Williams put it – just as, I have suggested, Marx understood Shakespeare.[92] Toward the still living hope of a world in which 'the free development of each is the condition of the free development of all', we, too, need to collect all the allies that we can.

Chapter 2

Marxism and Shakespeare

Jean E. Howard

The task we've set for the second part of this essay is to take up the question – not of how Marx read Shakespeare or what we can glean from Marx's reading of literature about what a Marxist aesthetics might entail – but, rather, how Anglo–American academic critics in the latter part of the twentieth and the beginning of the twentieth-first century have used the resources of the Marxist tradition in their work as Shakespeare critics. I argue that since the theoretical turn in Shakespeare studies in the late 1970s, Marxism, while far from the dominant critical paradigm, has been an important critical force. Its power has come not only from the many significant books of Marxist Shakespeare criticism that have been written during this time, many of which I discuss below, but also from its imbrication with, and sometimes its critique of, other forms of political criticism.[1] Not only Marx's own writings, but also the work of Lukács, Brecht, Macherey, Althusser, Delphy, Barrett, Jameson, Williams, Adorno, Horkheimer and others have been important to the Marxist and Marxist-influenced Shakespeare criticism of the last 40 years. Studies of genre, popular culture, historical reception, performance and appropriation are but a few of the arenas where the effects of this dense and varied Marxist literary tradition can be felt.

In what follows, I begin by examining some of the self-identified Marxist critics who have importantly shaped the course of current Shakespeare studies, and then trace the ways in which Marxism has played a role in the development of various forms of political criticism including new historicism, cultural materialism, feminism, political forms of poststructuralism and presentism. I can't catalogue all those critics influenced by Marxism or map all the territories where Marxism and Shakespeare have met in the last 40 years; instead, I focus on what seem to me some of the most important *kinds* of Marxist Shakespeare criticism currently practised and on those forms of political criticism where the impress of historical materialism is most pronounced or most lacking.

I do not want to suggest, of course, that Anglo–American Marxist Shakespeare criticism began in the 1970s. The Great Depression of the 1930s and the run-up to World War II, for example, called forth a wave of Marxist literary study, including the extensive writings of Christopher Caudwell, a member of the British Community Party who died fighting Fascism in the International Brigades in Spain. His flat reflectionist criticism, which assumed that literature directly reflects socio-economic forces external to itself as represented in the world view of particular classes, did little to inspire faith in the explanatory power of Marxist cultural analysis. A more explicit focus on early modern drama and a more flexible critical practice were exemplified by the work of L. C. Knights. His *Drama and Society in the Age of Shakespeare* provided a Marxist-influenced analysis of the rise of city comedy in relationship to the development of the changing commercial culture of early modern England.[2] Knights, however, had little to say there about Shakespeare, who largely avoided the genre of city comedy with its explicit thematizations of urbanization, market relations, long-distance trade and the changes in social relations attendant upon the emergence of a proto-capitalist economy.

Rather than rehearse in detail this earlier history of Anglo–American Marxist literary criticism, I have instead taken the 1970s as my launching point. This is in part because, in both the United States and Europe, that decade was one of significant political and cultural change. It saw, for example, the end of the Vietnam War, in part as a result of popular protest, but also the election of Ronald Regan and a rightward turn in American politics; the faltering of the British Labour Party, which after 1979 did not regain power until 1997; and, in both academies, the stirrings of a theory revolution that was to include work in structuralism, poststructuralism, feminism and psychoanalysis. Whether embraced or derided, this theoretical work was to remain central to humanistic study for several decades to come. Marxism's role in this period of theoretical activity and its aftermath is the focus of the rest of this essay; and while there are a number of important Marxist critics of the early modern period who do not work primarily on Shakespeare, including Crystal Bartolovich, David Hawkes, James Holstun and Christopher Kendrick, it is the impact of Marxism on Shakespeare studies that will be my focus here.[3]

Tracing a rough chronological arc from the 1970s to the present and looking at various critical movements in this period and their relationship to Marxism, I argue that an important factor distinguishing one form of political criticism from another is how each theorizes history's relationship to the present and to the future. We have lived through at

least three decades when various kinds of historical criticism have flourished. For some, as I will show below, the alterity of the past has become
an end in itself, marked by a desire to speak with the dead.[4] For others,
although historical difference remains of great importance, part of the
past's significance lies in the critical purchase it allows on the present or
the glimpses of utopian futurity it makes possible. Marxism is a dialectical
historicism that situates the past in a relationship both to the present
and to the future. I would argue that there can be no purely antiquarian
Marxist criticism, nor a Marxist criticism that is not in part oriented
toward the horizon of a more just future. At a time when new historicism
has increasingly dwindled into an antiquarian and oddly positivist mode
of inquiry, it is important to remember other ways of honouring historical
distance while paying attention both to present imperatives and the future
that might be.

Popular Performance Traditions and Generic Forms

One of the most important Marxist literary studies of the 1970s did not
originate in the United States or Britain, but in the German Democratic
Republic, though its influence on the English-speaking world has been
considerable. I refer to Robert Weimann's *Shakespeare and the Popular
Tradition: Studies in the Social Dimension of Dramatic Form and Function*, first
available in German in 1967 but expanded and translated into English
in 1978.[5] It is useful to start with Weimann's book because it gives the
lie to popular caricatures of Marxist criticism as reductive and reflectionist. While it locates the achievement of the Shakespearean stage in
the specific historical conditions of Elizabethan and Jacobean England,
Shakespeare and the Popular Tradition eschews the view that literature simply
reflects historical events or is determined purely by the economic mode
of production. Rather, Weimann argues that the drama of late sixteenth-
century England was itself 'a potent force that helped to create the specific
character and transitional nature of that society' (xii). What it helped to
bring into being, in Weimann's view, was nothing less than the idea of a
nation in which the interests and voices of various classes were held in rich
contrapuntal tension (103). Eschewing purely formalist and ahistorical
modes of criticism, Weimann argues that literature not only arises from a
particular set of historical circumstances, but also contains the capacity to
produce new meanings at future moments of reception and interpretation,
in part because it helps to produce and to anticipate the futures in which

it will be read (xiii). A dialectic conception of the relationship of past, present and future is thus built into Weimann's theoretical model.

When he analyses the particular features of Elizabethan theatre, Weimann puts special emphasis on the popular performance traditions that formed one strand of the complex mixture of cultural forces present during the transition to a capitalist social formation. He singles out the popular tradition because, as he says, it was rooted in performance practices that involved embodiment rather than in strictly literary culture and because it 'reflected the attitudes of those sections of society engaged in labor and production that were in closest contact with the physical world' (xviii). To a certain extent Weimann sentimentalizes 'the people' and idealizes the relationship between their physical labour and the greatness of the drama to which he argues they contributed; nonetheless, he makes a convincing case that it is from the vernacular performance tradition embodied in medieval mysteries and moralities, Robin Hood pageants and May games, that Shakespeare and his contemporaries took many of the specific conventions and dramatic structures underpinning their practice in the Elizabethan commercial theatres. At the same time, Weimann argues that Shakespeare also embraced humanist learning and the literary culture of the English Renaissance. The complex interplay between popular performance traditions and the poetic density of humanist literary culture explains, for Weimann, the peculiar balance and inclusiveness that he sees exemplified in the Elizabethan theatre.

For Weimann, the authority of popular culture is embodied with particular force in figures such as the clown or the fool who often speak directly to the theatre audience, providing a counterpoint to and a critique of elite figures and their values. Lear's all-licensed fool, Dogberry in *Much Ado* or the Falstaff of the *Henry IV plays* are varied examples of the type, sometimes shrewd and biting, sometimes simple and comic, but always offering an alternative to the ideologies of the powerful. For Weimann, the Elizabethan theatre was at its most resonant when the improvisation, unscripted clowning and acrobatic display associated with the festive and popular aspects of culture vied for pre-eminence with what he sometimes refers to as the authority of the scripted word. Weimann argues that in the late sixteenth century the author had not yet assumed its ascendancy as anchoring authority for textual production.[6] This was to happen only later in the seventeenth century, a change accompanied by the gradual eclipse of many elements of the popular performance tradition.

Weimann, however, is also a formalist who pays careful attention to the ideological implications of a play's internal structures and conventions, and in that regard he weds the best of New Critical practice to his more overt sociological and historical interests. He notes, for example, not only the centrality of the multiple plot to Elizabethan theatre, but focuses in on the counterpoint between the perspectives of different classes that it permits. One of his most striking observations involves the spatial dimensions of Elizabethan performance. Partly as a heuristic device and partly as an actual mapping of stage action, Weimann argues that there was a constant tension in Elizabethan performance between the upstage playing area, the *locus*, associated with political and social authority, and the downstage playing area, the *platea*, where the unscripted actions of the clown, the fool and the vice held sway.[7] This was where the popular performer could engage directly with the audience in asides or in assertive monologues, as when Iago reveals to the audience his intention to undo Othello or when Launcelot Gobbo confides in the audience his intention to leave his master, Shylock. Just as the clown speaks from the *platea*, seducing and entertaining those who have come to see the play, so the monarch speaks from the *locus*, embodying social authority but not able or not willing to silence the fool.

While Weimann has written several other important books, including *Authority and Representation in Early Modern Discourse* and *Author's Pen and Actor's Voice: Playing and Writing in Shakespeare's Theatre*,[8] his most fundamental contributions to the study of Shakespeare have remained remarkably consistent, rooted as they are in a Marxist commitment to the historicity of the material forms of the theatre and to the complicated links between those material forms and the social relations of early modern society. For him, jesting, jigging, scatological gesture and direct address to the audience form what Diana Taylor has described as an embodied repertoire[9] whose meanings would have been recognizable to an audience familiar with popular forms of festivity, and that could be set in various ways against the evolving representational and scripted practices of the commercial theatre. The historical juncture that produced the richest products of this theatre was, in Weimann's view, a fleeting one. If he sees the period from 1590–1610 as a Golden Age for the drama, this theatre's remarkable equipoise was soon lost when the authority of the author overpassed the authority of the common performer. In aesthetic terms, what ensued was a diminishment of the linguistic variety and contrapuntal tension built into the very fabric of Elizabethan drama; in political terms, what followed was a foreclosing of the social inclusiveness that marked Elizabethan theatre at its height.

What Weimann, then, bequeathed to subsequent Shakespeare studies, besides a commitment to exploring the sociology of the drama (i.e. its roots in a particular material stage of social and economic development), is his emphasis on the persistence and importance of popular elements in Elizabethan theatre, his identification of the material stage practices through which those popular elements were embodied, and an acute attention to the various ideological and class positions articulated through the rich contrapuntal structures of the particular mode of drama produced in the decades immediately before and after 1600. His emphasis on the political effects of material forms of performance practice has remained an important influence on critics such as Phyllis Rackin, who uses the distinction between *platea* and *locus* to talk about the dialectic interplay between clown, commoner and king in Shakespeare's histories,[10] and Douglas Bruster, William N. West and Terence Hawkes, all of whose work is represented in a volume dedicated to Weimann, *Rematerializing Shakespeare: Authority and Representation on the Early Modern Stage*.[11] Not all of those represented in that book are Marxists, but all have made compelling use of Weimann's materialist investigations of the performance traditions of the early modern stage and of the complex, historically-structured play of authorities apparent both in the represented world of Shakespeare's plays and also in subsequent interpretations of them.

The effects of popular culture on early modern theatre are also of concern to those Marxist critics particularly influenced by Mikhail Bakhtin's investigations of the carnivalesque.[12] Michael Bristol's *Carnival and Theater: Plebeian Culture and the Structure of Authority in Renaissance England*, for example, gives full weight to the popular dimensions of Shakespeare's theatre and is also interested in the glimpses of utopian futurity released by the energies of carnival inversion.[13] Bristol argues that there was a stubborn persistence to the material forms of plebeian culture experienced in everyday life throughout the early modern period. He does not see the transition to capitalism as a delimited and unified event, but argues for the coexistence of capitalist institutions and practices alongside earlier economic and social forms. For Bristol, the importance of the persistence of traditional forms of popular festivity in the deep structure of early modern drama is the basis they provide for resistance to oppressive forms of social authority. He shows, for example, how the drama draws on practices of travesty, misrule and topsy-turveydom to question established order and to offer alternative ways of organizing social experience based on the rhythms of agricultural production, Carnival and Lent, charivari and Saturnalia. In the drama, Bristol argues, clowning and devilment, the scatological exhibition of the material body and the subversive irreverent laughter they evoke materially express resistance and alterity. Like

Weimann, Bristol refuses to valorize the author over the performer and stresses the centrality of embodied performance to the potential of early modern theatre practice to enact misrule and subversion.

Peter Stallybrass and Allon White's *The Politics and Poetics of Transgression* also draws on Bakhtinian ideas of Carnival to highlight the power of the lower body, particularly in circumstances of heightened political antagonism, to subvert the authority of what a culture marks as 'high',[14] though they argue that the 'low' is always necessary to the self-definition of the high and often ambivalently desired by it (4). Drawing out the early modern theatre's connections to the fair, with its focus on consumption, excess and the grotesque, Stallybrass and White, like Weimann and Bristol, see the theatre as a place of potential plebeian resistance to the pieties of the godly and those entrusted with the maintenance of social order. By contrast, however, they also underscore the nostalgic and regressive potential of carnival and the danger of claiming that its effects are always progressive or subversive (19). Though aspects of their critical practice differ, Weimann, Bristol and Stallybrass and White all take seriously the role of popular or plebeian culture in the formation of early modern theatre and assign to these popular elements a potentially critical or subversive role. This emphasis was to be lost in much 'left' political criticism of the 1980s and 1990s as new historicism increasingly focused on how resistance is socially contained.[15] Increasingly attenuated, also, was Weimann, Bristol and Stallybrass and White's focus on performance and the body of the actor as critical interest shifted to the material history of the book and to the study of drama as text, not performance.[16]

Before turning to these developments, however, and the different kinds of Marxist work that flourished after 1980, I want to look at Walter Cohen's ambitious 1985 study, *Drama of a Nation: Public Theater in Renaissance England and Spain,* particularly for its focus on the grid of early modern theatrical genres as the vehicles through which class struggle was expressed and mediated in the 70 years leading up to the English Civil War.[17] Unabashedly reaching for a totalizing synthesis that would account, in the tradition of Lukács and Jameson, for the similarities between the Renaissance theatres in two countries and across all dramatic genres, and for what he argues was ultimately the revolutionary effects of that theatre, Cohen emphasizes the particular historical circumstances that brought together elite and popular elements on the early modern stage. In undertaking this ambitious project, Cohen acknowledges that his interest in it was spurred by 'the protest movements beginning in the 1960s' (9) and his sense that the revolutionary potential of early modern drama might find its most 'resonant context at least since the seventeenth century' in the social ferment of late twentieth century America (406). Though clearly interested, then, in the plays' original context of production, Cohen also cares about their political effects in the current historical conjuncture. For Cohen, as for Jameson, literary works play different roles at different times in the long struggle to wrest 'a realm of Freedom from a realm of Necessity' (Fredric Jameson, quoted in Cohen, 406). The past is never dead, but persists in the dialectical relationship of past, present and future.

In parsing the mixed nature of early modern theatre, Cohen does not assume the unvaryingly radical potential of popular culture, and he pays more attention than Weimann to the role of the state in setting the conditions of possibility for early modern theatre. In this regard, Cohen's work shows the strong influence of Perry Anderson who, in *Lineages of the Absolutist State*, argues that the centralized absolutist states that came into being in Western Europe in the sixteenth and seventeenth centuries represented an extension of the waning power of the feudal aristocracy but were also essential for the development of capitalism.[18] This state, Cohen argues, was a major factor in fostering the public theatre, but then also in undermining it. Despite their divergences, Cohen's work resembles Weimann's in several particulars, namely (1) in its assumption that the dynamism and inclusiveness of early modern public theatre in both Spain and England depended on the particular conditions attending the transition to a capitalist mode of production and (2) that this theatre drew powerfully on a mixture of elite and popular elements.

For Cohen, the early modern public theatre was thus a site of potential contradiction since many of the themes and concerns of the plays catered to the interests of the aristocratic classes, while the theatrical mode of production remained artisanal. As Cohen says: 'The total theatrical process meant more than, and something different from, what the dramatic text itself meant. The medium and the message were in contradiction, a contradiction that resulted above all from the popular contribution' (183). The history plays provide several illustrations of this point. For example, within the represented action, they depict stories centered on English monarchs, but in the playhouse they subject those fictions to the judgement of the common playgoer and their enactment to the skills of the common player. And within the represented action, a play like *1 Henry IV* sets as foil to the real King the corrosive words of Falstaff, playing king in a tavern.

However, Cohen's most important contribution to the Marxist study of Shakespeare may lie in his approach to genre. Rather than explicating individual plays in detail, Cohen reads broader generic formations and extrapolates from their structure and conventions, and then from what is unsaid or absent, evidence of the forms of class struggle and adaptation being enacted through them. He argues that in the 1580s and 1590s, through the genres of romantic comedy and the national history play, the ruling group accommodated itself to social change, for example, to the increasing power of the mercantile classes. Cross-class marriages, pervasive in 1590s comedy, mark that accommodation and acknowledge the growing power of social groups whose wealth sprang from traffic and trade. By contrast, the satiric comedies and tragedies prevalent after 1600 show what Cohen describes as 'aristocratic failure'; that is, the failure of the ruling class to come to terms with the challenges posed by the bourgeoisie with their mercantile values (as in *Timon of Athens* and *King Lear*) or by a politicized commons (*Coriolanus*). This view of Shakespearean tragedy resonates with Franco Moretti's powerful Marxist essay, '"A Huge Eclipse": Tragic Form and the Deconsecration of Sovereignty', in which he argues that in early modern tragedy the meaning of the absolute monarch was hollowed out and deconsecrated, stripped of its authority, leaving a void opening to a future in which its power could never be re-achieved. [19]

While Cohen's work in general operates at too high a level of abstraction to provide nuanced readings of individual plays, what he achieves instead is a comprehensive mapping of the totality of the early modern dramatic system in relation to the contending classes during the moment of the transition to capitalism. Like Weimann, he assumes the productive power of culture as a force in social struggles, and he retains Weimann's focus on the importance of popular elements in the drama and on the plays as both scripts for performance and as texts. Cohen's emphasis on generic forms as a vehicle for mediating social struggle has been influential with a number of critics including those associated with the 'historical formalist' movement of the past decade. While historical formalists are not always Marxist in orientation, they share with Cohen's brand of Marxist criticism the assumption both that literary forms have histories that affect the meanings they convey and that the formal features of different genres are key to their ideological functioning and their role in mediating competing social interests.[20]

New Historicism and Cultural Materialism

The work I have thus far described situates itself centrally in a Marxist problematic. Collectively, it locates early modern drama in determinate historical conditions, but stresses the relative autonomy of culture as a productive force in its own right; and it is sophisticated about the relationship of the historical past to present and future temporalities. The total picture of 1980s political criticism is more various. Of particular importance is the somewhat disparate work gradually consolidated under the name of the new historicism, though other political criticisms also flourished between 1980–2010. These include British cultural materialism, feminism, queer criticism, postcolonial criticism and presentism. Some of these movements, like feminism, are linked to activist projects of social change outside the academy. Others, like new historicism, were primarily developments within that academy, though spurred by what was happening in the outside world. In their academic forms, all focused on revealing literature's implication in reproducing or contesting power relations, whether those constructed by patriarchy, heteronormativity or a class system. In these varieties of political criticism, Marxism *per se* functioned variously – alive and well in the militant traditions of British cultural materialism – but in American criticism often functioning like a ghost in the background, haunting the critical scene.[21]

Explanations for this flourishing of political criticisms in the 1980s are numerous. In the US, the activism of the Vietnam era, coupled with the Civil Rights movement and then with the emerging forces of feminism, galvanized those who had been in college and graduate school during the 1960s and 1970s. Some kept their professional academic work separate from their social activism; some increasingly saw their academic work *as a form* of social activism; and they undertook, variously, to break down authoritarian modes of teacher-centered instruction, to broaden the canon to include writings by women, working class writers and people of colour, and to develop modes of critical reading that explored the political consequences of 'aesthetic' choices. Many of these critics had little familiarity with Marxism, partly as a legacy of the McCarthy era and the Cold War,[22] partly because of the New Critical principles that had dominated American literary study in the 1950s and 1960s, and partly because Marxist cultural criticism had a reputation for being dogmatic and reductive. Nonetheless, Marxism has continued, as I will show, to manifest itself in a variety of forms up to the present moment.

One of the dominant political criticisms of this period is undoubtedly the so-called new historicism. This is a fraught term, but it has displayed considerable staying power. In the US, it designates a varied body of work produced in its first generation by Stephen Greenblatt and a group of other critics including Louis Montrose, Leonard Tennenhouse and

Steven Mullaney, though none of them has consistently or wholeheartedly accepted that label. In the post-1990s years, a great many critics have been influenced by these first generation new historicists, but rather than trying to name them all and parse all the differences among them, it is perhaps more useful to focus on the primary assumptions and tendencies under-lying this general body of work.[23] As I will argue below, the overall trajectory of new historicism, despite its obvious virtues and the energy it has brought to the field, has bent, with some exceptions, toward political quietism and an undialectical mode of historical inquiry. This is at least partly because of its attenuated relationship to Marxism.

As a critical practice, new historicism involves first and foremost the analysis of power, particularly the role of the monarch and of institutions such as the court and the church in constructing subjects of limited agency. We can see these preoccupations and emphases in Stephen Greenblatt's *Renaissance Self-Fashioning from More to Shakespeare*, undoubtedly the most widely-read critical book to be published about early modern literature in the decade of the 1980s.[24] In taking up the seemingly tired topic of how selves are fashioned in the Renaissance, however, Greenblatt eschewed Jacob Burckhardt's aestheticized theory of a humanist self with self-knowledge and the power to shape itself. Instead, he posited a provisional and divided self, shaped by impersonal historical forces over which it has little control. Each chapter of this path-breaking book looks at how particular sixteenth-century selves were formed as subjects in relationship to specific authorities and their demonized antitheses. The selves Greenblatt examines were both historical, e.g., Sir Thomas More, and fictional, e.g., Shakespeare's Othello. In investigating 'both the social presence to the world of the literary text and the social presence of the world in the literary text' (5), Greenblatt thus suggests that the subjects of literature and of life are equally inscribed by historical forces and discourses. Famously, in the book's final pages he reveals his disconcerting conclusion concerning the un-freedom of the human subjects he has examined. 'In all my texts and documents, there were, so far as I could tell, no moments of pure, unfettered subjectivity; indeed, the human subject itself began to seem remarkably unfree, the ideological product of the relations of power in a particular society' (256).

Elsewhere in his early work, however, Greenblatt employs a somewhat different critical practice. In 'Murdering Peasants: Status, Genre, and the Representation of Rebellion', published in the first issue of *Representations*, Greenblatt comes much closer to a Marxist mode of analysis. Focusing not on individual subjects like More or Othello, but on a class (peasants and common labourers), 'Murdering Peasants' shows how genre can expose the violence visited upon common people who are viewed as rebels by nobles who 'bring order' by shedding their blood.[25] Greenblatt examines the various ways that Dürer, Sidney, Spenser and Shakespeare's task of condoning such bloodshed, if that is indeed their intention, is foiled by the generic templates with which they work, whether those templates are provided by the civic monument or the chivalric romance. The Marxist feel of this essay stems not only from Greenblatt's obvious sympathy for the murdered peasants and his revulsion at the inequalities of power that make their murders possible, but also from his recognition that genre is one of the sites where literature and other cultural productions encode social struggle, a struggle that can be parsed by a reading practice attuned to the contradictions embodied in the work. This essay also registers Greenblatt's characteristic recognition that it is impossible to separate his own location in the present from the history he is able to read off his chosen texts. He writes: ' ... in response to the art of the past, we inevitably register, whether we wish to or not, the shifts in value and interest that are produced in the struggles of social and political life' (14). What he elsewhere characterizes as the tragic impossibility of communing with the dead, he here accepts as the inevitable fact that all contact with the past is inevitably mediated through the present.

If Marxism, however, is discernible in some of Greenblatt's early essays, other influences eventually end up being more important, including the cultural anthropology of Clifford Geertz (from whom new historicists learned to approach the past as a foreign country inciting wonder and requiring interpretation) and above all from the work of Michel Foucault, especially the Foucault of *Discipline and Punish*. It is from Foucault that the new historicists took the idea of the epistemic breaks that supposedly separate one historical period from another, and from Foucault that they drew the idea of the discursive formations tying together different kinds of texts and connecting those texts to authorizing institutions such as the monarchy, the church, the new science. For a Marxist critic like James Holstun, Foucault was important to new historicists primarily because his work allowed them 'to do political criticism without using a Marxist vocabulary'.[26] It was not only a Marxist vocabulary that was missing, however, but also a sense that social struggle could ever be efficacious and that one should pay consistent attention to the dialectical processes linking the past that was the object of analysis, the present from which that past was observed, and the future to which the present might lead.

Of course, new historicism's Foucauldian premises produced many liberating and exciting consequences. New historicists saw themselves as breaking with an older historicism that presented literature as reflecting a stable background of political, religious and intellectual history. Like Marxists, they saw literature as part of what constitutes history, as a productive force in its own right. However, the idea of the epistemic break heightened their sense of the absolute alterity of the past, as did the anthropological investment in its strangeness. From its first moments, new historicism emphasized this 'strangeness' of early modern culture, whether considering the period's sex/gender system, its ways of under-standing the body, its organization of urban space, the rules governing the giving of gifts or the maintenance of social hierarchy. This emphasis on the difference of the past *can* be politically progressive; it can reveal how present social arrangements are contingent and can be changed since there is nothing permanent about human nature or the social structures humans create. But new historicists in general eschewed activist goals, settling instead for 'thick descriptions' of the past. Greenblatt, in fact, has sometimes preferred the term 'poetics of culture' to 'new historicism' to characterize his work, the former term evoking an intention not so much to analyse power relations as to identify the deep structures of a culture and interconnections visible only to the eye of the poet. As early as the intro-duction to *Renaissance Self-Fashioning*, Greenblatt called for a 'poetics of culture' (4–5), and in his later essay, 'Towards a Poetics of Culture', he tells a characteristically self-deprecating and wry story about how he stopped teaching courses in 'Marxist Aesthetics' at Berkeley. After a confrontation with a student about his political beliefs, he decided that 'I wasn't sure whether I was a Menshevik, but I certainly wasn't a Bolshevik', and he then began to teach courses on 'Cultural Poetics'. [27] In the same essay, he claims to be 'uneasy with a politics and a literary perspective that is untouched by Marxist thought, but that doesn't lead me to endorse propositions or embrace a particular philosophy, politics or rhetoric, *faute de mieux*' (2). An evasiveness or ambivalence about his attitude both toward Marxism and the political telos of his criticism remains a consistent feature of Greenblatt's work.

Rather than political optimism or activism, a political pessimism, as many have noted, eventually came to pervade much new historicist work.[28] By the time Greenblatt wrote *Shakespearean Negotiations*, a strong sense of the futility of social struggle was surfacing. In one of his most influential chapters, he looked at the Edgar scenes in *King Lear* to argue that they cite contemporary demonology and exorcism tracts in order to explore how the authority of religious belief was both evoked and evacuated of its power in the play.[29] Through the circulation of social energy, the charisma of the demystified exorcist is transferred to the theatre where it is used to create desire for the very religious certainties that the play has demystified. Spurred to love and desire what is revealed as fiction, the theatregoer is called, not to action, but to nostalgia. This is the mood that also dominates Greenblatt's later book, *Hamlet in Purgatory*, with its evocation of the lost world of Catholic ritual and belief that haunts the world of *Hamlet*.[30]

Of course, the energy released by new historical reading practices and by the compelling critical voice of figures like Greenblatt was considerable. 'The historicity of the text' and 'the textuality of history', in Louis Montrose's famous formulation, became a general rallying cry,[31] authorizing readers to link together familiar and unfamiliar texts, the 'real' and the fictive, and to explore the byways of the foreign land that was the past, often by recourse to the vivid anecdote that seemed to crystallize a moment of 'strangeness'. The less lionized work of Louis Montrose, however, shows a somewhat different potential within new historicism, one more persistently influenced by Marxist traditions, especially the later work of the humanist Marxist, Raymond Williams, whom Montrose uses to distance himself from a model that sees culture as a superstructural reflection of an economic base rather than a relatively autonomous zone within the social whole.[32] Such positions, along with his emphasis on the materiality of ideology, also implicitly link Montrose to an Althusserian problematic, though he also makes extensive use of the work of Victor Turner and Clifford Geertz in arguing that the early modern stage filled a void left in the Elizabethan social formation by the suppression of Catholic ritual and folk custom. In the wake of these suppressions, Montrose argues that the stage enacted 'rites of passages' which gave shape to the social existence of early modern subjects.[33]

A mixture of critical paradigms, then, subtend Montrose's essays, but the Marxist inflections in his work reveal themselves in his steady attention to the way in which literature produces, resolves or exposes the contradictions of a particular social formation. Like Walter Cohen, he sees genre or literary kinds as overarching vehicles for mediating intra- or inter-class struggles, though, unlike Cohen, he also does dazzling and extended readings of individual texts. Montrose is particularly illuminating on Renaissance pastoral, the genre which, in his view, mediates the anxieties of an Elizabethan courtier class fearful about its status and proximity to power.[34] Thus in *As You Like It*, the inequities of primogeniture find resolution through Orlando's marriage to the Duke's daughter, a marriage through which the gifts, patronage and favour of a benevolent ruler will erase the younger brother's former privations.[35] But unlike some examples of new historicist practice, Montrose's writing consistently focuses on the work of critique and eschews nostalgia or ambivalence. If for Montrose the literary text works both to produce and mediate the tensions of a social system, it is the job of the critic to reveal those workings, to examine the contradictions they encode and to reveal the ideological and interested status of the social relations they precariously attempt to naturalize.

As an overall movement, however, new historicism in all its guises stays safely within academic boundaries and is not linked to more overt forms of social activism, especially as successive generations of historical work have become notably more antiquarian and positivist. In that regard, new historicism differs from feminism and queer studies, and to a certain extent from the more overt and militant British cultural materialism often taken to be new historicism's transatlantic twin. Nothing could be less true, though many early accounts of political criticism in the 1980s did not distinguish between the two movements, and many excellent anthologies, even as late as Ivo Kamps's 1995 volume, *Material Shakespeare: A History*, mixed together Marxist and non-Marxist critics.[36] Like new historicism, cultural materialism arose as an extension of broader political developments, namely, as an angry protest against the Tory ascendancy of Margaret Thatcher and the gradual erosion of the power and achievements of the Labour Party. Thatcher's decision to launch the Falklands War, to privatize national industries, and to cut social services galvanized opposition, some of it located in the academy. But unlike American new historicists, British academics had a robust indigenous Marxist tradition upon which to draw.[37] They were not shy about claiming Raymond Williams, Christopher Hill or E. P. Thompson as inspiration, even when they quarrelled with some of the assumptions of their work. Moreover, they were not shy about calling for activism in the arena of the education system itself, a system in which Shakespeare, in their view, played a mystified role. Hence one of the key texts of cultural materialism, the influential anthology *Political Shakespeare: New Essays in Cultural Materialism*, ends with a quartet of essays that explicitly address current political issues concerning Shakespeare's use in the classroom, in the theatre, on film, and of a possible dialectical relationship between Brechtian theatre practice and modern stagings of Shakespeare. Though the book included essays by Greenblatt and Tennenhouse, its tenor was decidedly British and activist in tone. And the decision to include essays dealing with current appropriations and uses of Shakespeare effectively broke down the 'fourth wall' separating the study of past texts from the current moment. If Foucault argued that he was always providing a genealogy of the present, though not a history of continuities, much new historical work, in effect, surgically cut itself off from direct consideration of the 'now' of reception and historical reconstruction even as it in theory acknowledged the impossibility of accessing the present except from one's position in current history.

Not so for the cultural materialists. Jonathan Dollimore's introduction calls for a critical practice that seeks to break down the autonomy of the literary text; to link past and present struggles; to focus on popular and minority cultures rather than simply on dominant culture; to show how texts and social agents resist domination; and to free Shakespeare from the ways in which he has been positioned to reproduce and legitimize power and the powerful. Each of these goals serves the larger end of creating a political criticism that furthers progressive social change in all the institutions of culture where Shakespeare plays a role from government-sponsored theatre to A-level exams.

Dollimore's own highly influential study, *Radical Tragedy: Religion, Ideology and Power in the Drama of Shakespeare and His Contemporaries*, also differs markedly from new historicism in eschewing 'thick description' and an anthropological approach to the early modern as a foreign country.[38] Engaged in the practice of ideology critique, Dollimore enlists Renaissance tragedy as his accomplice. His book presses the case that in the early seventeenth century the theatre played a special role in undermining the legitimacy of key social institutions such as the church and the crown by subjecting them to 'skeptical, interrogative and subversive representa-tions' (4). Taking as his target Tillyard and Lovejoy's view of early modern England as dominated by an ideology of harmonious and hierarchical social order, Dollimore instead draws on Raymond Williams's view of the social formation as composed of residual, dominant and emergent elements to show conflicts within the culture and to point to ideological fissures and contradictions identifiable at the level of cultural representation.

For Dollimore, Renaissance tragedy is the example *par excellence* of a generic formation that by its skeptical highlighting of contradictions reveals, for example, the constructed and interested nature of religious truth and its role in securing the power of the clergy. In submitting the major tragedies of the English Renaissance to demystifying critique, Dollimore places those texts in conversation with skeptical figures such as Montaigne and Machiavelli, in particular, who seem to him to foreshadow Althusser's ideas about the legitimating and material force of ideology. Whether or not the tragedy of the period is as thoroughly saturated by a skeptical demysti-fication of the social order as Dollimore insists, it is certainly true that such demystification is the aim and end of Dollimore's own criticism which, eschewing new historicism's fascination with the corners and odd by-ways of obscure texts, takes head on the central canonical texts of the dramatic canon. Dollimore, however, is finally more interested in ideology than in history, and for the most part he says little about the actual material conditions in which his tragic texts were produced, received and reproduced. As others have noted, *Radical Tragedy* ends up being a surprisingly idealist account of the anti-idealizing tendencies in early modern tragedy. Invested in the history of ideas, it pays little attention to the cultural embeddedness or the performative elements of the works it studies.[39]

What perhaps most unifies the work of Dollimore, Alan Sinfield, Terence Hawkes and others who became identified with British cultural materialism is, however, their relentless critique of the idea of an unchanging human nature and an essential selfhood untouched by history or culture. As materialist critics, all find particularly pernicious the uses to which such ideologies can be put since they frequently are used to obscure the material conditions that create social identities and inequalities, and to underwrite the view that what is, is right. In *Radical Tragedy,* Dollimore see plays such as *King Lear* providing a skeptical critique of the central tenets of essentialist humanism and its Christian analogues, rather than a play about the persistence of a common humanity; *Lear* for him is a play about 'power, property and inheritance' (197).

In taking aim at essentialist humanism, the British cultural materialists attacked an ideology that only fully took root at a period much later than the Jacobean era, but the utilization of Shakespeare in reproducing this ideology was at the heart of their critique and of a piece with the presentist aims of much of their critical work. For them, engagement with past literature, and especially with canonical texts, was motivated by the desire to create change in the present, an aim seldom overtly articulated by American new historicists.

The 1980s, then, produced an outpouring of political criticism of Shakespeare, the forms of which varied. Some of it directly connected to Marxist modes of ideology critique and the material analysis of performance practices and literary genres, but much of it took the form of a politically deracinated 'poetics of culture' distanced both from activist agendas and from any overt affiliation with Marxism. There were, however, further developments within Marxism that next deserve attention.

Poststructuralism and Marxism

In the welter of theoretical discourses advanced in the 1980s, poststructuralism has an important place. Beginning as a critique of structural linguistics and anthropology, in particular, both of which attempted to identify the rules or structures underlying all cultures and languages, poststructuralism instead argues for the impossibility of such universals. It further posits that human subjects are not free originators of meaning but are themselves written or constituted by the discourses of culture (hence the 'death of the author'); and it shows, time and again, how the binaries structuring thought and representation turn into versions of one another, destabilizing meaning and opening space for linguistic play. Many of the political critics I have been discussing were affected to some degree by poststructuralist thought. Part of the pessimism about successful resistance to power in some new historicist work, for example, can be attributed to theories of language that see the subject inscribed, deterministically, by discourses of which he or she is not the origin nor in a position to resist; and part to the powerful effects on new historical thought of Foucault's writings on the disciplinary effects of power.

However, many critics have found poststructuralist thought compatible with their oppositional political agendas. For some Marxists, the poststructuralist work of Louis Althusser has been particularly important for developing a theory of the relative autonomy of the cultural sphere from the economic and political spheres, and in showing the way that subjects are hailed or interpellated by ideological state apparatuses and invited to accept as natural their roles in a society ordered by hierarchies of class, gender and race (though, because of their multiple interpellations, also positioned to discern contradiction and to exercise agency).[40] Critics like Dollimore reveal a clear debt to Althusser's work on ideology, and Marxist critics like Terence Hawkes mine the instabilities of Shakespearean language to unmoor his plays from the official, high culture uses to which they are frequently put and to reposition them in irreverent and oppositional ways.[41]

I want to focus here, however, on the publication of a particularly unusual and important book, Richard Halpern's *The Poetics of Primitive Accumulation*, that attempted both to take account of poststructuralist critiques of Marxism's reputed economic determinism and teleological view of history and also to put into dialogue Marx and Foucault, the lodestar of the new historicists.[42] The title of Halpern's book tips his hand. Referring to but revising Greenblatt's 'poetics of culture', Halpern insists that what interests him is the poetic or cultural dimensions of that aspect of the transition to capitalism that involves 'primitive accumulation'. By this he means the slow processes by which peasants and artisans were deprived of control of the means of production and transformed into wage labourers for the purpose of extracting profit from their work. Focusing on this fairly straightforward definition of the process of primitive accumulation, Halpern was able to talk about aspects of economic life not usually encompassed by the juridical and political models of power employed by new historicism: about, for example, enclosures, the accumulation of merchant capital, the transformation of the aristocracy from a warrior to a consuming class, the increasingly invisible extraction of surplus value from wage labourers. But the genius of the book, and a mark of its own participation in the postmodern disruption of totalizing narratives, is to argue (1) that the process of primitive accumulation involves more than economic accumulation and (2) that economic developments did not always precede the emergence of the political and cultural phenomena we associate with capitalism. In short, though his project involves a consideration of economic development, it does not reduce all other social phenomena to an effect of the economic. Moreover, it defines primitive accumulation not only as the accumulation of profit from the expropriation of labour power, but also as the accumulation of certain kinds of men with certain kinds of skills and capacities. In so doing, Halpern claims to be following up Foucault's throwaway remark that the histories of discipline and of capital supplement one another, the one involving transformation of subjects, the other the transformations of the mode of production in which those subjects learn to 'work by themselves'.

With this framework in place, Halpern goes on to look at what one could call instances of strangeness in early modern culture: the preoccupation in humanist pedagogy with questions of style rather than content; the puzzling disjuncture in Skelton's work between a slavish desire to serve Wolsey and the King and a mad attack on the persons and policies of both; the contradiction in More's *Utopia* between the emphasis on use value and a society based on socialist principles, and the many signs that what underwrites this utopia is the logic of capitalism itself; the gap in Spenser's *The Shepheardes Calender* between a text evincing nostalgia for the narratives that bind communities in common knowledge and the glosses that embody the logic of science and abstract reason. In each case, Halpern offers an explanation of the seeming anomalies and contradictions that takes into consideration the multiple processes of primitive accumulation that inform the transition to capitalism. In regard to Tudor pedagogy, for example, he discusses the way it does not so much inculcate ideology as instill habits of self-regulation and the production – through the loose imitation of masters – of the empty heterogeneity that will define the bourgeois subject. And in regard to Skelton, he discusses the way the mock-heroic sprawl of *Phyllyp Sparowe* constitutes resistance to the centralizing tendencies of Tudor absolutism, at the same time that Skelton was living the emergent side of the transition and fashioning himself – not as a feudal retainer, but as a useful civil servant.

Halpern's Renaissance is in many ways as strange as Greenblatt's, but it differs in several important ways, the most important being that for Halpern the strangeness is not the exotic otherness of a foreign land whose strange ways must be mapped by a poetics of culture, but rather the product of determinate historical conditions in which the several parts of the social whole – economic, political and cultural – relate, though not in a neatly determinative or homologous way. The move Halpern repeatedly makes is to go from a description of economic processes, such as the seizure of monastic lands by the crown or the development of proto-capitalist agricultural practices, to a consideration of political processes, such as the centralization of certain administrative powers under the Tudors, to an examination of a co-temporal cultural phenomenon, such as the development of humanist pedagogical practices or the layered construction of Spenser's *Fairie Queene*. This procedure assumes interconnections and determinate conditions of possibility for cultural productions, but not strict lines of determinism.

Ironically, new historicist accounts of early modern culture seem at once more random and more premised on a single all-controlling centre of power than Halpern's. The infamous new historicist practice of using an anecdote to begin an essay often seems random, yet the governing assumption behind the practice seems to be that there is no privileged point of access to a culture's practices, that careful reading at any point of entry is able to give evidence of the discursive rules governing that culture's sense-making procedures. In an important sense, the culture is conceived as a series of homologous layers, saturated with sameness, the law of the episteme.[43] And the theory of power that accompanies this account of culture is equally saturating. Nothing happens that is not eventually captured by the recuperative force of those on top. Hence, of course, the notorious difficulty new historicists have in explaining why things change.

Halpern's account of the social formation, though striving for a sense of interconnections, leaves a lot more room for randomness, dysfunction, dead ends and resistance than does Foucault's. For Halpern, certain

determinate conditions shape historical possibilities, but no single force
motors historical development and change. He is clear, for example,
about the limits of Tudor and Stuart absolutism. Whatever its pretensions, it did not have sufficient control of economic resources to free itself
from Parliament or to impose control over vast domains of culture. To
take another instance, humanist pedagogy, Halpern argues, also largely
developed outside royal control, and though one of its consequences was
the production of disciplined subjects set apart from popular culture and
suited for civil service, that was not the only or the inevitable effect of this
phenomenon. Such schooling also provided a route for upward mobility
and involved the development of a 'discourse of capacities', meaning a way
of sorting people in terms of their supposed innate abilities, regardless
of birth and background. In reality, this discourse of capacities could be
used to justify disposing of the culturally disadvantaged as lazy, just as in
modern high school tracking systems, but it could also be used to justify
cross-class mobility. It was, in short, a place where social struggle could and
did occur, with variable outcomes. Halpern gives us, then, a picture of early
modern England where real and not just pre-scripted resistance occurred
and *could* occur because of the relative autonomy of the various parts of the
social whole, the unevenness of capitalist development and the weakness
of political structures of control. High on sheer explanatory power, *The
Poetics of Primitive Accumulation* is one of the most important Marxist books
to emerge from the theoretical revolution of the 1980s. Influenced by
poststructuralist thought, Halpern nonetheless manages to keep Marxism
at the centre of his work.

Feminism and Marxism

If Marxism is a collective project that lives because it changes, some of the
biggest changes in Marxist Shakespeare criticism in the last three decades
have involved the incorporation of gender into materialist accounts of the
plays and their afterlives. It is fair to say that, before the 1980s, little Anglo–
American Shakespeare criticism written from a materialist perspective
emphasized the role of gender as a central category in social struggles, the
material practices through which gender difference was produced or its
role in the creation of surplus value and the social and biological reproduction of exploitable labour. This despite the fact that, from the time of
Engels's *The Origins of the Family, Private Property and the State*,[44] there had
been a discussion of gender, however underdeveloped, within the Marxist

tradition; and despite the fact that Alice Clark's early book, *The Working Life of Women in the Seventeenth Century,* had raised important questions about what the transition to capitalism meant for women's labour status, their role in guilds and professions, and their ability to assume authority outside the household.[45]

However, the renewal of feminism as a social movement in the 1970s and its incorporation into the academy by the 1980s made urgent the question of feminism's place among, and as part of, the decade's proliferation of political criticisms.[46] Many feminists objected to what they saw as new histor-icism's indifference to feminist issues and fascination with male-dominated court culture;[47] and many saw Marxism as dominated by veneration of theoretical fathers who at best paid lip service to the analysis of gendered exploitation.[48] Nonetheless, over the course of the decade, alliances were struck; feminism, shedding its residual essentialism, adopted and modified many of the practices of the new historicism even as new historicists began to take on board the analysis of gender; and many feminists came to see Marxism as an ally in its overt commitment to social change and its critique of existing material conditions. While some feminist work on Shakespeare retained a psychoanalytic underpinning, this was not universally true, though interest in the domestic sphere, in marriage and in genres such as comedy, all remain hallmarks of much feminist criticism.

Feminist work that affiliates itself with Marxism in the American context has often called itself materialist feminism, a term incorporated into the subtitle of Valerie Wayne's important 1991 anthology, *The Matter of Difference: Materialist Feminist Criticism of Shakespeare.*[49] In some ways, the term is an evasion, a way to avoid public alliance with Marxism, and sometimes the 'materialism' in materialist feminism can dwindle into a simple concern with material things or with raw matter rather than with the ambitious dialectical analytics of historical materialism. As Natasha Korda and Jonathan Gil Harris argue, while much 'material' or 'thing' criticism has focused on the physicality of objects, 'Marx, by contrast, understood the materiality of objects to embrace as well the domain of labor and *praxis*, and thus to entail social relations of *production* – relations, Marx argued, that are effaced in the commodity form'.[50] In the introduction to her anthology, Wayne stipulates that her collection embraces many kinds of feminist work and that many critics included in the book would not designate themselves either as Marxists or socialists. Nonetheless, Wayne identifies some characteristics that in her view bind together the essays included in this anthology: a focus on class and its role in constructing and dividing feminine subjects (5), an emphasis on women's work in all its forms from the reproduction of biological life to household labour to paid labour outside the household (6), an acknowledgement that class-based and patriarchal modes of oppression intersect, though the priority assigned to one over the other varies from critic to critic (7), and a concern with the materiality of ideology as it both effects women's oppression and exploitation and also provides an arena for its disruption (8).

In the volume itself, these principles lead to various critical practices. Cristina Malcolmson, for example, deftly examines how class and gender are interconnected in a play like *Twelfth Night* in which, she argues, ideol-ogies of love become the model for imagining master–servant relationships and naturalizing exploitative hierarchies. She performs a familiar kind of ideology critique, but one made particularly compelling by its simulta-neous examination of several kinds of social relations held in place and naturalized precisely *through* their mutual imbrication. She makes a good case that one can't really understand how ideology works to construct the common sense of a culture without recognizing the particular ways in which class and gender are deployed with and against one another.

Also in this volume, I take up issues of the materiality of ideology that I was to develop more fully in my 1994 book, *The Stage and Social Struggle in Early Modern England*.[51] By the mid-1990s, debates about subversion and containment had grown stale, and the rigid determinism informing certain uses of Foucault and Althusser had become apparent. In *The Stage and Social Struggle*, I do use Althusser's theory of ideological interpellation, but argue that interpellation 'is a process which not only subjects the subject but qualifies him or her for maneuver in the terrain of ideology' (81). Moreover, because subjects are never hailed by one ideology only, the multiple positions they occupy open the possibility for recognition of contradiction, for politicization and for resistance.

For me, the early modern theatre is a site of contradiction and multiple interpellations that make its political effects unpredictable and different for different subjects, partly as they are distinguished by gender. I argue that the ideological power of the stage resides not just in its fictions, but in the performance and institutional practices of the stage that form the matrix within which those fictions are experienced. I analyse, for example, the consequences for female theatregoers of the fact that boys played women's roles and that women were paying customers in a commercial institution that solicited their money and encouraged their spectatorship, but also barred them from acting.[52] In focusing on performance practices and on the contradictions that can open up between what is performed, by whom, and before whom, my work is indebted to Robert Weimann's, and also to Walter Cohen's, observation that while the fictions of the stage often catered to aristocratic subjects, the mode of theatrical production remained artisanal.

Thinking, however, in terms of gender and not just in terms of class expands the social relations implicated in theatregoing. I focused not just on the unmarked male theatregoer, but on the unnamed women for whom attendance at the theatre was an opportunity (1) for self-display, (2) for the exercise of spectatorship and critical judgement and (3) for an encounter with fictions that frequently condemned women for precisely such activities. I thus examined the nexus of ideological pressures and material practices in which various theatregoers were enmeshed. Not only were the plays themselves fissured by gaps in the sense-making structures of early modern culture, and thus open to a symptomatic readings of their contradictions and silences, but they were performed by certain kinds of actors in certain kinds of buildings before certain kinds of mixed audiences. These material conditions affected how audience members of different genders and classes were interpellated by their theatregoing experience and affected the possibilities for dis-identification and opposition that that experience enabled.

The importance of materiality was taken up in a different way by another feminist critic, Natasha Korda, in her influential book, *Shakespeare's Domestic Economies: Gender and Property in Early Modern England*.[53] Arguing that 'during the late sixteenth and early seventeenth centuries, relations between subjects within the home became increasingly centered around and mediated by objects' (8), Korda nonetheless carefully avoids the allure of objects-in-themselves, choosing instead to focus on 'the specific historical forms that women's subjection assumes with the rise of capitalism and development of the commodity form' (12). Reading a range of Shakespeare's plays from *The Taming of the Shrew*, *Othello*, *Measure for Measure* and *The Merry Wives of Windsor*, Korda argues that in them one can trace the gradual delineation of a household sphere filled with 'stuff' or material goods that it became the woman's task to supervise, maintain and display. Rather than primarily involved in the production of food and goods for immediate use, women of the middling sort, she argues, were increasingly positioned in the changing economy of early modern capitalism as consumers of luxury items and guardians of the household property by which their family's social status was signified. While women in this emerging economy were to maintain household property *as if* they owned it, Korda explores the tensions and contradictions that arose from the fact that they did not, under coverture, actually *own* household 'stuff', though in numerous ways they exercised daily control over it.

Refusing the view that women were simply the victims of a patriarchal culture that objectified them, Korda instead draws a much more complicated picture of the contradictory positioning of middling sort women within nascent capitalism and the ways in which they were both subjected by their roles as managers of household property and able to use that role in struggles against and resistance to England's patrilineal property regime. Korda is influenced by new historicism, feminism and Marxism in about equal proportions, but what is perhaps most interesting about her work from a Marxist perspective is the seriousness with which she confronts the consequences to female subjects of the intensification of commodity culture in early capitalism, and the way in which the stage not only thematizes that intensification and reveals the contradictions that emerge as a result, but also emblematizes the regime of the commodity by its use of stage properties. Arguing against the idea of a 'bare stage', Korda examines the things, from buckbaskets to handkerchiefs, that surround the female subject on the early modern stage and frequently became the means for revealing the contradictions in her social positioning.

There are a number of other feminists whose work is influenced by the conjunction of Marxist and feminist perspectives, including Rosemary Kegl and Dympna Callaghan,[54] and the collective achievement of this Marxist feminist work is to theorize and to demonstrate the interconnections between, and yet the unique specificities of, early modern class and gender struggle, and to open up the particular ways in which the transition to an emergent capitalist economy refigured the social relations between men and women as well as between classes. Ania Loomba, particularly in *Shakespeare, Race, and Colonialism,* produces an even denser analysis of early modern social relations by including race in her theoretical framework. A thoroughly dialectical critic, Loomba focuses 'not just on the distance, but also the very powerful connections, between "then" and "now"'.[55] Her work shows its debts to historical materialism not only when it directly engages Marx on the question of how colonialism and capitalism are imbricated (151–56), but also in her steady emphasis on the material practices that fuel transformations in the various regimes of difference (including religious difference) that mark the early colonial moment. In her careful attention to the multiple strands that feed into the creation of modern racial ideologies and her admirable specificity about the way race, gender and class interact in the making of the early modern social formation, Loomba is another critic who puts paid to the notion that Marxism can only produce a reductive account of culture.

Frankfurt School Marxism

If many forms of Marxist Shakespeare criticism prominent in the 1980s and early 1990s were influenced by the anti-humanist poststructuralist Marxism of Althusser, and if new historicism emphasized anthropological thick description and, drawing on Foucault, the absolute alterity of the past, then Frankfurt School Marxism offered an alternative to much of what was professionally fashionable during these decades and articulates a clear critique of antiquarian and undialectical approaches to history. I am going to focus here on the work of Hugh Grady as offering the most sustained example of this kind of humanist Marxism.

Grady has written four books, but there is considerable consistency among them, first, as to how he positions himself in relationship to other forms of political/historical criticism.[56] He was among the first to argue that new historicism had the capacity to become a sterile antiquarianism by emphasizing too absolutely the difference of the past and the absolute breaks between one historical period and another. Instead, he argues for the position that many new historicists articulate and then frequently suppress; namely, that every historicist is a 'presentist' in the sense that he or she cannot approach the past except from the vantage point of the present (*Universal Wolf*, 7). While that does not mean that one gives up the attempt to see the difference of the past, the attempt to do so is always imperfectly realized and, in fact, should be embraced as part of an inevitable and necessary renewal of past texts in light of present circumstances.

But Grady goes further, arguing that in the late twentieth century the 'modernist' Shakespeare has given way to the 'postmodernist' Shakespeare (*Modernist Shakespeare*, 190–246) and that that transformation allows the critic better to see a pre-modernist Shakespeare, one who does not yet exemplify Enlightenment ideas about the unity of the art work or the singularity of authorship (*Universal Wolf*, 8). In short, to use Foucault's terms, our situation at the end of the Age of Man permits critics to see new aspects of cultural works produced before its inauguration, our 'presentism' allowing an importantly *historical* view of the pre-Enlightenment Shakespeare to emerge.[57] When, in *Universal Wolf*, Grady does look back at the early modern Shakespeare, what he sees is a pervasive and constitutive tension between what he calls pre-Enlightenment aspects of the plays and elements that look ahead to the reification and instrumental reason we associate with the Enlightenment.

Reification is thus a key term for Grady, and drawing on Horkheimer and Adorno, he uses it to describe the 'property of social systems to act through

their own objective logic, as if they possessed an autonomous intentionality' (*Universal Wolf,* 19), a regime connected with the emergence of
commodity culture and the abstract rationality and scientism that supplants
a theocentric religious culture. The split he sees in Shakespeare's work is
important to Grady because it allows the pre-Enlightenment elements of
Renaissance culture to act as an anticipatory critique of reification. Thus,
for example, he argues that figures like Edmund in *King Lear* or Iago in
Othello are emergent examples of instrumental reason and cold scientism
critiqued by the archaic heroism of an Othello, while in the playful leisure
of a play like *As You Like It* he sees a utopian response to new market
pressures, enclosure and reification. Grady's readings of plays like *Troilus
and Cressida,* from which he takes his book's title, are smart and compelling,
and they challenge new historicism's emphasis on Shakespeare's conservative alignment, especially in his tragedies, with aristocratic power and
nostalgia for a feudal past, by arguing that the 'pre-Enlightenment'
elements of his dramatic vision actually often function as denunciations,
before the fact, of reification or serve as intimations of a different, more
utopian future.[58]

This point brings me to two other important aspects of Grady's Frankfurt
School Marxism: its retention, and indeed its valorization, of the category
of the aesthetic, and its embrace of a conception of the subject as capable
of critical rationality and some degree of autonomy. Just as Grady rejects
Foucault's notion of absolute critical breaks between one historical period
and another, he rejects with more vehemence what he sees as Althusser's
anti-humanism and denial of the subject's agency. He parts company, in
particular, with the Althusserian bent of much British cultural materialism
on this score and follows Habermas in positing a more flexible and autonomous subject (*Shakespeare, Machiavelli, and Montaigne,* 10–14), though
not one possessed of an unchanging human nature. For Grady, humanism
is a complex and varied ideology and not simply the enemy of a robust
historical materialism.

Similarly, the aesthetic for Grady is not a discredited category. Rather,
he uses Adorno to argue that art does not equal ideology, but instead has
a capacity to critique the empirical world and to set free what capitalism
represses. In his most recent book, *Impure Aesthetics,* Grady struggles hard
to free himself from the Kantian, transcendental view of aesthetics in which
the Frankfurt School is implicated by positing an 'impure' aesthetics that
is both of the world and apart from it, infiltrated by ideology but capable
of distance from it, an historical construction that nonetheless retains
an essential capacity for both critique and utopian revelation. Eager not

simply to condemn the theoretical developments of poststructuralism and other forms of Marxism, Grady works to modify the Frankfurt School theoretical model that serves as his critical foundation while retaining its embrace of the categories of the aesthetic, critical rationality and the partially autonomous subject. If his work cannot entirely escape the transcendentalism from which he strives to free himself, nor completely reconcile his deep humanism with recognition of the validity of critiques of essentialist humanism, his body of work nonetheless demonstrates an admirable consistency, a capacity to reveal new facets of the 'postmodern' Shakespeare, and a compelling critique of aspects of both the British cultural materialism, the new historicism and the Althusserian Marxism with which it is in constant conversation.

Presentism

Recently, Grady's name, along with that of Terence Hawkes and others, has come to be associated with the critical movement within Shakespeare studies known as 'presentism', though it may be inaccurate to describe this as a unified phenomenon. Grady has been calling attention to the presentist dimensions of his work since at least 1996, and often, for him, the term marks his difference, as I have indicated, from an historicism that stresses the absolute alterity of the past and masks the critic's roots in contemporary culture. But the term has come to carry even more polemical punch in the writings of Terence Hawkes, in particular. As a critic, Hawkes is somewhat *sui generis*, and though he clearly considers himself a Marxist, in his writing he largely eschews abstract theorizing for a dazzling performative practice that strives to embody the 'jouissance' of jazz and enacts as much as it announces its critical programme.

When Hawkes does make programmatic pronouncements, they tend to emphasize the creative aspects of criticism. In various ways, he repeatedly asserts: 'Our "Shakespeare" is our invention: to read him is to write him.'[59] And to write him, for Hawkes as for Grady, is to begin from the present.[60] In a revision of Stephen Greenblatt's famous desire to speak with the dead, Hawkes and Grady argue:

> If an intrusive, shaping awareness of ourselves, alive and active in our own world, defines us, then it deserves our closest attention. Paying the present that degree of respect might more profitably be judged, not as a 'mistake', egregious and insouciant, blandly imposing a tritely

modern perspective on whatever texts confront it, but rather as the basis of a critical stance whose engagement with the text is of a particular character. A Shakespeare criticism that takes that on board will not yearn to speak with the dead. It will aim, in the end, to talk to the living.[61]

Presentism, then, is perhaps most usefully seen as a direct riposte to the increasingly antiquarian, positivist drift of new historicism and the hegemony it established.

Such a critical stance is easily accused of irresponsibility to 'facts' and to history. In the end, however, Hawkes is quite interested, not in facts in and of themselves, but in facts as they are marshalled by a critical perspective into a narrative that exposes the workings of power in both past and present. His criticism is, indeed, 'of a particular character', returning repeatedly to how Shakespeare has been used to justify current or past political positions, many of them rebarbative. Consequently, many of the essays in *That Shakespeherian Rag* unearth the unacknowledged political effects of the work of eminent Shakespeareans such as A. C. Bradley, Sir Walter Raleigh and G. Wilson Knight. The 'facts' of their lives and works are carefully sought out, not as ends in themselves, but as part of a narrative about the exclusionary and nationalist consequences of the rise of English studies and the role of Shakespeare and of Shakespeareans in that narrative. In *Shakespeare in the Present,* many chapters comment on the present devolution movement in Great Britain both by investigating the representation of the Irish and the Welsh in Shakespeare's plays, and by exploring how a disturbing Irishness erupts as the '*unheimlich*' within discourses of Englishness.[62] In practice, Hawkes's Marxism and his presentism are inseparable. He takes up classic Marxist questions like the effects of early modern enclosures on the writing of a play like *The Tempest,* but starts and ends his investigation by contemplating the effects of the Shakespeare industry on present-day Stratford (*That Shakespeherian Rag,* 1–26). Each, he implies, along with Shakespeare's own possible involvement in enclosing land near Stratford, reveals variations on the theme of expropriation and displacement. There are no innocent uses of Shakespeare, perhaps especially when he has become part of the national culture industry.

It is in their co-edited volume, *Presentist Shakespeares,* however, that Grady and Hawkes attempt to give shape to or define a larger presentist movement within current Shakespeare criticism. The volume contains many smart and provocative essays, but the aggregation of voices does not quite add up to a coherent theoretical programme, and certainly not one consistently in conversation with Marxist work. Hawkes and Grady's short introduction summarizes their wish to move beyond the moment of new historicism; to speak to the living, not the dead; and to find in the late works of Jacques Derrida, and in the writings of Heidegger, Adorno and Benjamin, fresh theoretical resources for thinking of Shakespeare in the present. Hawkes and Grady each contributes an essay that extends the particular brand of Marxist-indebted presentism to which they have dedicated their careers. Hawkes uses the transatlantic career of Allardyce Nicoll, founder of the first International Shakespeare Conference, to deliver one of his character-istically mordant and witty critiques of the entanglements of Shakespeare, Stratford-upon-Avon, a particular Shakespeare play (in this case *Timon of Athens*) and a modern cultural issue (in this case, the shifting terms of the British–American 'alliance' in the past 100 or so years). Grady elegantly traces the various aesthetic paradigms through which *Hamlet* has been acted and interpreted over the course of its 400-year history with the aim of revealing the 'inevitable "presentism" of all critical discourse' (142).

But the presentism encompassed by the volume invokes a rather eclectic range of projects, and not all of them, certainly, see presentism as an extension of historical materialist analysis. Catherine Belsey, for example, offers a genuinely original and absorbing account of why, in her view, new historicism is not indebted to poststructuralism so much as to the functionalist social theory of Talcott Parsons, which she sees as also informing the cultural anthropology of Clifford Geertz (27–45). Michael Bristol quarrels with the term 'presentism' because in his view it makes an 'ism' of an uncontroversial and necessary assumption, namely, belief in 'the possibility of making general interpretations about the way people think and act that would be valid in different historical contexts' (48 and 47). Ewan Fernie makes the case that we need to revive the concept of presence, which in this essay he connects with action, and specifically with the way action operates in *Henry V* as an example of the 'fierce agency' and 'terrible energy' of King Henry, an energy that is theatrically compelling, if ethically problematic (96-120). And Kiernan Ryan argues, using the prescience of *Troilus and Cressida* as his example, that critics must not just read Shakespeare's texts in terms of present needs and interests, but must entertain the possibility that they anticipate a future that might radically, and positively, refigure the present (164–83).

The book contains other impressive essays, but they don't exemplify a methodology or a theory so much as a general commitment to acknowledge the present as the starting point for engagement with the many forms of 'Shakespeare' that are possible. 'Presentism' expresses, I think, a desire to extend the political criticism of the 1980s and 1990s forward in time, to find new ways to argue that editing, acting, reading and interpreting Shakespeare are historical and political acts, and involve much more than the recovery of originary meaning or the sheer assembly of 'facts'. To that extent, 'presentism' is allied with Marxist traditions of thought, though a number of 'presentists' would undoubtedly eschew or be mystified by any more rigorously theorized affiliation.

It is, of course, possible to do work on Shakespeare in periods later than the early modern or even in the current moment without necessarily embracing the presentist label. Richard Halpern, for example, has written a probing examination of how the moderns read and performed Shakespeare in the moment of imperialist or monopoly capitalism, a project that he opposes to those forms of historicism 'which rejects all contexts or meanings other than the original ones as "ahistorical" or "anachronistic"'.[63] I want to close by focusing, however, on another American critic, Denise Albanese, who in *Extramural Shakespeare* imaginatively uses the trans-disciplinary techniques of cultural studies to push Marxist analysis of Shakespeare into the 'now' of what she calls 'perimillennial culture'.[64] Albanese's work self-consciously casts itself as an attempt to continue, but in crucial ways to update, the cultural materialist project of the 1980s and 1990s, which drew part of its inspiration from Raymond Williams, Stuart Hall and the Birmingham Centre for Contemporary Cultural Studies. Albanese argues that earlier cultural materialist work engaged in a form of ideology critique that assumed that Shakespeare was inevitably connected with high culture, elite institutions and the hegemony of a ruling class. It saw Shakespeare primarily as a force of oppression that could only be refigured by appropriations that were, in essence, a form of theft (17). Albanese argues, however, that this was always more true for Britain than for the United States, and, to the extent it was true in the US, by the year 2000 historical forces had brought about a new conjuncture in which Shakespeare could no longer be considered solely the property of high culture.

The reasons for the absorption of Shakespeare into what Albanese calls 'public culture' (thus avoiding the antinomies of 'high' and 'low') have primarily to do with American mass education and, since early in the twentieth century, Shakespeare's incorporation into the educational apparatus at every level. Mass education, Albanese argues, has made Shakespeare part of mass culture, and with unpredictable results. She suggests that it is wrong to think of Shakespeare as contained or constrained by the walls of academia – Shakespeare both has a life beyond those walls, and the walls themselves are increasingly permeable. To continue to associate Shakespeare only with high culture and with repression is to deny a truly dialectical reading of his uses in culture and to 'fix' his essence in a way that denies historical change. Her evidence for these claims rests on a series of incisive case studies, each of which examines the contradictory ways that various institutions such as the NEA, the Shakespeare film industry and the American educational apparatus position Shakespeare as both a demotic part of a widely-shared public culture and simultaneously as a figure apart from and above that culture.

Particularly telling examples of the schizophrenia surrounding the use of Shakespeare in contemporary culture are afforded by Albanese's juxta-position of the opposing assumptions about Shakespeare that motivated two 1996 films: Kenneth Branagh's *Hamlet* and Baz Luhrmann's *William Shakespeare's Romeo + Juliet*, and the contradictory impulses behind the NEA's 'Shakespeare in American Communities' project, which both claimed that Shakespeare needed to be 'brought' to the heartland and small towns of America and that Shakespeare was already part of an authentic America separate from the big cities and elite cultural institutions they house. The real importance of the book, however, resides not in the individual case studies, but in its insistence that a genuinely Marxist criticism will not endlessly repeat the insights of a particular historical moment, but will, instead, constantly remake itself to meet the demands of a changing social formation. Otherwise, Marxism will become just another reified system of thought and the Shakespeares it produces will cease to matter in urgent cultural struggles and in what Albanese in her last chapter calls 'social dreaming', Ernest Bloch's term for the necessary Marxist project of imagining a refigured world (121).

Chapter 3

Afterword

Crystal Bartolovich and Jean E. Howard

While the foregoing overview of Marxist Shakespeare criticism since the 1970s shows the persistence of some outstanding work being written from within this tradition, it is nonetheless true that the field's current centre of gravity lies elsewhere. As we write in 2011, we are at the tail end of a moment in which critics devote impressive attention to the material text and to material objects – the so-called 'New Materialism' – but most often fail to do so within a historical materialist frame of reference. The kin of the New Materialism, the 'New Economic Criticism', is less interested in 'things', but is more apt to focus on economic metaphors than on structures of oppression. Religion remains a prime topic of investigation, and its role as a culturally dominant discourse in the early modern period is readily acknowledged, but seldom in terms of its interactions with other elements of the social formation. The same could be said of historicized explorations of affect, emotion and cognition. Political criticism in general still commands significant attention, encompassing, at the least, presentism, early modern postcolonial and race studies, work on global cultural exchanges, green criticism and queer and feminist work, though both of the latter appear somewhat attenuated since the 1980s and 1990s. Only in a few instances does any of this work self-consciously enter into conversation with Marxist modes of analysis.

It could be different. If utilized, Marxist theorizations of the commodity form and discussion of the social relations of production could deepen discussion of the coins, books, clothes, household movables, props and other objects that have become the centre of so much recent critical interest. Similarly, Marxist analyses of primitive accumulation – especially in Halpern's nuanced and expanded sense – could inform green work on land use, the built environment, urbanization during the transition to capitalism and the role of literary genres in mediating that transition. Furthermore, we could continue to expand the way that Marxist categories can have meaning in a world that is changing and in which Shakespeare still has a central place. While many acknowledge that Shakespeare is constantly remade in performance and criticism, the same is much less true for Marx in Shakespeare Studies, where Marxism is often reduced to a handful of clichéd abstractions (e.g. economic determinism) that are assumed never to be contested or to change. One point of this essay has been to suggest otherwise, and to remind readers of the rich array of analytic categories and reading practices Marxism has developed and is still developing for both social and literary analysis. These resources have the potential both to produce new avenues of work and to reconfigure existing bodies of criticism, including those less obviously open to an historical materialist analysis.

In the world of Shakespeare studies, where Marx is often marginalized, these chapters on 'Marx and Shakespeare' attempt to put Marx at the centre, where, in our view, he belongs. In Chapter 1, 'Marx's Shakespeare', the goal was to open up new ways of thinking about Marxist Shakespeares by showing how varied, clever and insightful Marx's own uses of Shakespeare actually were. He resisted the attempts of so many others in his time to yoke Shakespeare to nationalist or elitist cultural politics, consistently deploying the plays in ways that indicate their usefulness to liberatory social struggle, which meant that they did not belong to any one group, in global or class terms. In *Capital*, Marx writes an unBildungsroman, to educate workers (and anyone else who cared to listen) in the concepts that would help them see that the contradictions with which they were continually buffeted – desire and privation, freedom and constraint, and so on – were an effect of capitalist social relations, not of their own internal lacks and limits. In the *Eighteenth Brumaire*, he instead used Shakespeare to think through the relations of past and present, rupture and repetition, directed toward breaking the cycle of oppression and opening social relations to a liberatory future. To these ends, Marx did not produce 'readings' of Shakespeare, but reconstellated textual fragments in contexts in which they could challenge blindness, hypocrisy and other impediments to revolution.

Chapter 2's overview of Marxist criticism since the 1970s suggests that Marxism has remained uniquely alive to the imperatives of the historical conjuncture in which texts are written, while retaining a vibrant sense of the dialectical relationship of past to present and of the present to possible futures. While new historicism drifted into an antiquarian relationship to the past and fell prey to the idea of its absolute alterity, Marxist critics continued to unpack the ways in which both the works of Marx and of Shakespeare arise in determinate historical conditions but are remade in the new historical conditions in which they are read and used. This is as true of Denise Albanese as of Robert Weimann. Moreover, Marxist critics have developed a set of concepts and techniques of analysis that, far from reducing literature to a flat reflection of objective fact, allow them to analyse the ways it participates in history. These include concepts such as commodity fetishism, reification, mediation and ways of reading that focus on the analysis of literary form as a site for mediating the contradictions of a social formation; ideology critique to reveal the interests informing naturalized and supposedly neutral ideas and practices; and symptomatic reading for speaking the unsaid of texts, the repressions marking the site of ideological struggles.

As we write in the summer of 2011, we are in real danger of entering a second recession: the official unemployment rate is well over 9 per cent (including the disaffected, who have stopped seeking work, it is closer to 15 per cent); and the under-employed, unwilling part-time workers or those whose jobs are entirely inadequate to their needs, form an invisible underclass. We are writing in a country in which the richest 20 per cent control 85 per cent of the wealth, and the only thing that the government can agree to do is make still deeper cuts in social services. This as Verizon and other major employers such as Walmart are working hard at union-busting, while continuing to contribute to the demise of small family businesses. California, New York, Illinois and Wisconsin university systems – among too many others – are in crisis. At a time in which every aspect of our lives is affected by the economy, and when the ills of this economy are crying out for Marxist analysis, such analysis is strikingly absent from most public discourse. Shakespeare criticism may seem far from this arena, but while 'Shakespeare' is still publicly situated at the centre of 'English', and while 'English' is still viewed as a site in which values and ethical concerns are raised, then there are compelling reasons to allow the present moment of political and economic crisis to motivate new conjunctions of Marx and Shakespeare that can speak to the past, the present and the more just future that might be.

Part II

Freud

Chapter 4

Introduction: Freud and Shakespeare

David Hillman

Being invited by the editors of this series to write an essay on Freud and Shakespeare put me in mind of the old joke about the proverbial American tourist who, upon first going to see *Hamlet*, exclaimed that the play was so darn full of quotations; for one could equally imagine the newcomer to Freud reading a chunk of his work and complaining about its being so full of clichés. Freudian slips, Oedipus complexes and mother fixations, narcissists and fetishists, anal characters and penis envies and numerous other notions that populate Freud's writings have become part of our everyday language as well as of the nearly inescapable ways we in the West conceive of our psychic worlds. Our world has become not only (to quote Emerson) 'Shakespearized', but also, now, 'Freudianized'; as W. H. Auden put it, Freud has become 'no more a person / Now but a whole climate of opinion'.[1] Alongside a powerful resistance to psychoanalytic ideas, there is the (apparently) nearly contrary problem of overfamiliarity. And this is true in a twofold way: in a popular sense, some of Freud's ideas are almost too well-known for their own good, subject to parody and reductive reformulation, so that it can seem that most people are at once both too knowing and too ignorant in relation to Freud; and in a deeper sense, Freudian concepts have so permeated the realms of theory and criticism that it is hard to imagine any structuralist or poststructuralist thought existing in the form it does without the influence of these omnipresent notions. Freud, as Paul Ricoeur writes, 'is nowhere because everywhere'; his impact, says George Steiner, is 'enormous, all-pervasive'.[2] So that a full evaluation of Freud's influence on the reception of Shakespeare would entail not much less than a coming-to-terms with the main strands of Western intellectual history of the past 100 years; and this of course lies well beyond the scope of this essay. Even were one to leave out of the account the many major non-psychoanalytic literary critics strongly influenced by Freud, a summary of the existing psychoanalytic criticism of

Shakespeare would fill several volumes. Comprehensiveness is out of the question – and so too any claim to authority. Since, apart from anything else, 'we inhabit psychoanalysis, living with it, in it, around it, or beside it' (to quote Jacques Derrida),[3] it is not at all clear that it is possible to find a position sufficiently outside the Freudian universe from which to evaluate the difference Freud has made to our habits of mind – or to our reception of Shakespeare.

Nor, on the other hand, is it possible to imagine Freud's understanding of the psyche without the profound influence of Shakespeare's works. It may be something of an overstatement to declare simply, as David Willbern does, that 'Shakespeare dramatizes what psychoanalysis theorizes',[4] or – as Harold Bloom contends – that Freud's theories are, in essence, 'prosified Shakespeare'.[5] But there is more than a grain of truth in Bloom's argument that 'Freud's vision of human psychology is derived, not altogether unconsciously, from his reading of the plays', and it is certainly the case that, as Meredith Anne Skura puts it, 'Freud internalized Shakespeare's dramas', and that, as Philip Armstrong suggests, 'at every critical moment of his "discovery", Freud finds Shakespeare there before him'.[6] Indeed, the writings of Freud and Shakespeare may seem to be tied together like a dream and its constituent materials; so central is Shakespeare to Freud's thinking, at a subterranean level, that it is surely the case that his plays were amongst the most important of the raw materials out of which Freud constructed the dream he called 'psychoanalysis', second only perhaps to the clinical input from his patients. References to Shakespeare are scattered everywhere in the psychoanalyst's writings, though – interestingly – only a very small proportion of these directly interpret the playwright's works. The influence of the latter on the former – like that of Freud on the reception of Shakespeare – is pervasive, but diffuse, and not at all easy to disentangle. 'The question is by now familiar', writes Joel Fineman: 'is Shakespeare Freudian or is Freud Shakespearean?'[7] To which we could respond: is any of us anything but both?

It is for these reasons that it is not so much difficult as practically impossible to fulfil the task proposed by this series: to 'assess the double impact of Shakespeare on the figure covered and of the figure on the understanding, interpretation and appreciation of Shakespeare ... including comparison with other figures or works within the same field'.[8] In this case, what we are dealing with is, in both directions, mostly indirect, sprawling and radically amorphous. And the difficulties are exacerbated by other factors: first, Freud's own multiplicity and elusiveness – not only does he write about a huge range of topics, but (as we shall see) his thinking is not of a piece; it is constantly evolving and, at almost every turn, at odds with itself – and so too the wide variety of psychoanalytic theories for which his writings have acted as catalysts and which are so diverse in part as a result of his own multiplicity. And second, the controversial nature of Freud's writings and legacy, not excluding his influence on the reception of Shakespeare.[9] That these have been highly contentious from the outset is to some extent the result of his theories being, to quote Auden again, 'often ... wrong and, at times, absurd'.[10] We could assign this problem to the vulgarity (in every sense of the word) of so much psychoanalytic criticism, but, beyond this, the repudiation should be attributed to the unsettling nature of psycho-analytic forms of thought. At the heart of Freud's work lies the concept of the unconscious (*das Unbewusste*) – that 'Which, look'd on as it is, is nought but shadows / Of what it is not' (*Richard II*, 2.2.23–4).[11] This, according to Freud, is the profoundly elusive and chaotic part of the mind that is the home of suppressed energies and repressed ideas; unobservable and unrestricted, it is, in Cynthia Chase's words, 'definable only as what it is not'.[12] In the unconscious, says Freud, there is a complete indifference to reality, there is no negation, no morality, no sequential temporality, no doubt or logic; there is only endless desire and mobile energy.[13] It is 'the Realm of the Illogical',[14] 'Where every something, being blent together, / Turns to a wild of nothing' (*The Merchant of Venice*, 3.2.181–2).

With such a concept at the heart of his thinking, the resistance to Freud's work is hardly surprising. The indignation his ideas evoke is largely a result of their propensity to unveil, with astonishing, unsentimental frankness, the hidden (Freud would say repressed) energies and desires of the psyche, as well as their promotion of a vertiginous sense of depths within the human subject. But – one might immediately wonder – are these not things that Shakespeare's works similarly explore? While their methods, genres and aims are of course quite dissimilar, the writings of Freud and Shakespeare share a great deal: a fascination with the vagaries of desire (above all, sexual desire), a candour about the central role of aggression in human relations, a preoccupation with the dynamics of the family, a delight in the endless playfulness of language (and the ways in which it both shapes and reveals our deepest selves) and a pervasive sense not only of the inevitable limitations upon human fulfillment, whether in the realms of love or of knowledge, but also of the many ways we try to escape these limitations. Yet Shakespeare has, at least since the mid-eighteenth century, elicited little other than adulation, while Freud has given rise to tides of virulent, almost allergic, hostility: Hyperion to a satyr. Freud's writings evoke – they may almost be said to solicit – heated resistance; whereas

Shakespeare's provoked – in their own time as well as over the centuries since – relatively little controversy or opposition, despite their interest in no less inclusive an index and obscure prologue to the history of lust and foul thoughts, and indeed despite their implicit interventions in political and religious debates of his time.

That literature (and Shakespeare pre-eminently) managed to evade censorious criticism was a fact that interested Freud, who had his own ideas about the ways in which literary pleasure compensates for its transgressiveness. As Freud puts it in his essay on 'Creative Writers and Day-Dreaming': 'many things which, if they were real, could give no enjoyment, can do so in the play of phantasy, and many excitements which, in themselves, are actually distressing, can become a source of pleasure for the hearers and spectators at the performance of a writer's work'.[15] The casual reference (in an essay on 'creative writers') to 'the *performance* of a writer's work' can give us a hint as to just how central drama, and particularly Shakespeare's drama, was to Freud's thinking. The fact that many of Shakespeare's contemporary playwrights did spend time in prison as a result of their writing is suggestive of Shakespeare's remarkable adroitness in dodging authority's censorship; in taking on taboo subjects, Shakespeare, like Freud, had to find ways of overcoming powerful censoring mechanisms. It is, in any case, of no small interest that for both these writers – albeit in very different ways – censorship and its evasion were matters of great consequence.

One of my aims throughout this essay will be to meditate upon the radically different reactions evoked by Shakespeare and Freud, a division between what might perhaps best be thought of as the positive and negative transferences – the love and hate – instigated by these two writers. 'Transference' in Freud's writing refers to the passage of pre-existing affects and ideas from one context to another (most immediately, to the figure of the analyst, but more generally, on to any figure or object to which the emotion doesn't 'rightfully' belong); it is almost always split into positive and negative poles. (Jacques Lacan helpfully characterises these poles in an uncharacteristically understated way: 'The positive transference is when you have a soft spot for the individual concerned, the analyst in this instance, and the negative transference is when you have to keep your eye on him'.)[16] Freud's so-called 'cure through love' is thus also a cure through hate; and this is surely not unconnected to the hostility he evokes. At several points in this essay, I will be equally concerned with these opposed reactions – with the way originally ambivalent emotions can become increasingly polarised over time.

I begin by giving an overview and an interrogation of Freud's writings on Shakespeare, and proceed in the following chapter to tease out some of the more compelling connections between the two. Freud was a great thinker, a great theorist, a great searcher after truth; and certainly he has been hugely influential in the ways we have come to read Shakespeare's texts – indeed any literary text – and perhaps even more influential in the ways we have come to think of ourselves in relation to these texts. But a great *Shakespearean*? The first part of this essay argues that he is not (not, that is, if 'Shakespearean' is understood as a noun); the second suggests that he is (taking 'Shakespearean' as an adjective). That is to say: he is assuredly not a careful, scholarly, attentive reader of Shakespeare's texts; but he is, I argue, powerfully attuned to Shakespearean ways of thinking. Freud is deeply Shakespearean; Freud's Shakespeare is hardly Shakespeare at all.

Chapter 5

Freud's Shakespeare

David Hillman

… My hereditary claim on life runs out, as you know, in November. I would like to be able to guarantee it up till then, but I really do not want to delay any longer than that, for everything around us grows ever darker and more ominous and the awareness of one's own helplessness ever more pressing. And so I do not wish to be fobbed off with the thought of your making your visit to Europe any later. So do not postpone it. We will have a lot to discuss about Shakespeare. I do not know what still attracts you to the man of Stratford. He seems to have nothing at all to justify his claim, whereas Oxford has almost everything. It is quite inconceivable to me that Shakespeare should have got everything secondhand—Hamlet's neurosis, Lear's madness, Macbeth's defiance and the character of Lady Macbeth, Othello's jealousy, etc. It almost irritates me that you should support the notion.

– Freud, Letter to Arnold Zweig, 2 April, 1937[1]

It would not be accurate to call Freud's explicit treatment of Shakespeare an interpretation of the playwright's works; it would be more correct to refer to his appropriation of some fragments of these works. For, in a sense, Freud never actually takes on Shakespeare: he generally takes hold of an element – a few words or lines, a character, a scene – and uses these to bolster his psychoanalytic understanding of a wider structure; he has something of a scavenger's attitude to the writer he acknowledges to be his greatest predecessor in matters psychological. The gaps in his writing about Shakespeare are immeasurably larger than the engagements. Nowhere does he work with a Shakespearean text on what we might think of as its own terms or in anything approaching its entirety (as he does, more or less, with E. T. A. Hoffmann's 'The Sandman' or Wilhelm Jensen's 'Gradiva' – though in these cases, too, his interpretations are tendentious and almost entirely uninterested in aesthetic or formal issues). Like Marxism, Freudian psychoanalysis is a methodology which, as C. L. Barber has suggested, 'it is one's constant effort to avoid being trapped in, because being trapped in [it] leads you to be unable to get at the work of art; the work of art becomes an illustration of the theology, ceases to matter as a separate fact'.[2] In this regard, Freud set the tone for one of the more problematic aspects of so much psychoanalytic literary criticism.

Indeed, one could say that Freud's bizarre disavowal of 'Shakespeare' as the author of the works during the latter part of his life is of a piece with his turning-away from the plays themselves. For it is a notable irony of Freud's thinking about Shakespeare that, while his overall method acts powerfully as an impetus to close reading of latent content, he himself practically never turns this kind of attention to Shakespeare's words, but rather comes up with speculative interpretations of structures and characters; his comments on Shakespeare's language are almost always aimed at decontextualised snatches. It is also the case that Freud's oversights when it comes to Shakespeare are quite as fascinating as his positive contributions. From childhood, Freud could recite large swathes of Shakespeare by heart (in English);[3] amongst his psychoanalytic circle of colleagues, 'Shakespeare was the most frequent topic of our discussions when they turned to literature'.[4] Given his thoroughgoing knowledge of and intense admiration for the works, Freud's omissions are nothing if not strange – and, as strangers, I would like to spend some time in this chapter 'giving them welcome'. At one point in his *Introductory Lectures on Psycho-Analysis,* Freud asks rhetorically, 'Can it be that we have left the most important item out of our account?'[5] Of course, he has; here as elsewhere Freud highlights the crucial significance of apparent omissions, forgettings and distortions – the way such 'mistakes' are structured by unconscious repression. Here, we can turn to Shakespeare's plays and note that it is not just through a Freudian lens that we now see the significance of such moments; which is to say that Freud could have learnt this from Shakespeare. Think, for example, of the telling incident in *Coriolanus* where the protagonist cannot recall ('By Jupiter, forgot!' – 1.9.89) the name of the impoverished man in Corioles who gave him succour in time of need; the forgetfulness reveals not just Coriolanus's attitude to those socially inferior to him but, more interestingly, his occlusion of any sense of his own vulnerability or indebtedness to others. Freud is particularly interested in the forgetting of proper names, and devotes a long section of *The Psychopathology of Everyday Life* to the topic. *Coriolanus,* incidentally, is a play Freud never once mentions – this despite his lifelong obsession with Rome and his more than passing interest in the significance of a boy's love for his mother (and the play's

close linking of these two matters). Such omissions tempt one to follow
Harold Bloom in accusing the father of psychoanalysis of being so anxious
about the priority and influence of Shakespeare as to be unable to bring
himself to acknowledge the extent of the dramatist's role in his thinking:
'Shakespeare is everywhere in Freud, far more present when unmentioned
[– and perhaps even more so when mentioned obliquely, as if merely in
passing –] than when he is cited'.[6]

The Bradleyesque list in the letter to Zweig quoted in the epigraph
to this chapter – 'Hamlet's neurosis, Lear's madness, Macbeth's defiance
and the character of Lady Macbeth, Othello's jealousy' – includes
pretty much everything substantial that Freud had to say directly about
Shakespeare – and more: he has practically nothing to say (in his
published writings, at least) about the last of these four tragedies, and
never mentions Othello (or Iago, or Desdemona) in his various writings
about sexual and delusional jealousy.[7] Whereas much of his writing on
art and literature focuses on analyses of the psychology of the artist,
what Freud is primarily after in his commentary on Shakespeare is (in a
nutshell) the analysis of dramatic character as neurotic type. The word
'type' recurs in his writings on Shakespeare – as we shall see in our
discussion of 'Some Character-Types Met with in Psycho-Analytic Work'
– highlighting a tendency towards generalization in his thinking, a more
than occasional effacement of unique individuality, complexity, nuance.
What Shakespeare offers Freud in his analysis of character is, most
obviously, prestige and discretion – the backing-up of clinical observation
through 'high' culture and the obviating of the problem of indiscretion
regarding real people. But at another level, several of Shakespeare's plays
– and above all *Hamlet, King Lear* and *Macbeth* – become potent catalysts,
instigators of rhizome-like thoughts recurring throughout Freud's work
and bringing out connections between a number of his most primal
themes: fatherhood and childhood; authorship and creativity; conscience,
ambition and ambivalence; death and mourning. The plays work upon
him at strata that go well beyond his avowed readings and aims; all of
these are used by Freud to help him think through two central issues:
familial structures, and the relation between what is 'actual' and what is
'fantasized' (external and internal events). Reading these plays, Freud is
working out notions of what it means to be a member of a family: a son,
a father, a childless couple – I refrain from saying 'respectively', because
Freud sees, if not always lucidly, that Shakespeare's plays never stop at
singular identification; in their polyvocality and in their multiple layers
of identification it becomes impossible to pin down the primary familial

position a given play, or even a given character, is 'about'. He also finds himself confronted with and musing about the immense difficulties of pinning down 'reality' – a past event, an actual identity or a character, an empirical explanation of human psychology.

It is no coincidence that the plays that fascinate Freud are all tragedies. The preoccupation bespeaks something about Freud's view of life – set out most explicitly in *Civilization and Its Discontents* – as tragically shot through with irreconcilable desires: as he repeatedly points out, our desires, whether we act upon them or not, cause us to feel profound guilt; and often enough (and paradoxically enough) this guilt itself causes us to transgress – a process acutely portrayed by Nietzsche (who, along with Shakespeare, is the most notorious and powerful occluded influence on Freud.). Freud could have derived such insights from, say, *Measure for Measure*, another play we might have expected to hear more about in his writings – set as it is in Vienna, and centrally concerned as it is with the incompatibility of libidinal desire and the constraints of 'civilization'. *Measure for Measure* could be said to give a fine sense of how, for instance, 'The sexual behaviour of a human being often lays down the pattern for all his other modes of reacting to life';[8] of how 'virtuous renunciation' only ends up reinforcing an attitude of 'severity and intolerance' (and guilt) towards one's own sexual and aggressive drives;[9] and perhaps also of how, in the last analysis, 'destructiveness is constitutive of sexuality'.[10] (Freud might have also gained something from spending more time than he does with Falstaff, who can be seen to be posing a challenge to many of these ideas: much virtue in id.) The analyst, though, pays little attention to the comedies – and even less to the histories. Though he quotes from both tetralogies at various points, the histories are, as a genre, so occluded throughout Freud's work that in his 1930 speech accepting the Goethe prize he refers to 'the author of the Comedies, Tragedies and Sonnets of Shakespeare'.[11] The *Sonnets* seem to have interested him only in so far as they cast light on the authorship controversy, and the narrative poems appear to have remained something of a terra incognita. It is not hard to imagine him deriving a good deal from – to suggest a few of the more obvious possibilities – *Twelfth Night* (vis-à-vis, say, his understanding of narcissism or the endless mobility and contingency of desire); or *As You Like It* (in relation to, for example, his theories of innate bisexuality); or *1 Henry IV* (as something like an allegoresis of ego, super-ego and id). But even when ostensibly writing an essay on *The Merchant of Venice* ('The Theme of the Three Caskets'), Freud spends much of his time thinking about *King Lear*.

***

It is, of course, *Hamlet* that shaped Freud's thinking far more than any
other play. His (Coleridgean) identification with the protagonist is already
evident in 1872 (at the age of 16), when he writes to a friend of 'the
nonsensical Hamlet in me, my diffidence';[12] at the end of his life he is still
representing himself through the words of the Danish prince, ending one
of his last letters (to his brother) with 'The rest – you will know what I
mean – is silence'.[13] *Hamlet* haunts Freud at almost every turn in his writing;
yet his analysis of the play is both exceedingly selective and – given the
almost crushing influence of his Oedipal reading of the play over the past
hundred years – startlingly truncated: it emerges in no more than half a
dozen skirmish-like paragraphs, footnotes and asides. Perhaps it is precisely
the extreme compression, the simplicity of the basic outlines of the interpretation, that has fostered the power of the reading, which constitutes his
most famous (and infamous) contribution to the reception of Shakespeare.
So well known as barely to require reiteration, these outlines have by now
grown perilously close to becoming an almost literally stupefying cliché.

Nevertheless: Freud's reading of *Hamlet* is inseparable from the inaugural
moment of psychoanalysis, generally located in the famous letter of 15
October 1897 to Wilhelm Fliess. Here, Freud writes that 'a single idea
of general value dawned on me. I have found, in my own case too, [the
phenomenon of] being in love with my mother and jealous of my father,
and I now consider it a universal event in early childhood'; 'If this is so, we
can understand the gripping power of *Oedipus Rex* [...] Everyone in the
audience was once a budding Oedipus in fantasy and each recoils in horror
from the dream fulfillment here transplanted into reality, with the full
quantity of repression which separates his infantile state from his present
one'.[14] And Freud continues:

> A fleeting idea has passed through my head of whether the same
> thing may not lie at the bottom of *Hamlet* as well. I am not thinking of
> Shakespeare's conscious intention, but I believe rather that here some
> real event instigated the poet to his representation, in that the uncon-
> scious in him understood the unconscious in his hero. How can Hamlet
> the hysteric justify his words 'Thus conscience does make cowards of
> us all', how can he explain his hesitation in avenging his father by the
> murder of his uncle—he, the same man who sends his courtiers to
> their death without a scruple and who is positively precipitate in killing
> Laertes? How better could he justify himself than by the torment he

suffers from the obscure memory that he himself had meditated the same deed against his father from passion for his mother, and—'use every man after his desert, and who should 'scape whipping?' (2.2.530). His conscience is his unconscious sense of guilt. And is not his sexual alienation in his conversation with Ophelia typically hysterical? and his rejection of the instinct which seeks to beget children? and, finally, his transferring the deed from his own father to Ophelia's? And does he not in the end, in the same remarkable way as my hysterical patients, bring down punishment on himself by suffering the same fate as his father of being poisoned by the same rival?[15]

It is remarkable how many of the central elements of Freud's thinking emerge here in relation to Shakespeare's play, condensed in these few lines. First: Freud implicitly asserts the importance of early childhood in the formation of the (adult) subject, suggesting that the passions of this period of life are not so much abandoned as hidden, and leaving us in no doubt as to the unashamedly sexual and unmistakably hostile content of these passions. Second, and closely connected to this: the 'discovery' (Freud's term) of the Oedipus complex, the 'nuclear complex [*Kernkomplex*]' of the subject.[16] The specifics of the original formulation of the complex – murderous wishes aimed at the father, sexual desire directed at the mother – are undoubtedly reductive, as Freud himself came to recognize. But in its essential form (and it takes many shapes in the later development of his own and more broadly psychoanalytic thought), the complex involves nothing more than the triangular position of the self in relation to a desired object and a prohibiting object: a powerful mythology, as Wittgenstein (though himself no adherent of psychoanalysis) was wont to point out; whether we accept the specifics of the reading or not, it is worth acknowledging its tremendous explanatory force. The supposed universality of the complex means that it is a straightforward matter for Freud to suggest that both Shakespeare and Hamlet show their Oedipality in the play: 'the unconscious in him understood the unconscious in his hero'. This partakes of a long tradition of seeing something essential of the playwright limned in the Danish prince, though here the identification is at a subterranean level: the Schlegel–Coleridge notion of a 'tragedy of thought' here becomes a tragedy of unconscious thought. Third: the concept of repression – the operation constitutive of the unconscious – a notion central to Freud's thinking; as he writes in *On the History of the Psycho-Analytic Movement*, 'the theory of repression is the corner-stone on which the whole structure of psycho-analysis works'.[17] Fourth: the passage begins with a quintessentially Freudian sense ('a fleeting idea has passed through my head') that the most ephemeral ideas are worthy of note, and that in giving voice to these apparently trivial, inappropriate or incoherent materials, one can come closest to the core of the unconscious self; it is this notion that becomes the principle of free association, which Freud called 'the fundamental rule'[18] of psychoanalytic treatment and 'the methodological key to its results'.[19] What repression buries – above all, the Oedipus complex – free association can disinter (like a ghost).

The emergence of psychoanalysis is here unmistakably an intertextual event – it is first spelled out in an epistolary conversation, and it is formulated in relation to the Sophoclean and Shakespearean dramas. There is a convergence and layering of autobiography, literary biography, mythography, psychological intuition and literary criticism in the genesis of the theory, without Freud ever spelling out the relative (empirical or interpretive) weight that should be given to each. Freud's 'solution' has an element of enacting an Oedipal relation to figures of authority – the art of Sophocles and Shakespeare is mastered, even overcome, in the unveiling of the underlying themes. And here, again, we can ask: is Shakespeare, in this play at least, inadvertently Freudian, or is Freud, at the heart of his theory, unconsciously Shakespearean? Did Freud bring out – 'discover', as he claims – the hitherto-hidden Oedipal aspect of *Hamlet*, or did *Hamlet*, in its intertextual conjunction with *Oedipus Tyrannus*, suggest the complex to Freud? And how could Freud, or we, ever be sure?

Finally, we should note Freud's assertion that 'some real event instigated the poet to his representation'. It is a view that leads eventually, inexorably, to Freud's insistence that Shakespeare could not have written the plays, for, as he puts it in the letter to Zweig: 'It is quite inconceivable to me that Shakespeare should have got everything secondhand'; firsthand experience of 'real' events alone, it appears, can explain the understanding evinced by the playwright – an astounding position for the originator of psychoanalysis to take. We will revisit the question of authorship, but for now we can note that the oscillation between an attempt to pin down the origins of psychic creations and structures in 'real' past events and a privileging of the autonomously engendering power of the imagination or fantasy is a thread that runs through all of Freud's work, from the abandonment of the seduction hypothesis a few months before the letter to Fliess (his assertion that the lion's share of what his patients told him about past sexual and other traumatic events was attributable to their own fantasies),[20] through the uncertainty in his writing about the aporetic status of primal scenes (are these memories of actually experienced events or retrospective fantasies?),[21] and on to the ostensible 'original murder' of the father by the 'primal horde' in *Totem and Taboo*. Just as he is torn between emphasizing a unitary and identifiable concept of the self and an idea of the self as fragmented, infinitely constructed and mysterious – so too Freud is never quite sure whether to insist upon traceable, empirical aeteologies or to accept that fantasy, imagination, the life of the mind can be as 'real', or at least as effectual, as material actuality. So, on the one hand, we have (in *Oedipus*) 'the dream fulfillment here transplanted into reality', and, on the other, (in *Hamlet*) 'some real event' inspiring the representation. There is a move from fantasy to reality and back. Freud is as always in two minds, never quite sure how to face the problem that (in Wallace Stevens's famous words) 'We do not know what is real and what is not'.[22]

***

It is through Freud's understanding of dreams – 'a model of all the disguised, substitutive and fictive expressions of human wishing or desire'[23] – that this issue becomes most acute. Dreams hold a pivotal and privileged place in his work – as they do in that of Shakespeare. 'We are such stuff / As dreams are made on' (*The Tempest*, 4.1.156–7): Prospero's poignant words express a deep sense of the shimmering relation between waking reality and dreaming that informs Shakespeare's writing; hence the resonance of Christopher Sly's questions, in the (notably unclosed) framing-scene to *The Taming of the Shrew*, 'do I dream? Or have I dream'd till now?' (Induction, 2.69); of Antipholus of Syracuse's wondering, 'What, was I married to her in my dream? Or sleep I now and think I hear all this?' (*The Comedy of Errors*, 2.2.182–3); of Demetrius's 'Are you sure / That we are awake? It seems to me / That yet we sleep, we dream' (*A Midsummer Night's Dream*, 4.1.193–4); of Leontes' response to Hermione's 'Sir, / You speak a language that I understand not. / My life stands in the level of your dreams': 'Your actions are my dreams' (*The Winter's Tale*, 3.2.79–82); and of Imogen's 'The dream's here still; even when I wake, it is / Without me, as within me; not imagin'd, felt' (*Cymbeline*, 4.2.306–07). Posthumous's long speech upon awakening from his familial dream puts things in ways Freud might have recognised as positively Freudian:

> Sleep, thou hast been a grandsire and begot
> A father to me; and thou hast created
> A mother and two brothers. But (O scorn!)
> Gone! they went hence so soon as they were born.

And so I am awake. [...]
'Tis still a dream, or else such stuff as madmen
Tongue and brain not; either both or nothing,
Or senseless speaking, or a speaking such
As sense cannot untie. Be what it is,
The action of my life is like it... (5.4.123–49).

Yet throughout his writings, Freud is stunningly indifferent to Shakespeare's implicit understanding of dreams; nor does he appear to notice that the plays are populated by a variety of individual narrated or performed dreams. *A Midsummer Night's Dream*, the play that is most deeply involved with the intertwined notions of dreaming and theatricality – and that includes two significant relations of apparent dreams (Hermia's and Bottom's) – gets barely a mention; full and apparently eminently interpretable dreams such as those of Posthumous, *Richard III*'s Clarence, *Julius Caesar*'s Calphurnia, *The Winter's Tale*'s Antigonus, or *Henry VIII*'s Queen Katherine (whose 'good dreams / Possess' not just her 'fancy' (4.2.93–4) but the stage itself) are altogether ignored;[24] Hamlet's comment on his 'bad dreams' – 'I could be bounded in a nutshell, and count myself a king of infinite space – were it not that I have bad dreams' (*Hamlet*, 2.2.254–6) – is disregarded, in spite of Freud's obsession with this play (and in spite of the ease with which he might have linked these nightmares with Hamlet's supposed Oedipal distress); Mercutio is mentioned only in the context of politics, with Freud quoting his 'A plague a both your houses' (*Romeo and Juliet*, 3.1.106) as his own view on the choice of parties in Austria in 1934;[25] had he been inclined to, he could easily have used Mercutio's Queen Mab speech as support for his wish-fulfilment theory of dreams; for Mab, catalyser of dreams,

                          gallops night by night
Through lovers' brains, and then they dream of love;
[O'er] courtiers' knees, that dream on cur'sies straight;
O'er lawyers' fingers, who straight dream on fees;
O'er ladies' lips, who straight on kisses dream...

                                        (*Romeo and Juliet*, 1.4.70–4)

Or as Sonnet 87 has it:

Thus have I had thee as a dream doth flatter:
In sleep a king, but waking no such matter (ll.13–14).

That literary works – but not the dreams in them – should be susceptible of analysis is one of the many imponderables in Freud's thinking. Perhaps Freud felt that Shakespearean dreams are too literary, or (as Cleopatra says) 'past the size of dreaming' (*Antony and Cleopatra*, 5.2.97), or perhaps he was heeding Bottom's warning that 'Man is but an ass, if he go about [t'] expound this dream' (*A Midsummer Night's Dream*, 4.1.206–07). Certainly it is the case that Freud repeatedly insisted that a dream can only properly be interpreted in the context of the particular (free) associations of the dreamer – the analyst can only work with 'all the story of the night told over'; but none of this prevented him from reading works of literature as if they were the writer's (aesthetically-moulded) dreams, or indeed from commenting – albeit somewhat hesitantly – upon some fragments of dreams of Descartes when these were sent to him by an acquaintance.[26]

Shakespeare does, however, make his way indirectly into Freud's thinking about dreams. For one thing, Freud's own dreams are liberally sprinkled with Shakespearean associations; a couple of examples here can suffice: sparked by the mention of Henry VIII, an allusion to flowers in one dream is 'a striking reminder of the scene in one of Shakespeare's historical plays [*3 Henry VI*, 1.1] which represented the beginning of the Wars of the Red and White Roses';[27] regarding a dream about his social aspirations, Freud has associations to different types of caviar, remarking pithily, '"caviare to the general", aristocratic pretensions' (*Hamlet*, 2.2.437);[28] in analysing a dream about his ambitions for promotion and success, Freud recalls the scene from *2 Henry IV* in which Hal takes the crown from his father's pillow as an example of (in this case, parricidal) 'wishes that call for suppression':

Shakespeare's Prince Hal could not, even at his father's sick-bed, resist the temptation of trying on the crown. But, as was to be expected, [my] dream punished my friend, and not me, for this callous wish. 'As he was ambitious, I slew him.' As he could not wait for the removal of another man, he was himself removed.[29]

Somewhat oddly, though, Freud does not quote Henry IV's 'Thy wish was father, Harry, to that thought' (*2 Henry IV*, 4.5.92) in this context: as so often, Shakespeare had got there first, and Freud appears chary of admitting too much (of leaving the crown on his precursor's pillow). Elsewhere, in discussing whether 'background thoughts would have sufficed to evoke a dream' – his own highly significant 'dream of the botanical monograph' – he quotes Horatio's 'There needs no ghost, my lord, come from the grave / To tell us this' (*Hamlet*, 1.5.124–5).[30] *Hamlet*, indeed, looms large throughout *The Interpretation of Dreams*, especially when Freud wants to show the underlying order in the apparently chaotic world of dreams:

> [Dreams] are often most profound when they seem most crazy. In every epoch of history those who have had something to say but could not say it without peril have eagerly assumed a fool's cap. The audience at whom their forbidden speech was aimed tolerated it more easily if they could at the same time laugh and flatter themselves with the reflection that the unwelcome words were clearly nonsensical. The Prince in the play, who had to disguise himself as a madman, was behaving just as dreams do in reality; so that we can say of dreams what Hamlet said of himself, concealing the true circumstances under a cloak of wit and unintelligibility: 'I am but mad north-north-west: when the wind is southerly, I know a hawk from a hand-saw!'
>
> (*Hamlet*, 2.2.378–9)[31]

Indeed, in describing the central mechanisms of disguise employed by dreams (the 'fool's cap' or the 'cloak'), Freud again has recourse to Shakespearean examples: he writes that Hamlet's comment about 'the funeral bak'd meats', which fuses the funeral of his father and the remarriage of his mother, epitomises the 'economy' or 'Thrift, thrift' (*Hamlet*, 1.2.180) inherent to condensation (the process of forming new unities out of materials our conscious minds would prefer to keep separate);[32] and one illustration Freud gives of displacement (the transfer of intense emotions from one object or person to a (less revealing) substitute) is: 'when, in *Othello*, a lost handkerchief precipitates an outburst of rage'.[33]

Dreams adopt these 'disguises' in order to evade our internal censors – to hide us from ourselves: the ostensible connection between dreams and insanity is thus deceptive; and Freud in fact seems to have – again, strangely, we might think – no doubts at all about Hamlet's sanity. Though it is hard to think of any play by Shakespeare in which the boundaries of sanity are not blurred or unpicked, Freud is generally unconcerned with the question of madness in the playwright's works. He is ever eager to discern method in apparent nonsense or madness, which is why he keeps returning to Polonius's well-worn formulation: in insisting that 'the psychical anarchy and disruption of every function that prevail in dreams' is no reason to dismiss them as absurd, he writes: 'It seems, however, to have dawned upon some other writers that the madness of dreams may not be without method and may even be simulated, like that of the Danish prince on whom this shrewd judgement was passed';[34] again, in his late essay 'Constructions in

Analysis', explaining how repressed material from the past resurfaces in delusional states, Freud writes: 'The essence of [delusion] is that there is not only *method* in madness, as the poet has already perceived, but also a fragment of *historical truth*'.[35]

***

Freud's insistence here upon the significance of some 'fragment of *historical truth*' corresponds to his pinpointing of the 'real event [that] instigated the poet to his representation' in *Hamlet*. By the time he published his views in *The Interpretation of Dreams*, he believed he knew what this 'real event' was: it was the death of Shakespeare's father in the lead-up to the writing of the play. Oddly – and this again evinces his anxiety about Shakespearean influence – in the first edition of *The Interpretation of Dreams* the presentation of the reading was relegated to a lengthy footnote; it was only inserted into the text proper in 1914 (after the publication of Ernest Jones's elaboration of Freud's theory).[36] The paragraph, famous though it is, is worth quoting in full:

Another of the great creations of tragic poetry, Shakespeare's *Hamlet*, has its roots in the same soil as *Oedipus Rex*. But the changed treatment of the same material reveals the whole difference in the mental life of these two widely separated epochs of civilization: the secular advance of repression in the emotional life of mankind. In the *Oedipus* the child's wishful phantasy that underlies it is brought into the open and realized as it would be in a dream. In *Hamlet* it remains repressed; and—just as in the case of a neurosis—we only learn of its existence from its inhibiting consequences. Strangely enough, the overwhelming effect produced by the more modern tragedy has turned out to be compatible with the fact that people have remained completely in the dark as to the hero's character. The play is built up on Hamlet's hesitations over fulfilling the task of revenge that is assigned to him; but its text offers no reasons or motives for these hesitations and an immense variety of attempts at interpreting them have failed to produce a result. According to the view which was originated by Goethe and is still the prevailing one to-day, Hamlet represents the type of man whose power of direct action is paralysed by an excessive development of his intellect. (He is 'sicklied o'er with the pale cast of thought'.) According to another view, the dramatist has tried to portray a pathologically irresolute character which might be classed as neurasthenic.

The plot of the drama shows us, however, that Hamlet is far from being represented as a person incapable of taking any action. We see him doing so on two occasions: first in a sudden outburst of temper, when he runs his sword through the eavesdropper behind the arras, and secondly in a premeditated and even crafty fashion, when, with all the callousness of a Renaissance prince, he sends the two courtiers to the death that had been planned for himself. What is it, then, that inhibits him in fulfilling the task set him by his father's ghost? The answer, once again, is that it is the peculiar nature of the task. Hamlet is able to do anything—except take vengeance on the man who did away with his father and took that father's place with his mother, the man who shows him the repressed wishes of his own childhood realized. Thus the loathing which should drive him on to revenge is replaced in him by self-reproaches, by scruples of conscience, which remind him that he himself is literally no better than the sinner whom he is to punish. Here I have translated into conscious terms what was bound to remain unconscious in Hamlet's mind; and if anyone is inclined to call him a hysteric, I can only accept the fact as one that is implied by my interpretation. The distaste for sexuality expressed by Hamlet in his conversation with Ophelia fits in very well with this: the same distaste which was destined to take possession of the poet's mind more and more during the years that followed, and which reached its extreme expression in *Timon of Athens*. For it can of course only be the poet's own mind which confronts us in Hamlet. I observe in a book on Shakespeare by Georg Brandes (1896) a statement that *Hamlet* was written immediately after the death of Shakespeare's father (in 1601), that is, under the immediate impact of his bereavement and, as we may well assume, while his childhood feelings about his father had been freshly revived. It is known, too, that Shakespeare's own son who died at an early age bore the name of 'Hamnet', which is identical with 'Hamlet'. Just as *Hamlet* deals with the relation of a son to his parents, so *Macbeth* (written at approximately the same period) is concerned with the subject of childlessness. But just as all neurotic symptoms, and, for that matter, dreams, are capable of being 'over-interpreted' and indeed need to be, if they are to be fully understood, so all genuinely creative writings are the product of more than a single motive and more than a single impulse in the poet's mind, and are open to more than a single interpretation. In what I have written I have only attempted to interpret the deepest layer of impulses in the mind of the creative writer.[37]

Again pairing (as he does throughout his work) *Hamlet* and *Oedipus*, Freud here marks out the former as emblematic of an epochal watershed in the development of civilization ('the secular advance of repression in the emotional life of mankind'). The hallmark of modernity for Freud involves the repression of primal drives, and hence the creation of the split, self-alienated modern subject. Henceforth, psychoanalysis will be needed in order to unearth the 'inhibiting consequences' of repressed desire. The work of repression means that Oedipus does what Hamlet cannot even know he wants to do. As Cynthia Chase drolly points out, 'Sophocles' play portrays Oedipus as the one person in history *without* an Oedipus complex in the conventional sense', since the complex involves a *repressed* fantasy (a 'complex', psychoanalytically speaking, is a connected group of repressed ideas), not its enactment.[38] Repression – like sleep, or like drama – keeps dangerous things in the realm of the unreal(ized).

Freud's argument is elegant in its streamlined contours: Hamlet cannot bring himself to kill Claudius because that would amount to punishing the character who embodies (by having fulfilled) his deepest desires. In relation to *Hamlet*, Freud never advanced beyond the outlines of this argument, never returned to the play in any substantial way except to reiterate this reading in increasingly atrophied ways.[39] But the streamlining goes along with a quite remarkable distance from the text – a text which Freud knew intimately and quoted from copiously throughout his work. In the long paragraph above there is just one quotation – 'sicklied o'er with the pale cast of thought' (3.1.84) – and this is adduced in support of Goethe's rejected argument; nor are the quotations from *Hamlet* in the letter to Fliess pertinent to Freud's central case, which in fact includes, bizarrely, *no* close reading of the play's language – reading of the kind at which Freud repeatedly shows himself so brilliantly adept in his analyses of dreams and jokes. Indeed, elsewhere Freud explicitly rejects the notion that *Hamlet*'s 'magical appeal rests solely upon the impressive thoughts in it and the splendour of its language': 'we feel the need of discovering in it some source of power beyond them alone'.[40] We might say that this is the equivalent of insisting on 'some real event' as a catalyst for the creative mind: there must be something *behind* the mere surface of words and thoughts. As a result, Freud leaves out material he might have used to support his reading. To take an obvious instance: when Hamlet bemoans his lack of vengeful action with the words 'How stand I then, / That have a father kill'd, a mother stain'd' (4.4.56–7), the ambiguous syntax allows for either a passive or an active construal of the verbs in the second line; and Freud might have made a case for the passive mood as (barely) covering up the active to argue that the latter reveals 'what was bound to remain unconscious in Hamlet's mind'.

His distance from the play emerges too in the mistake (in the letter to Fliess) over the prince's 'killing Laertes': it is of course Polonius whom Hamlet is 'positively precipitate' in killing. While the mistake is corrected in *The Interpretation of Dreams*, it is nonetheless telling that there had been confusion in Freud's mind about a father and a son. Freud wants to have it both ways here – to show, on the one hand, how '*Hamlet* deals with the relation of a son to his parents' (and to bolster this argument through the analogy between the author's and the character's recently-bereaved situations), and, on the other, to lend further support to his thesis through Shakespeare's loss of his son Hamnet. If 'the unconscious in [Shakespeare] understood the unconscious in his hero', it is not through a one-to-one correspondence. In any case, given the centrality of the notion of ambivalent feelings towards a recently-dead father to his interpretation, it is remarkable – indeed almost unbelievable – that Freud's realization that the loss of his own father informed the writing of *The Interpretation of Dreams* only apparently came to him some time after completing the book. Freud only inserted the following admission in the preface to the 1908 edition:

> [T]his book has a further subjective significance for me personally—a significance which I only grasped after I had completed it. It was, I found, a portion of my own self-analysis, my reaction to my father's death—that is to say, the most important event, the most poignant loss, of a man's life. Having discovered that this was so, I felt unable to obliterate the traces of the experience.[41]

The admission opens up a sudden sense of infinite regress, with layers upon layers of identification and loss – along the lines of Claudius's 'you must know your father lost a father, / That father lost, lost his' (1.2.89–90). Freud's father had died towards the end of 1896, setting in motion an emotional and intellectual upheaval in his son that culminated in many of the central insights of psychoanalysis. His magnum opus thus shares something crucial with what he thinks of as 'Shakespeare's masterpiece':[42] at a profound level, their 'common theme / Is death of fathers' (1.2.103–4). But the 'most poignant loss' is also a huge gain – for both Shakespeare and Freud: in both cases it is intimately connected to the genesis of what is perhaps their 'most important' work. And indeed ambivalence in relation to loss is one of the main lessons of 'Mourning and Melancholia', where Freud writes of mourning as always enacting both a preservation (through memorialization) and a destruction (through gradual disengagement), and where the pain of loss of the loved object is matched by the way 'the ego becomes free and uninhibited again' at the end of the process.[43]

In *Hamlet*, both Claudius and Gertrude insist that the death of a father is 'common' (1.2.72, 103): 'Thou know'st 'tis common', says Gertrude; 'Why seems it so particular with thee?' (75). Hamlet is scathing in his response ('Ay, madam, it is common' – 73) and adamant ('I have that within which passes show' – 85) about his uniqueness. Freud's flat assertion that the loss of a father is 'the most important event, the most poignant loss, of a man's life' generalises from a particular example – is the 'man' *every* man, or is this Freud? The leap from a 'subjective significance for me personally' to this generalization is akin to the rapid jump from 'my own case' to 'a universal event' in the letter to Fliess. We are back in the realm of autobiography or self-analysis as somehow (but how? – as evidence? catalyst? analogy?) related to 'universal' theory. In 'Mourning and Melancholia', Freud writes of the self-castigations of melancholics: 'there can be no doubt that if anyone holds and expresses to others an opinion of himself such as this (an opinion which Hamlet held both of himself and of everyone else), he is ill, whether he is speaking the truth or whether he is being more or less unfair to himself.'[44] We could say that the Oedipal hypothesis, like the assumption about the most poignant loss in a man's life, is 'an opinion which [Freud] held both of himself and of everyone else'; but the labelling of Hamlet as 'ill' is perhaps even more problematic than this. Whenever Freud uses locutions such as 'undoubtedly' or 'there can be no doubt' – as he very frequently does – it is worth stopping and considering what doubt he may be suppressing at that juncture in his argument, or whether he is in fact drawing attention to a doubt, challenging the reader to face it. So the reduction of Hamlet to a 'world-famous neurotic', a 'hysteric', or 'typically hysterical' should not be taken entirely at face value.[45]

Nevertheless, these labels highlight Freud's tendency to come up with diagnostic typologies – a tendency that seems, at a minimum, short-sighted in relation to so utterly distinctive and elusive a character as Hamlet. Though he repeatedly claimed to have 'solved the riddle' of 'our Prince Hamlet' through the discovery of the Oedipus Complex, Freud admits that such diagnoses have their limits. Indeed, the analyst at one point quotes at length Hamlet's sparring with Rosencrantz and Guildenstern in order to underline just how difficult such knowledge always is: 'You would pluck out the heart of my mystery ... *'Sblood, do you think I am easier to be played on than a pipe? Call me what instrument you will, though you can fret me, [yet] you cannot play upon me*' (3.2.364–72; Freud's italics): 'it is not so easy to play upon the instrument of the mind'.[46] In 'Mourning and Melancholia', Freud labels Hamlet a neurotic based in part on his use of the phrase 'Use every man after his desert, and who shall 'scape whipping';[47] in doing so, he seems to forget that Hamlet speaks these words not so much to condemn humanity, not in bitterness (let alone illness), but out of a generosity of spirit: he is responding to Polonius's sniffy, snobbish 'I will use them [the Players] according to their desert':

> God's bodkin, man, much better: use every man after his desert, and who shall scape whipping? Use them after your own honor and dignity: the less they deserve, the more merit is in your bounty.
>
> (*Hamlet*, 2.2.529–32)

Late in his life, in trying to dissuade his friend Arnold Zweig from writing a biography of him, Freud wrote: 'Truth is unobtainable; humanity does not deserve it, and incidentally, wasn't our Prince Hamlet right when he asked whether anyone would escape a whipping if he got what he deserved?'[48] His use of the quotation has come full circle.

***

It is impossible to ignore the strange gender bias of Freud's comment that the loss of a father is 'the most important event, the most poignant loss, of a man's life' – not just the assumption of a male subjectivity, but also of male objecthood; it is almost as if one's maleness receives its confirmation in finding the loss of a father more poignant and significant than any other loss. As throughout so much of Freud's work, here the figure of the mother is strikingly absent.[49] She returns – unexpectedly, hauntingly – in 'The Theme of the Three Caskets', Freud's (1913) essay which offers an implicit answer to the question of why the death of a father should appear to Freud 'the most poignant loss': because for him, it seems, the mother is never lost – only ever, in effect, returned to. 'The Theme of the Three Caskets' is the only one of Freud's essays that announces itself in its title more or less explicitly as being about Shakespeare; it is also, not coincidentally, one of the few places in Freud's work where mothers and daughters take centre stage – in the words of Julia Lupton and Kenneth Reinhard, it marks 'a momentary mutation of the phallic economy in Freud's writing, an aberration'.[50] The essay is manifestly *not* a reading of *The Merchant of Venice*, and only very partially a reading of *King Lear*, nor does Freud make any attempt at integrating his interpretation of the casket scene into a

wider reading of the earlier play. Here, for once, Freud is not interested
in character, in neurosis and diagnosis, but pursues rather a thematic
issue. He follows a winding path of connections between various mythological, fairy tale and literary scenes depicting the choice between three
options (astral myths of sun, moon and stars; the judgement of Paris; three
sisters in the tales of Cinderella and of Psyche), deploying this material to
underpin the provocative proposition that the opening scene of *King Lear*
is 'linked by many hidden similarities to the choice of the casket in *The
Merchant of Venice*'.[51] Taking 'the three caskets symbolically as three women'
(293), Freud suggests that in both cases it is the third of three female
figures who, it transpires, is 'the best, the most excellent one' (293), but
who is also associated – via the idea of silence or hiddenness – with death:
thus the three figures are closely related to the three Fates, 'the third of
whom is called Atropos, the inexorable' (296). He continues:

> On our supposition the third of the sisters is the Goddess of Death,
> Death itself. But in the Judgement of Paris she is the Goddess of Love, in
> the tale of Apuleius she is someone comparable to the goddess for her
> beauty, in *The Merchant of Venice* she is the fairest and wisest of women, in
> *King Lear* she is the one loyal daughter. We may ask whether there can
> be a more complete contradiction (298).

Since, however, in dreams 'replacements by the precise opposite' (298)
are common enough, Freud argues that the substitution of the goddess of
death with 'the fairest and wisest' (and, simultaneously, of the inevitability
of death with an ostensibly free choice) is a 'reaction-formation' (299): 'No
greater triumph of wish-fulfilment is conceivable. A choice is made where
in reality there is obedience to a compulsion; and what is chosen is not a
figure of terror, but the fairest and most desirable of women' (299).

How, then, has Shakespeare used the theme? Freud suggests that in *King
Lear* (*The Merchant* has pretty much dropped out of the picture by this
point), Shakespeare permits a sense of the original significance of the myth
to show through the distortion; it is precisely 'by means of this reduction of
the distortion, this partial return to the original, that the dramatist achieves
his more profound effect upon us' (300). It is Lear's refusal to 'renounce
love, choose death and make friends with the necessity of dying' (301) that
is dramatized in the opening scene of the play. By using the mythological
and fairy tale material to link the casket scene in *The Merchant* and the
opening scene of *King Lear*, Freud unearths an important undercurrent
in the latter play; he also implies how confused the categories of mother,

wife and daughter are for Lear – even though he again ignores the textual evidence which might have supported his claim.[52]

Freud's essay ends with some of the most plangent words in his entire corpus: 'But it is in vain that an old man yearns for the love of woman as he had it first from his mother; the third of the Fates alone, the silent Goddess of Death, will take him into her arms' (301). This, implies Freud, is what Shakespeare's play is really about: the way in which Lear vainly tries to avoid the inevitable 'embrace' of death. While the pathos of the ending comes from the contrast between this inevitability and Lear's refusal to 'make friends with the necessity of dying', the personification and eroticization of the 'Goddess of Death' here act as mitigating factors; as Nicholas Royle puts it, Freud's prose here performs 'a demystification that is also a sort of remystification'.[53] Throughout the essay, Freud links eros and thanatos, imbuing desire with death and vice versa; though he only fully theorises it seven years later, he is already moving – under the influence of *King Lear* – beyond the pleasure principle and towards the idea of the death instinct (though, again, Freud signally fails to consider, for example, the importance of 'nothing' in *King Lear* in this context.) The death instinct – the hypothesis of an inherent drive towards quietude – becomes in *Beyond the Pleasure Principle* increasingly inseparable from the erotic drive and is associated with muteness or silence – though in this later formulation, the figure of the goddess and the role of the woman have disappeared (as Elizabeth Bronfen has pointed out, 'both "death" and "woman" function as Western culture's privileged tropes for the enigmatic and for alterity'.)[54] 'Desire is death' (Sonnet 147.8): Shakespeare's works played no small part in impelling Freud to think about the relations between the pleasure principle and the inexorability of our fates – our desire to return (as Freud puts it in *Beyond the Pleasure Principle*) to inorganic nothingness.[55]

Tracing the roots of the essay back to the various triads of significant women in his life – Freud's father's three wives; Freud's three daughters, the third and last of whom (Anna) was the one closest to him ('my faithful Anna-Antigone', he called her)[56] – as well as to Freud's propensity to address his fiancée (Martha Bernays) as 'my Cordelia-Marty' or his 'sweet Cordelia'[57] – recent critics have convincingly shown how 'The Theme of the Three Caskets' can be read as one of Freud's most revealing autobiographical pieces. And there is – as Lupton and Reinhard have suggested[58] – another autobiographical fold here, derived from an earlier part of the famous letter to Fliess in which the Oedipus complex was first proposed. Here, Freud describes one of his earliest memories:

a scene occurred to me which in the course of twenty-five years has occasionally emerged in my conscious memory without my understanding it. My mother was nowhere to be found; I was crying in despair. My brother Philipp (twenty years older than I) unlocked a wardrobe [*Kasten*] for me, and when I did not find my mother inside it either, I cried even more until, slender and beautiful, she came in through the door. What can this mean?[59]

Without belabouring the possible connections between this 'scene' and 'The Theme of the Three Caskets', it is worth simply noting that the essay gives a sense of how Freud's methodology – mixing memory and desire – can lead to a significant intuition about *King Lear*.

While 'scientifically' unsound, autobiographical input opens the door for some of Freud's most interesting theoretical insights – and for some of his most remarkable oversights. Two in particular come to mind here: Shylock and Prospero. We might have expected to hear more in this essay, preoccupied as it is with older fathers and their daughters, about Prospero (and indeed about Shakespeare's late plays more generally); but Freud seems to have been singularly uninterested in the figure who, along with Hamlet, was so often considered to be the one most closely associated with the playwright himself. As Norman Holland points out, 'curiously, although [Freud] thought *The Tempest* autobiographical like the *Sonnets*, he never analysed, only quoted it'.[60] And we would certainly have expected to hear more about Shylock in an essay ostensibly on *The Merchant of Venice*. Yet Freud is completely silent about this character, whom we might think of as both relevant to the essay and in certain ways close to its author: another aging father whose precious daughter becomes a signifier of loss, a conspicuous figure of the Jew as lonely outsider – a figure of whom one is put in mind by the closing sentences of Freud's 1925 essay, 'The Resistances to Psychoanalysis':

Finally, with all reserve, the question may be raised whether the personality of the present writer as a Jew who has never sought to disguise the fact that he is a Jew may not have had a share in provoking the antipathy of his environment to psycho-analysis. ... To profess belief in this new theory called for a certain degree of readiness to accept a situation of solitary opposition—a situation with which no one is more familiar than a Jew.[61]

The position of the outsider is one by which (as we shall see in the next chapter) Freud, like Shakespeare, is continually fascinated. Freud kept

returning to the figure of Moses, 'the lonely man',[62] eventually concluding
– infamously and almost certainly incorrectly – that Moses was not Jewish
but Egyptian. So there are internal connections between the turning-away
from figures of potential identification with Freud (Shylock) and with
Shakespeare (Prospero). Perhaps Freud needed to distance himself from
characters who might tarnish the reputation of his fledgling 'science'
with its aspirations to objectivity: the bloodthirsty usurer and the angry
magus who share a barely controlled (or uncontrolled) desire for revenge.
Certainly, we can say that Freud is more willing to use his insights into
his own psyche to interpret works of art and literature than vice versa. In
any event, it is hard not to feel that, in the occlusion of both Shylock and
Prospero from both this essay and his work more generally, *something* is
being kept at bay.

***

Freud's most extended treatment of Shakespeare's plays comes three years
after the 'Caskets' piece, in an essay entitled, with a certain insouciance,
'Some Character-Types Met with in Psycho-Analytic Work' (1916).[63] Like so
much else in Freud, the essay is tripartite; it outlines three kinds of patients
the analyst has encountered repeatedly in his work, described in the
titles of the essay's three sections: 'The Exceptions' (those who consider
themselves so exceptional as to be exempt from the rules constraining
others); 'Those Wrecked by Success' (those who collapse psychically upon
attaining a long-wished-for achievement); and 'Criminals from a Sense of
Guilt' (those who, paradoxically, relieve their conscience by committing
crimes, thereby giving themselves a form of objective correlative to match
their pre-existing sense of guilt). The first two sections focus on literary
exemplars of each 'type': Richard III in the first case, Lady Macbeth and
Ibsen's Rebecca (in *Rosmersholm*) in the second. The third and shortest
section addresses no literary material (one could say that Freud returned to
the central motifs of this section in his essay on Dostoyevsky a decade later).

Freud never explains the principle of selection of the 'character-types'
in his essay, but only states that he intends to trace 'a few … surprising
traits of character' (311) that pose particular problems of resistance to
psychoanalytic treatment; the three 'types' could surely have been supple-
mented by numerous others. In all three cases, though, transgressiveness is
a central concern; if the first 'character-type' asserts that 'I may do wrong
myself, since wrong has been done to me' (315), we could say that the
second declares that 'I must do myself wrong, since I have done wrong';

and the third: 'I must do wrong, since I have (already) done wrong'. There is in all these cases a relation between transgression projected outwards and wrongdoing turned inwards. But one could also argue that the essay is a meditation on diverse fantasies of escape from a circle of commonality and community: an escape, as it were, outwards (through exclusion from normative standards), upwards (through kingship or transcendent success) or downwards (towards criminality). The title of the essay cuts these fantasies down to size, bringing them back within the sphere of the familiar and the common – these are, in the end, no more than 'character-types' we can all recognise. As so often in Freud's work, the (underlying) notion of repetition undermines pretensions of all kinds: we may think we are exercising free will, but in fact we are (unconsciously) repeating a script composed during our childhoods; we may think we are embracing love, but in fact we are in death's grip; we may think we're exceptional, but we're just 'types'. There is scepticism verging on cynicism here, but it is always paradoxically balanced by a powerful sense of the unique patient or character Freud is discussing: Freud was fond of quoting his old teacher Jean-Martin Charcot: '*La théorie c'est bon; mais ça n'empêche pas d'exister*'.[64]

It is no coincidence that an essay on 'Character-*Types*' begins with a section entitled 'The Exceptions': for Freud's writing, as we have already seen, is always pulled simultaneously in two directions – towards the generalizing or typologizing tendencies of his scientific ideals, and towards an absolute concentration on the unique person or character before him. Nor does he come close to resolving the matter here: for Freud's central example, Shakespeare's Richard III, becomes, in this essay, at once the most exceptional and the most normative of characters: extraordinary in his utter rejection of social norms, and quite ordinary (almost pathetically so) in his need to be extraordinary. 'Observation teaches us that individual human beings realize the general picture of humanity in an almost infinite variety of ways. If we yield to the legitimate need to distinguish particular types in this multiplicity...':[65] so begins Freud's essay on 'Libidinal Types' (with the analyst sounding not a little like Dr Johnson). We might discern a nod here to Enobarbus's characterization of Cleopatra's 'infinite variety' (*Antony and Cleopatra*, 2.2.235); the latter is another of Shakespeare's characters whom Freud ignores completely. If it seems strange that characters of such mythic proportions as Cleopatra, Shylock and Prospero are ignored by Freud, it seems no less remarkable that characters as utterly distinctive as Richard III, Lady Macbeth and Hamlet should be upheld as particular neurotic 'types'. (It is worth contemplating the paradoxical notion that while Freud's Montaignean self-exposure is placed at the service of his universalizing aims,[66] Shakespeare's exemplary blankness becomes the vehicle for utterly distinct individuality; as Dogberry puts it, 'but God is to be worshipp'd, all men are not alike' – *Much Ado About Nothing*, 3.5.39–40.)

Unlike the 'Caskets' essay, 'Some Character-Types' does in fact address the topic of revenge – if indirectly – portraying it in the opening section as a form of resistance to the need to bow to 'the exigencies of life'.[67] (The half-buried link between fantasies of revenge and of exceptionality returns in the second section, where Freud writes of 'the avenger, Macduff, who is himself an exception to the laws of generation, since he was not born of his mother but ripp'd from her womb' (321): it is possible to dream of escaping from these exigencies at the beginning as well as at the end of life.) Those who consider themselves exceptional often feel that life has short-changed them, writes Freud; they say to themselves (and this is how Freud reads Richard's opening soliloquy, after quoting it at length): "'I have a right to be an exception, to disregard the scruples by which others let themselves be held back. I may do wrong myself, since wrong has been done to me'" (314–15). Freud's archetype here is 'a figure in whose character the claim to be an exception is closely bound up with and is motivated by the circumstance of congenital disadvantage' (313): in Richard III, we find a 'magnification' of a common 'demand [for] reparation for early wounds to our narcissism, our self-love' (315). His deformity provides him with a kind of alibi. There are people – and indeed 'whole nations' – who feel that they are, as Freud writes (with perhaps a nod to *Hamlet* – 5.2.219–20), 'watched over by a special providence' (313). But, it turns out, these supposed 'exceptions' aren't really exceptional after all; for, as Freud asserts, 'we *all* demand reparation for early wounds to our narcissism' (315).

There is a democratizing impulse in Freud's work, which finds us all to be both implicitly neurotic – 'we are all to some extent hysterics', as he once put it[68] – and fantastically creative. As Rieff writes, 'in Freud's conception of the normal man, there is a certain echo of the Romantic idea of genius – the ideal man who attains to the self-expression that other men, intimidated by convention, weakly forgo'.[69] Nevertheless: 'the incomparable Shakespeare'[70] *is* for Freud this ideal man, the exceptional genius. So it is particularly striking that, in spite of his enormous admiration, Freud never identifies himself with Shakespeare; he seems to feel that the dramatist is literally (as Dr Johnson said of Falstaff) 'unimitated, unimitable', a figure of *non*-identification.[71] In fact, Freud does not tend to align himself with poets and artists in general but rather with conquistadors and military or public leaders (Hannibal, Julius Caesar, Napoleon, Moses) or with riddle-solving characters *in* literature (Oedipus, Hamlet, Sherlock

Holmes). In his interpretations of Shakespeare (as elsewhere), Freud always plays the detective. To his brief reading of *Richard III*, he adds that the opening soliloquy 'merely gives a hint, and leaves us to fill in what it hints at' (314); Shakespeare 'does not permit his hero to give open and complete expression to all his secret motives. By this means he obliges us to supplement them'; he thereby 'keeps us firmly identified with his hero' (315). It is a claim he will repeat often: that creative writers engage our sympathies by withholding full disclosure of the motives of their protagonists. Freud's psychoanalysis precisely reverses this process, and in this sense openly pits itself against art.

The contention is reiterated in the next section, on *Macbeth* – but here it borders on accusation. 'Those Wrecked by Success' offers Freud's most detailed reading by far of a Shakespearean text. Freud begins with the problem that neurosis is usually caused by 'an external frustration' – that is to say, when a 'satisfaction is withheld *in reality*' – whereas, in certain cases, it is precisely upon the removal of external impediments to the fulfilment of a wish that breakdown occurs.[72] Freud takes Lady Macbeth as his exemplar, and attempts to solve the conundrum of why it is that she 'collapses on reaching success, after striving for it with single-minded energy' (318). What was it, asks Freud, 'that broke this character which had seemed forged from the toughest metal?' (319). His answer – coming as it does from such a proud riddle-solver – is unexpected: 'It seems to me impossible to come to any decision' (320). Nevertheless, Freud resolves to have a stab (or, as it transpires, two or three stabs) at the problem; he turns to 'external' materials – first the historical background of the (heirless) end of Elizabeth's reign and the accession of James I, then the primary source of the Macbeths' story in Holinshed's *Chronicles* – in order to argue that the idea of childlessness is contextually crucial, as well as thematically at the heart of the play itself. Freud reaches the assessment that 'Lady Macbeth's illness, the transformation of her callousness into penitence, could be explained directly as a reaction to her childlessness' (321–2). Shakespeare, by massively accelerating the time frame of the original tale from Holinshed's ten years (which would allow the frustration of not having any children to set in) to 'about one week' (322),[73] has cunningly obscured the effects of Lady Macbeth's barrenness and thereby created the mystery that draws the audience in – but, at the same time, has 'take[n] the ground from under all our constructions of the motives for the change in the characters of Macbeth and his wife' (322). The protagonists' frustration in their hopes for succession are thus echoed in Freud's (and the audience's) sense of impotence in his hopes for comprehension.

Shakespeare's play is thus, according to Freud, not so much 'a tragedy of ambition' (320) as a tragedy of sterility; the issue at its heart is the protagonists' 'fruitless' (3.1.60) condition. On this reading, the Macbeths are 'wrecked by success' because their idea of 'success' (the word is repeated four times in the first act of the play) emphasizes the wrong meaning of the word; and the famous sibilance of Macbeth's 'catch / With his surcease, success' (1.7.3–4) resonates so powerfully because it catches his anguish at the juxtaposition of 'surcease' (ending, cessation) and 'success' (having an heir).[74] In effect, Freud shifts the focus from the apparent cause, openly averred by Macbeth at the end of his great soliloquy of 1.7 –

> I have no spur
> To prick the sides of my intent, but only
> Vaulting ambition... (25–7).

– back a few lines to the mysterious, powerful (and similarly semi-equestrian) image of 'pity, like a naked new-born babe / Striding the blast' (21). Macbeth sets these metaphors in opposition – one rider pushes him towards the murder of Duncan, the other urges desistance; the horseriding image, like the Porter's drink, 'provokes, and unprovokes' (2.3.28). But Freud's interpretation suggests that the two urges have the same source – that Macbeth spills blood in order to obscure the absence of his bloodline, as it were by way of revenge. Becoming king and queen has merely sharpened the pain of being 'unlineal' (3.1.62): the 'internal frustration' of being childless 'has only made its appearance after an external frustration has been replaced by fulfilment of a wish' (317). Freud implies that the story of ambition is a cover story for the question mark hanging over the (non-existent) 'babe' (and, indeed, along the same lines, we could even tentatively suggest that in the many images of breath and wind punctuating Macbeth's soliloquy, culminating in the 'sightless couriers of the air' (23), there may be a suppressed reference to his own (missing) heir; the pun is common enough in Shakespeare's work).

Freud's reading of *Macbeth* provides an insight into the imaginative power of the theme of childlessness – while repeatedly reaching an interpretive impasse; as Ned Lukacher puts it, 'theoretical barrenness and the barrenness of the Macbeths are ... never far apart in Freud's thinking'.[75] Towards the end of the section on *Macbeth*, Freud writes:

What, however, these motives can have been which in so short a space of time could turn the hesitating, ambitious man into an unbridled tyrant, and his steely-hearted instigator into a sick woman gnawed by remorse, it is, in my view, impossible to guess (322).

And after half-heartedly offering another possible avenue of interpretation – following Ludwig Jekels's suggestion that the Macbeths are split and complementary 'parts of a single psychical individuality' (324) – he concludes the section by, in effect, throwing up his hands and turning away from the play: 'If we have been unable to give any answer to the question why Lady Macbeth should collapse after her success, we may perhaps have a better chance when we turn to the creation of another great dramatist…' (324).

One oddity about Freud's essay is the omission of any mention of the Doctor who witnesses Lady Macbeth's sleepwalking. It is as if Freud is avoiding the obvious identification here with the character who is charged with diagnosing and curing Lady Macbeth – and who also acknowledges his inability to do so, to 'Cleanse the stuff'd bosom of that perilous stuff / Which weighs upon the heart' (5.3.44–5).[76] 'My mind she has mated, and amaz'd my sight. / I think, but dare not speak' (5.1.78–9): one can see why Freud may have wanted to steer clear of the suggestive association. Elsewhere in his use of *Macbeth* in his dreams and associations, Freud identifies with the protagonist: he ends one letter to a colleague with: 'In the words of King Macbeth, let us die in harness' (5.5.51);[77] and another (to Jung) with: 'all in all, it is better "to die in harness"'.[78] In an early letter, while still a student of neurophysiology, Freud gives a sense of the magnitude of his ambitions for publication:

> I am also sending you herewith my collected works, not my complete ones as I have reason to suspect, for I am awaiting the correction of a third, and a fourth and fifth keep appearing in my prescient mind, which is startled by them like Macbeth by the ghosts of the English kings: "What! Will the line stretch out to the crack of doom?" (4.1.117).[79]

The 'line' referred to is, of course, the vision of non-Macbeth-engendered kings, so that it is a strange association indeed: through it, Freud's ambitions for his collected works seem at once crowned with everlasting success (they will 'stretch out to the crack of doom') and doomed to failure (they will, apparently, not be his own brainchildren). 'Those Wrecked by Success' indeed.

It may well be the case that *Macbeth* worked upon Freud's mind more profoundly than any other work of literature – more, indeed, than *Hamlet*, which he felt he could set aside once he had 'solved' it:

> Let us consider Shakespeare's masterpiece, *Hamlet*, a play now over three centuries old. I have followed the literature of psycho-analysis closely, and I accept its claim that it was not until the material of the tragedy had been traced back by psycho-analysis to the Oedipus theme that the mystery of its effect was at last explained.[80]

The hilarious 'acceptance' of his own claims vis-à-vis *Hamlet* bespeaks a kind of hubris: it is as if Freud felt that he had mastered 'Shakespeare's masterpiece'. In his *Introductory Lectures on Psycho-Analysis*, on the other hand, Freud briefly revisits *Macbeth* in his discussion of the meaning of dreams:

> Dreams do not simply reproduce the stimulus; they work it over, they make allusions to it, they include it in some context, they replace it by something else … Shakespeare's *Macbeth*, for instance, was a *pièce d'occasion* composed to celebrate the accession of the king who first united the crowns of the three kingdoms. But does this immediate historical occasion cover the content of the tragedy? Does it explain its greatnesses and its enigmas? It may be that the external and internal stimuli, too, impinging on the sleeper, are only the *instigators* of the dream and will accordingly betray nothing to us of its essence.[81]

A dream's meaning, like that of a work of literature, invariably exceeds the grasp of its raw materials, its '*Stoff*'.[82] And Freud at times doubts the efficacy of his hermeneutic attempts to plumb the psyche's depths. At several points, he asserts that all such interpretation is destined to reach an impasse – most notably, in his much-quoted declaration that

> there is often a passage in even the most thoroughly interpreted dream which has to be left obscure; this is because we become aware during the work of interpretation that at that point there is a tangle of dream-thoughts which cannot be unravelled and which moreover adds nothing to our knowledge of the content of the dream. This is the dream's navel, the spot where it reaches down into the unknown.[83]

In spite of the force of repression, one can come to know certain aspects of the unconscious; but there will always be, as Freud repeats at a different point in *The Interpretation of Dreams*, 'a navel, [a] point of contact with the unknown'; 'the deepest layer of impulses' can never be reached.[84] Like 'Bottom's dream', which 'hath no bottom', it is, Freud sometimes suggests, 'past the wit of man' (*A Midsummer Night's Dream*, 4.1.214; 205) finally to unravel the meaning of a dream – or of a Shakespearean text. *Macbeth* marked for Freud the most powerful literary example of a piece of literature that stymied all hermeneutic efforts to explain its enigmas.

***

Given this sense of the open-endedness and unknowability of the sources of creativity, Freud's engagement with the authorship controversy is truly bizarre: if the aporia at the heart of *Macbeth* stung Freud, the uncertainty surrounding the identity of Shakespeare himself seemed to make him positively apoplectic.[85] Having noted how Freud's interpretation of *Hamlet* is doubly staked upon the identification of Shakespeare with the man who lost both a father and a son in the years preceding the composition of the play, it is startling to watch his struggle, over the course of the four decades following the publication of *The Interpretation of Dreams*, to undo the Stratfordian identity of the author of the plays. As a young man, Freud had steadfastly rejected the hypothesis that the true identity of 'Shakespeare' was Sir Francis Bacon: had Bacon written the plays, wrote Freud to his fiancée Martha Bernays, he 'would have been the most powerful brain the world has ever produced'; 'there is more need to share Shakespeare's achievement among several rivals'.[86] Freud's first known pronouncement on the topic thus opens up a possibility not that far removed from the idea of collaborative authorship promoted by recent scholarship on early modern practices. Indeed, given the constant interanimation of ideas within Freud's circle of followers, collaborative work was something about which Freud came to know a good deal. In any case, it is striking that from the very beginning, Freud strained against the idea of Shakespearean authorship.

The comment in the letter to Bernays reveals an ambivalence towards Shakespeare – unbounded admiration on the one side, along with what could be understood as a form of (Orphic) *sparagmos*, or a kind of will-to-revenge against the irreducible greatness of the dramatist – an ambivalence discernible (as many scholars have noted) almost everywhere in Freud's attitude towards his predecessor. We could set his remark that 'there is more need to share Shakespeare's achievement among several rivals' side by side with his (much later) description of the primeval attitude towards the totem. Indeed, in *Totem and Taboo*, Freud draws attention to 'the killing and tearing in pieces' of Orpheus in his discussion of the totem meal, going on to suggest that

> an event such as the elimination of the primal father by the company of his sons must inevitably have left ineradicable traces in the history of humanity; and the less it itself was recollected, the more numerous must have been the substitutes to which it gave rise.[87]

To this sentence Freud attaches an odd footnote quoting (without explication) Ariel's song from *The Tempest* –

> Full fathom five thy father lies;
> Of his bones are coral made;
> Those are pearls that were his eyes:
> Nothing of him that doth fade,
> But doth suffer a sea-change
> Into something rich and strange.[88]

Ariel's words cannot be taken to offer much reinforcement to Freud's point; it is more in the nature of a free association, connecting fathers, death, transformation – and Shakespeare.

These elements – and especially paternal figures – keep coming back to haunt Freud whenever he turns to Shakespeare's identity. By the turn of the century, as we have seen, it served Freud's purposes to accept the Stratfordian identity of the playwright, since Georg Brandes's influential book dated the composition of *Hamlet* in the year following John Shakespeare's death.[89] Within a few years, though, Freud was already entertaining doubts; having suggested to Ernest Jones that Shakespeare's name might derive from the French 'Jacques Pierre', and having received a reply to the effect that 'Jacques père' was unlikely since 'père' was not usually integrated into French names, Freud wrote back:

> A slight misunderstanding has crept in between us regarding the derivation of Shakespeare's name. I did not mean Jacques *père* but Jacques Pierre, which is not an uncommon combination of two forenames. The derivation was given to me by a very erudite old gentleman, Prof. Gentilli, who now lives in Nervi.[90]

Is it specious to suggest that the idea of the father is here first cast out ('I did not mean Jacques *père*), only to reappear in the guise of a 'very erudite old gentleman'?

Perhaps Gentilli the gentleman (and scholar) had the advantage of being quite unlike Shakespeare the glover's son and actor; but 'Jacques Pierre' had nothing on Edward de Vere, seventeenth Earl of Oxford, whose candidacy for the authorship of the plays, once he had embraced it after reading Thomas Looney's book,[91] Freud found utterly compelling, promoting it – against the better judgement (and advice) of almost all his various correspondents and followers – for most of the last two decades of his life. As he wrote to a colleague: 'I have been troubled by a change in me … I no longer believe in the man from Stratford'.[92] In the 1930 edition of *The Interpretation of Dreams*, after the passage on the death of Shakespeare's father, Freud inserted a notorious footnote: 'Incidentally, I have in the meantime ceased to believe that the author of Shakespeare's works was the man from Stratford'; and in 1935 he 'corrected' his comments on the relation of Shakespeare's biography to the composition of *Hamlet*:

> This is a construction which I should like explicitly to withdraw. I no longer believe that William Shakespeare the actor from Stratford was the author of the works which have so long been attributed to him. Since the publication of J. T. Looney's volume *'Shakespeare' Identified* (1920), I am almost convinced that in fact Edward de Vere, Earl of Oxford, is concealed behind this pseudonym.[93]

By the time he wrote the letter cited in the epigraph to this chapter – 1937 – Freud was positively irritated that 'the man of Stratford' 'still attracts' his friend Zweig: 'He seems to have nothing at all to justify his claim, whereas Oxford has almost everything'.[94] 'Stratford' had become little more than a term of dismissal for Freud, and the idea of Oxford's authorship almost delusional in its power.

How is it possible that the man who wrote (to the same friend, Zweig, a few months before this last letter) that 'biographical truth does not exist, and if it did we could not use it'[95] could become so irked when his friend refused to accept the Oxfordian hypothesis? How can one explain the fact that anyone so unflinchingly aware of the self-deceptions and distortions to which the psyche resorts (especially in relation to figures of authority) could fail to turn his analytic powers to his own attitude to the authorship question? Freud should have been able to see better than anyone that the fantasy of Shakespeare-as-Oxford had the structure of a family romance or, even better, of a dream – working, quite precisely, through mechanisms of condensation and displacement, and that (therefore) this idea was practically crying out to be interpreted as in some sense Freud's own wish fulfilment. I do not propose to offer an analysis of the underlying wish – only to indicate the way Freud's own powerful methodology transcends the specifics of the mythologies he created. Freud had already decided that 'Shakespeare' was Oxford when he wrote, near the beginning of *Civilization and Its Discontents*:

> We do not think highly of the cultural level of an English country town in Shakespeare's time when we read that there was a big dung-heap in front of his father's house in Stratford; we are indignant and call it 'barbarous'...[96]

'Stratford', again, comes across as almost disreputable here, and Freud presents the 'dung-heap' as somehow inimical to high culture. But how exactly? Elsewhere, Freud repeatedly embraces the notion that it is precisely in what is usually discarded that we may find the deepest truths. Dreams recycle 'the day's residues'[97] to do their work, and the psychoanalyst turns his or her attention 'precisely to those associations which are "involuntary", which "interfere with our reflection", and which are normally dismissed by our critical faculty as worthless rubbish'.[98] And again:

> the technique of psycho-analysis ... is accustomed to divine secret and concealed things from despised or unnoticed features, from the rubbish-heap, as it were, of our observations.[99]

The psyche, Freud suggests, can transform 'indifferent refuse'[100] into precious matter; so somewhere in Freud's quoting of Ariel's song there must be the sense that that which is lost, discarded or decayed can become as gorgeous as coral and pearl. Just as he knew that dreams are created through the metamorphosis of 'despised' matter, Freud must have known that the son of a glover with a dungheap outside his door could transform those 'secondhand' ideas, so curtly dismissed in the letter to Zweig, 'Into something rich and strange'.

Freud's final pronouncement on the authorship controversy hints at this knowledge. In the late *An Outline of Psychoanalysis*, he writes that 'the name *William Shakespeare* is very probably a pseudonym behind which a great unknown [*ein grosser Unbekannter*] lies concealed'.[101] Psychoanalysis finds 'secret and concealed things' in 'the rubbish-heap, as it were, of our observations'; for Freud, in the end, 'the name *William Shakespeare*' marks 'the dream's navel, the spot where it reaches down into the unknown' – the spot where 'a great unknown lies concealed'.

It is in this sense that Freud can be termed a 'Great Shakespearean' – not in his comprehension of Shakespeare, but in his apprehension of that '*grosser Unbekannter*', the unconscious.

Chapter 6

Shakespeare and Freud

David Hillman

> The times are dark, fortunately it is not my task to put them right.
> – Freud, Letter to Arnold Zweig, 2 May 1935[1]

'They have seem'd to be together, though absent; shook hands, as over a vast; and embrac'd as it were from the ends of oppos'd winds' (*The Winter's Tale*, 1.1.29–31): we might begin by considering Shakespeare and Freud as bracketing the so-called 'Enlightenment project' that dominated much of the gap between the early seventeenth and late nineteenth centuries.[2] If Shakespeare can be understood (as Stanley Cavell among others has done) as pre-emptively reflecting upon this Enlightenment project *avant la lettre*, Freud can be seen as both its product and one of its greatest demolishers. In his thinking about thinking, he effectively undermines the notion of a rational, controlled, self-identical human subject, a model that received its paradigmatic or emblematic characterization in the Cartesian cogito. Freud suggests that this subject is illusory, based on a radically inaccurate expectation that we can fully know what we think, let alone why we think what we think. Our conscious selves are, according to him, but a small part of who we are; the latter is determined by forces and effects of which we are anything but fully conscious, so that even as we (overtly) believe we are doing, or aiming to do, one thing, we are always (covertly) doing, and aiming to do, other things at the same time.

The essential and formative role of the unconscious in Freud's work means that rationality has been severely overrated. For Freud, as for Shakespeare, madness and truth are often close allies, and dreams are the royal road to knowledge of the unconscious; for Descartes, madness and dreams are the epitomes of dismissable phenomena, nothing but paths to error and confusion. Descartes sought certain, rational knowledge about the world, while psychoanalysis constitutes a critique not only of the stability of such knowledge, but also of the search itself; where Cartesian epistemology was founded upon a proprietary relation to the body and an assumption that nature is the object of knowledge, Freud shows how fundamental a misconception it is to posit the body or nature as an object susceptible of being mastered. From a psychoanalytic perspective, certainty – that which Descartes sought through, and in arriving at, the *cogito* – is a mirage, one based largely on the strict differentiation of subject and object; and Freud repeatedly shows just how tenuous and complex the subject–object split always is. But, as recent scholars have argued, this epistemological dualism was only beginning to be rigorously conceptualized and enforced during the course of the sixteenth and seventeenth centuries. Shakespeare was therefore in a privileged position from which to comment on the signs of its emergence – signs such as the increasing reliance of early modern selfhood upon 'The eye of reason' (*1 Henry IV*, 4.1.72) – that 'sovereign eye' (*Sonnets*, 33.2) of Cartesian vision which, as a number of psychoanalytically oriented critics have argued, Shakespeare did more than anyone to subvert.[3]

Freud had a particular interest in the early modern period, having frequent recourse to Renaissance writers (notably Rabelais, Tasso, Ariosto and Cervantes – though it is noteworthy that he never mentions the one writer closest to him in spirit – the spirit of self-scrutiny, self-exposure and dispassionate analysis: Montaigne),[4] artists (most prominently Leonardo and Michelangelo, to each of whom Freud dedicated a substantial essay, but also Giotto, Raphael, Signorelli, Verrocchio, Rembrandt) and historical figures (e.g., Ferdinand and Isabella, Henry VIII, Cardinal d'Este, Oliver Cromwell) alongside his unwavering interest in Shakespeare. Though Freud is essentially anything but a historiographical thinker, in an important sense his work looks back to and draws on pre-Enlightenment thought. Freud seemed to feel – without ever stating it explicitly – that in early modernity he could discern the contours of modern subjectivity *in statu nascendi*; at times his work implies that looking at materials from this earlier period can allow a more direct access to the workings of the mind, 'much as a vein of pure metal may sometimes be struck which must elsewhere be laboriously smelted from the ore'.[5] Indeed, it is to early modernity – and to Shakespeare in particular – that scholars have traced the inauguration of a notion of the self as interiorized and having impenetrable depths. But here we can already begin to see how multilayered or even paradoxical Freud's thinking so often is. On the one hand, Freud implicitly views the period between the middle ages and Enlightenment as the central turning point in the birth of the modern individual – the self-determined and independent figure espoused by the influential nineteenth-century historian Jacob Burkhardt (one of Freud's favourite authors)[6] as epitomizing the Renaissance; on the other hand, this recognizably 'modern' form of selfhood is, according to Freud, so complexly related to the external world and so inwardly riven that any possibility of autonomy, intentional agency and independence is radically undermined. In a Freudian world, the self is made up of internally contradictory parts, and is therefore inherently – constitutively – out-of-control and inescapably transgressive rather than self-determined.[7]

It may be that Freud returns to the Renaissance again and again in his writings precisely because the undermining of the autonomous individual is indeed co-extensive with its emergence. Individuality and self-division are intimately linked; for once one begins to conceive of the self as truly separate from the world, one is inevitably driven to consider the unwanted and disowned parts of the self – those parts that previous eras could assign to devils, for example – as internal. In *Civilization and Its Discontents*, Freud remarks on the illusion that the ego 'appears to us'

> as something autonomous and unitary, marked off distinctly from everything else. That such an appearance is deceptive, and that on the contrary the ego is continued inwards, without any sharp delimitation, into an unconscious mental entity which we designate as the id and for which it serves as a kind of façade—this was a discovery first made by psycho-analytic research.[8]

The opening sections of *Civilization and Its Discontents* suggest, however, that not only the sense of internal unity but also the ability to differentiate 'more sharply'[9] one's own body from other bodies in the environment are not simply a given but a cultural (and individual) achievement; and if, as Freud's writing elsewhere implies, the Renaissance marked a significant advance in the development of 'civilization', 'us' (in 'appears to us' above) is, I suggest, best understood as 'us modern subjects'. From this perspective, the use of the word 'individual' in the seventeenth century to denote a separate entity – rather than, as previously, a part of a larger whole, a member of a community 'undividable, incorporate' (*The Comedy of Errors*, 2.2.122) or indivisible from that whole – is something like an act of repression, an attempt to hide both the divided nature of the self and the inseparability of self and environment by labelling that self an 'individual' or non-divisible and autonomous thing.[10] (And we might here recall that 'analysis' derives from the Greek for 'breaking up' or 'undoing'.) The most extreme version of such an argument follows Lacan in suggesting that what we find emerging at this period, and especially in Shakespeare, is (in Christopher Pye's formulation) 'the pure nonsubject of early modernity'.[11] Lacan himself, in his influential discussion of anamorphosis in Hans Holbein's painting 'The Ambassadors', writes: 'At the very heart of the period in which the subject emerged' – the Renaissance – 'Holbein makes visible for us ... the subject as annihilated'.[12]

In his essay 'A Seventeenth-Century Demonological Neurosis' (1923), Freud uses a little-known treatise describing the demonic possession of an obscure early modern painter to elucidate his theories about the aetiology of mental illness. Freud writes:

> The demonological theory of those dark times has won in the end against all the somatic views of the period of 'exact' science. The states of possession correspond to our neuroses, for the explanation of which we once more have recourse to psychical powers. In our eyes, the demons are bad and reprehensible wishes, derivatives of instinctual impulses that have been repudiated and repressed. We merely eliminate the projection of these mental entities into the external world which the middle ages carried out; instead, we regard them as having arisen in the patient's internal life, where they have their abode.[13]

Freud here claims to be at least partially reverting to an earlier theory of the ways in which our minds become haunted by demons: where 'the middle ages' made of mental troubles entities out there in the external world, science in the intervening (eighteenth and nineteenth) centuries has blamed these troubles on bodily disturbances; and, argues Freud, the older theory is in a sense more accurate – 'exact' science has got it wrong. (Elsewhere, Freud lectures a group of medical students: 'psychological modes of thought have remained foreign to you. You have grown accustomed to regarding them with suspicion, to denying them the attribute of being scientific, and to handing them over to laymen, poets, natural philosophers, and mystics. This limitation is without doubt detrimental to your medical activity'.[14]) The issue, Freud suggests, is psychic ('having arisen in the patient's internal life') rather than somatic. It is a strange claim. As with so much of Freud's writing, there are oddities and interesting slippages going on here (and again, this is one of the continuing pleasures in reading Freud: although his theories can usually be reduced to straightforward, positivistic statements, the more one looks at his writing, the more unexpected things one finds; in fact, the more unexpected things he himself has taught us how to find). To begin with, as Freud surely knew,

possession throughout the medieval and early modern periods was understood to be nothing if not a somatic state, so that to say that 'we once more
have recourse to psychical powers' is somewhat disingenuous; and in fact
the relation between the somatic and the psychic is a lifelong preoccupation
of Freud's, from the early years of his studying neurophysiology to his final
writings. Indeed, I would suggest that it is precisely his preoccupation
with this conundrum – the *problem* of the relations between psyche and
soma, or language and the body – that Freud shares with early modernity
in general and Shakespeare's writings in particular; it is arguable that
modern subjectivity emerged in no small part out of the intense pressure
placed upon the relation of body and self.[15] Freud's interest in possession
precisely interrogates this problem, while also highlighting his sense of the
conscious self as inhabited by something alien – having an unconscious is
like having a 'foreign body' inside one, as he puts it elsewhere;[16] this sense
lies at the heart of his conceptualization of selfhood. One implication in
this passage is that in getting rid of the supernatural dimension science has
gone too far, so to speak, towards the natural; it has displaced the mental
with the purely physical. Psychoanalysis balances things out; it reinstates a
'daemonic' dimension to our relation to the world while retaining the idea
that there is no supernatural element meddling with our fates. As with his
understanding of dreams, Freud saw himself as returning to a pre-modern
point of view.

Indeed, Freud's labelling the period of the demonological treatise's
publication (1677) as 'the middle ages' is worth pausing over: a (Freudian)
slip, one might say, and *therefore* (again: this is one of the many ways Freud
has himself helped us to see how we can read with a certain kind of
attention) not merely a (dismissable) mistake but a point of some interest.
The Renaissance seems to have vanished mysteriously here in the transition
from 'the middle ages' (long gone by 1677 by most accounts) to the age
of science (well advanced, of course, by this point: the Royal Society, for
example, was founded in 1660). It is almost as if Freud's writing here
allows free reign to what he elsewhere describes as the 'timelessness' of
the unconscious, partaking of the mechanisms of dreams, where 'simul-
taneity in time' is the equivalent of a logical connection.[17] And we might
here mention Shakespeare's notorious propensity to ignore chronological
exactitude – his anachronisms, his playing fast and loose with temporal
sequences in his plays; these may perhaps best be explained by reference
to Freud's suggestions about the non-linearity of time in the unconscious;
indeed Freud himself writes (in relation to the strange temporality
of *Macbeth*) that 'a dramatist is at liberty to shorten at will the natural

chronology of the events he brings before us, if by the sacrifice of common probability he can enhance the dramatic effect'.[18] Perhaps Freud is hinting at the persistence of 'primitive' modes of thought into the later period, at the ways in which dimness and demons – 'the dark backward and abysm of time' (*The Tempest*, 1.2.50) – still unavoidably haunt the period of the birth of modern selfhood, and the ways in which these things of darkness must be acknowledged. In the life of the mind, 'nothing which has once been formed can perish'; 'everything past is preserved'.[19] It is clear everywhere in Freud's work that, for him, our deepest strata are utterly resistant to any notion of progress: 'Our unconscious is just as inaccessible to the idea of our own death, as murderously minded towards the stranger, as divided or ambivalent towards the loved, as was man in earliest antiquity'.[20]

As Freud once said in a public lecture: an idea should not be dismissed (murderously) merely because it appeared to be raised 'from the tomb of the past, like the Ghost in *Hamlet*'; rather, he insisted, 'as a stranger give it welcome' (*Hamlet*, 1.5.165).[21] And the analogy is one that (like a ghost, or like the repressed) keeps returning in his work: 'In an analysis … a thing which has not been understood inevitably reappears; like an unlaid ghost, it cannot rest until the mystery has been solved and the spell broken'.[22] The metaphor of buried matters coming back to haunt the present like unfinished business was one of Freud's perennial favourites – hence his fondness for the analogy of archaeology and psychoanalysis, both of which uncover layers of the past. In his late work 'Constructions in Analysis', Freud draws out this parallel at some length, going on to argue that there is no danger of leading the patient astray with such 'reconstructions' of the past, since in the end 'the false construction drops out, as if it had never been made; and, indeed, we often get an impression as though, to borrow the words of Polonius, "our bait of falsehood had taken a carp of truth"' (*Hamlet*, 2.1.60).[23]

For Freud, then, the past is always with us. In *Inhibitions, Symptoms and Anxiety*, he writes about the various 'useless … ceremonials' deployed by obsessional neurotics in order to try to efface the past.[24] One of the main techniques he describes is a form of 'negative magic' in which a person 'endeavours […] to "blow away" not merely the *consequences* of some event (or experience or impression) but the event itself'; Freud terms this 'undoing what has been done [*ungeschehenmachen*]'.[25] We might be reminded here of Lady Macbeth's obsessive attempts to erase the traces of Duncan's murder: though she may try to insist that 'what's done, is done' (*Macbeth*, 3.2.12), it is precisely this phrase that returns to haunt her in the sleepwalking scene, when she repeats the resolute sentiment in a more regretful key: 'What's done cannot be undone' (5.1.68).[26] Not only this: in her reiteration of the phrase, the very name of what she least wants to remember 'inevitably reappears ... like an unlaid ghost': for bubbling up in the middle of 'What's *done can*not be undone' is the name *Duncan*. Like Freud, Shakespeare knows that we can never be done with the past.

***

In relation to our pre-modern past, Freud seems divided: on the one hand, he is intent on showing the way scientific, rational thought can advance our understanding of the world; this is a triumphal model of human history, which sees reason and progress as interlinked, and it is one to which Freud was passionately committed. (It is worth remembering that he is always willing to admit that advances in knowledge may yet radically modify his theories of human nature, that his own ideas might eventually come to be considered, as it were, pre-scientific). On the other, he is as ever profoundly aware of how the present is 'made and moulded of things past' (*Troilus and Cressida*, 3.3.177) – phylogenetically (that is, across the generations) and ontogenetically (within an individual's life): the dark ages inhabit the Renaissance and indeed the present, just as our childhoods form (and trouble) our adulthoods. The achievements of '"Reason and Science, the highest strength possessed by man"'[27] can, from this perspective, only ever be fragile and limited, held in suspension with what Freud calls 'some sort of "other world", lying beyond the bright world governed by relentless laws which has been constructed for us by science'.[28] We may have moved from the so-called 'Dark Ages' ('those dark times') through the En*light*enment to an (even brighter) present, but at the same time – to continue with this chiaroscuro sense of the history of thought – 'it must follow, as the night the day' (to quote Polonius again – *Hamlet*, 1.3.79), that we have returned to a darkness constitutive of who we are.

The sense that our occult selves flourish at night, and a feeling for the way 'death's dateless night' (*Sonnets*, 30.6) haunts our daytime selves, are present throughout Freud's work. Even as he was at constant pains to differentiate his new 'science' from anything remotely occult or disreputable, he freely admitted that 'unconscious mental activity deserves to be called "daemonic"'.[29] Hints of the scandalous alignment of psychoanalysis with sorcery or the supernatural come through particularly clearly in some of Freud's early epigraphs – for example, the epigraph to *The Psychopathology of Everyday Life* (from Goethe's *Faust*):

Now fills the air so many a haunting shape,
That no one knows how best he may escape.[30]

Or, more famously, the epigraph to *The Interpretation of Dreams* (from Virgil's *Aeneid*):

If I can't bend those above, I'll stir the lower regions.[31]

Freud's language is frequently medieval or early modern in its free use of such demonic metaphors: 'No one who, like me, conjures up the most evil of those half-tamed demons that inhabit the human breast, and seeks to wrestle with them, can expect to come through the struggle unscathed', he wrote in his early description of the Dora case;[32] or: 'To urge the patient to suppress, renounce or sublimate her instincts the moment she has admitted her erotic transference would be … just as though, after summoning up a spirit from the underworld by cunning spells, one were to send him down again without having asked him a single question';[33] or again, in the *Introductory Lectures on Psycho-Analysis*: 'in thus emphasizing the unconscious in mental life we have conjured up the most evil spirits of criticism'.[34] Indeed, both Freud's understanding of fetishism (the word itself derives from the Portuguese *feitiço*, meaning 'sorcery' or 'magical practice', and – as Ann Rosalind Jones and Peter Stallybrass have shown – 'the concept of the fetish emerged in the Renaissance')[35] and his late, extravagant theory of the death drive (the exposition of which prompted Freud to describe himself as an '*advocatus diaboli*')[36] must owe something to this Medieval or early modern habit of thought. Of the 'compulsion to repeat' (the most palpable manifestation of the hypothetical 'death drive'), Freud writes: 'It may be presumed, too, that when people unfamiliar with analysis feel an obscure fear – a dread of rousing something that, so they feel, is better left sleeping – what they are afraid of at bottom is the emergence of this compulsion with its hint of possession by some "daemonic" power'.[37]

Over and over throughout his work, Freud 'give[s] the devil his due' (*1 Henry IV*, 1.2.119). 'Occultism asserts that there are in fact "more things in heaven and earth than are dreamt of in our philosophy"', writes Freud (citing lines that immediately follow Hamlet's 'therefore as a stranger give it welcome'):[38] given his persistent (if equivocal) belief in the limitations of 'rational' scientific knowledge, it is perhaps unsurprising that Freud's 'favourite quotation' (according to his biographer Ernest Jones) was Hamlet's remark to the tellingly-named Ho*ratio*:

In the years before the great war I had several talks with Freud on occultism and kindred topics. He was fond, especially after midnight, of regaling me with strange or uncanny experiences with patients, characteristically about misfortunes or deaths supervening many years after a wish or prediction. He had a particular relish for such stories and was evidently impressed by their more mysterious aspects. When I would protest at some of the taller stories Freud was wont to reply with his favourite quotation: 'There are more things in heaven and earth than are dreamt of in your philosophy.' [39]

The oscillation between 'our philosophy' (the Folio version) and 'your philosophy' (the Quarto version) in Freud's various recyclings of this sentiment bespeaks his bifold or ambivalent relation to rational systems of philosophy such as that of science.[40] Yet again, there is for all intents and purposes more than one Freud; the one who wants to take possession, and the one who allows himself to be possessed. Though he wanted to be one of those 'philosophical persons' who 'make modern and familiar things supernatural and causeless' (*All's Well that Ends Well*, 2.3.2–3), there is throughout Freud's writings an acute awareness that we are still haunted by inexplicable and ineffable forces – and that, however 'civilized' we may become, we cannot simply get rid of our gods and devils without taking note of the immense human needs addressed by the idea of these supernatural entities: 'in past times religious ideas, in spite of their incontrovertible lack of authentication, have exercised the strongest possible influence on mankind. ... We must ask where the inner force of [these ideas] lies and to what it is that they owe their efficacy, independent as it is of recognition by reason'.[41] This last sentence is a sentiment Shakespeare might have shared; certainly both writers have in common a fascination with the role of religious belief in society and culture, with the way 'worship shapes, blocks and transforms desire'.[42] Yet both seem to be in an important way 'post-religious' – quoting 'What's Hecuba to me?' was on one occasion Freud's jokey way of dismissing the hold of religious belief on his own life.[43] Both appear ultimately to be concerned with human motivations, relations and potentialities (with the stories we tell ourselves and the language we use to tell these stories) rather than with otherworldly interventions and hopes. It is hard to escape the implication, in every appearance of equivocally supernatural forces in Shakespeare, that what we are watching is an externalized manifestation of the unknown forces within the self – though of course this may be in part an effect of the Freudian lens through which Shakespeare is now viewed. In this regard, both these writers participate in the Enlightenment project that undermines the validity of religious belief, even as they are also both part of the anti-Enlightenment project that undercuts all pretensions to rational mastery.

Freud is thus nothing if not ambivalent about the status of the '"exact" science' (Freud's inverted commas are telling) that dominated the period between the mid-seventeenth century and his time. When he famously referred to his contribution to human knowledge as a second 'Copernican revolution', he was implicitly drawing another (ambivalent) line of affinity between the Renaissance and his own historical emplacement. In the *Introductory Lectures on Psycho-Analysis*, Freud claimed that his was the third of the three major blows dealt by science to the notion of anthropocentric mastery and 'the *naïve* self-love of men'. The first was the Copernican displacement of 'man' from the centre of the cosmos; the second, Darwin's destruction of 'man's supposedly privileged place in creation' and portrayal of 'his ineradicable animal nature'; and 'the third and most wounding blow', Freud's own 'psychological research of the present time which seeks to prove to the ego that it is not even master in its own house, but must content itself with scanty information of what is going on unconsciously in its mind'.[44] (That this third blow was the 'most wounding' of all is of particular interest if we recall that Freud, in 'The Theme of the Three Caskets', associated the third amongst three with the figure of Death;[45] so that Freud's contribution to the historical process was implicitly fatal to human narcissism.)[46] The historical dislocation of the human subject takes the form of what Freud dubs the 'cosmological', 'biological' and 'psycho-logical' wounds to the arrogant idea of human centrality. The implication here is that the brackets around the Enlightenment opened by Copernicus have been doubly shut by Darwin and Freud himself. All three, to judge by the powerfully hostile responses they evoked, were shocking in their own time.

'To prove to the ego that it is not even master in its own house': throughout Freud's writings, the idea of mastery is at once powerfully attractive ('To *prove* to the ego...'!) and constantly undone: what Freud calls 'the instinct for mastery, or the will to power' – over the self, over nature (human or otherwise), over one's relations with others, over a text or a meaning.[47] In all three cases – Copernicus, Darwin, Freud – there is a tension between the loss of dignity in terms of self-image and a gaining of dignity in the form of empirical knowledge; there is loss, but there is also a compensatory mastery. It is a familiar Freudian story. But whereas the Copernican and Darwinian wounds were to the human position vis-à-vis an external placement in the cosmos (and were therefore, to some extent, healable, if not reversible), Freud's portrait of dislocation is radically placeless – the mind is ex-centric to itself, not just to the surrounding world – and thus past all cure. One can see, though, why Freud wants to align his theories with those of Copernicus: the sixteenth-century figure was after all a great scientist, and one whose findings were controversial – and nevertheless turned out to have been right. But, in so far as the primary alignment here is between Copernicus and Darwin (rather than Copernicus and Freud), perhaps there is, in addition, an underlying suggestion that we can find affinities between Freud's coming in the wake of the nineteenth-century scientist and Shakespeare's coming in the immediate aftermath of the sixteenth-century discoverer: from this perspective, the alignment would seem to be of two creative thinkers each writing in the wake of a tremendous shock to human self-conception, each both building upon and assuaging the concomitant narcissistic wound. As so often, Freud's affiliations are divided: there is what he himself calls (in describing Leonardo da Vinci) a 'vacillation between art and science'.[48] Freud wants the prestige of both; and there is no greater literary prestige than that of Shakespeare. Nor, I would suggest, is there any literary figure who more consistently shows pretensions to mastery receiving their comeuppance at every turn. Is there a single head of a household (or family) in all of Shakespeare who comes close to being master in his own house?

***

Shakespeare seems to share with Freud an awareness of the absurdity or irony in our attempts to master all things – our desires, our relations with others, our understanding of the world. In Shakespeare, Freud could find paths to think about the ways in which we are blind, not in control of our selves, our words, our relations with the world. And both writers show us not only the frailty of rationality, but also its potential deployment as a cover story, an avoidance of certain unwanted, and therefore 'unknown', truths about ourselves and others, all of us – to quote Lafew's resonant phrasing in *All's Well that Ends Well* again – 'ensconcing ourselves into seeming knowledge when we should submit ourselves to an unknown fear' (2.3.4–5).[49] Freud wrote that his analysands often 'give intellectual reasons for their affective rejections of my ideas ... and the arguments advanced – arguments are as common as blackberries, to borrow from Falstaff's speech (*1 Henry IV*, 2.4.239) – were the same and not exactly brilliant'.[50] Freud makes use of Falstaff's witticism several times in his writing in order to show how limited 'intellectual grounds' can be in their purchase on truth: beyond a certain point, 'logical arguments are impotent against affective interests, and that is why disputes backed by reasons, which in Falstaff's phrase are "as plenty as blackberries", are so unfruitful in the world of [affective] interests'.[51] For both these writers, 'reason' is heavily compromised; throughout their work, 'seeming knowledge' and rationality struggle to assert their claims in the face of the 'unknown fear' of the mind's passions and madnesses and the body's desires and appetites.

Reason in Shakespeare's plays is always compromised, partly by its perpetual tug-of-war with desire: 'If the [beam] of our lives had not one scale of reason to poise another of sensuality, the blood and baseness of our natures would conduct us to most prepost'rous conclusions; but we have reason to cool our raging motions, our carnal stings, our unbitted lusts' (*Othello*, 1.3.326–9):[52] the sentiment is altogether traditional – the espousing of the need for the rational will to 'cool' sensuality is omnipresent in the Renaissance; but both the fact that it is the duplicitous, manipulative, malevolent Iago who speaks these words, and the context of the play as a whole, reveal how limited a counterweight reason may be. Iago succeeds in instilling in Othello precisely an over-reliance on a bogus rationality ('Give me the ocular proof'; 'give me a living reason' – 3.3.360, 409), and it is this that leads the protagonist to his 'most prepost'rous conclusions'. Over and over, Shakespeare's plays show how reasoning the need can only offer a very partial perspective on human existence; how (as Bottom says) reason and love keep little company together; and how, as Hamlet puts it, 'reason [panders] will' (*Hamlet*, 3.4.88) – that is, rationality can act as a go-between or procurer for sheer desire, especially, it seems, sexual desire: 'reason is the bawd to lust's abuse' (*Venus and Adonis*, 792). There is a repeated link in Shakespeare's plays between reason and the regulation of our bodies' temperature (and hence also between reason and clothing). Reason can appear 'to cool our raging motions, our carnal stings, our unbitted lusts', but often enough it merely serves to heat them further. ('In psychology, unlike physics', writes Freud, 'we are not always concerned with things which can only arouse a cold scientific interest'.)[53] Troilus's scathing accusation to his brother – 'You fur your gloves with reason' (*Troilus and Cressida*, 2.2.38) – brings out the way rationality in Shakespeare's plays can work as one more layer in which we clothe ourselves to feel more comfortable or protected against the cold truth. And Lear's

O, reason not the need! our basest beggars
Are in the poorest thing superfluous...

If only to go warm were gorgeous,
Why, nature needs not what thou gorgeous wear'st (2.4.264–9),

points to the limitations of what Theseus (in *A Midsummer Night's Dream*)
terms 'cool reason' in comprehending our 'shaping fantasies'. Reason in
Shakespeare is no match for the 'seething' of our brains (5.1.5–6), and
nowhere in his plays does the mastery reason tries to exert ever succeed in
taking over the whole self. 'My reasonable part produces reason', says the
grieving Constance (*King John*, 3.4.54); but that is but one part of her, and
far from the strongest.

***

If, for the Enlightenment Freud, 'there is no appeal to a court above
that of reason',[54] for the anti-Enlightenment Freud reason itself isn't
a unitary thing: and though there may be no higher court, there are
other ones. Here, as so often in Freud, a doubleness emerges. As we saw
in the previous chapter, Freud's work manifests a classificatory impulse
which comes up against a fascination with the idiosyncracies of individual
personality. But the ambivalence runs much deeper; reading Freud,
in fact, can be a bit like looking at one of those perspectival paintings
so popular in the Renaissance: 'One face, one voice, one habit, and
two persons, / A natural perspective, that is and is not!' (*Twelfth Night*,
5.1.216–7). It is this doubleness that allows Lacan to portray his own
theories as a return, in the face of a false psychoanalysis based on a kind
of impostor-Freud, to a more faithful or 'rigorous' Freudianism, and that
provides the basis of much of the work of Jean Laplanche, who shows
the ways in which Freud's conceptual apparatus is internally conflicted,
forever 'going astray' from itself.[55] Several recent scholars have read Freud
along these lines; a sample of such views might include Mark Edmundson,
who refers to 'the normative Freud' and 'the Romantic Freud', and labels
this 'Freud's double-writing'; Adam Phillips, who suggests that there is
an 'Enlightenment Freud' and a 'post-Freudian Freud'; Leo Bersani,
who offers a reading of the 'domesticating' Freud and the 'celebratory'
Freud whose text 'dismantles its own discourse'; and Shoshana Felman,
who suggests that Freud's teaching 'turns back upon itself so as to subvert
itself'.[56]

This self-subversion is quintessentially represented in the differing
interpretations of Freud's famous motto, 'Where id was there ego shall
be [*Wo Es war soll Ich werden*]': is this a conquistador's triumphal slogan,

implying that the ego (aided by psychoanalysis) will slowly but surely take control of the unconscious, or is it rather – as Lacan avers – a tragedian's realization that the ego or 'I' is doomed forever to struggle to maintain its footing on the quicksand of the id?[57] Like the awakening lovers of *A Midsummer Night's Dream*, Freud seems to 'see these things with parted eye, / When every thing seems double' (4.1.188–9); perhaps this is just what 'natural[ly]' happens when 'every thing' is seen through the prism of dreams, which, we could say, 'rightly gaz'd upon, / Show nothing but confusion; ey'd awry, / Distinguish form' (*Richard II*, 2.2.18–20). Broadly speaking, we could say that in all these descriptions the opposition is between a practical rationalist whose posture is one of hermeneutic authority, committed to the idea of efficient knowledge and insisting upon the need for sublimation and an acquiescence in the dictates of the reality principle,[58] and (or perhaps we should say: in response to) an 'extravagant and wheeling' (*Othello*, 1.1.136) writer whose objective is, as Freud himself puts it at one point, 'far-fetched speculation',[59] a thinker who is drawn to the idea of the unknowable and the excessive. Throughout his work, the two sides of his thinking keep making accommodations to or contaminating each other; we are not seeing merely a development in his views but a constant competition or *agon*. As Freud himself wrote in describing Empedocles of Acragas, 'one of the great thinkers of ancient Greece':

> His mind seems to have united the sharpest contrasts. He was exact and sober in his physical and physiological researches, yet he did not shrink from the obscurities of mysticism, and built up cosmic speculations of astonishingly imaginative boldness.[60]

Freud is turning here to Empedocles for 'confirmation' of his binary theory of the instincts. In doing so, he claims that he is 'very ready to give up the prestige of originality for the sake of such a confirmation';[61] but throughout his work it is evident that this is not the whole truth – that he is, so to speak, not altogether willing (no more, perhaps, than is Othello) to put his 'unhoused free condition … into circumscription and confine' (*Othello*, 1.2.26–7). It comes as no surprise that towards the end of his life, Freud is reported to have said: '*Je ne suis pas un Freudiste*'.[62]

Freud's 'cause' – to borrow Troilus's formulation – 'sets up with and against itself'; his thinking embraces a

> Bi-fold authority, where reason can revolt

Without perdition, and loss assume all reason
Without revolt.

                                        (*Troilus and Cressida*, 5.2.143–6)

'Our views have from the very first been *dualistic*', wrote Freud in acknowledging his controversially binary conceptualization of life and death drives
in *Beyond the Pleasure Principle*, but dualistic also accurately describes his
thinking about thinking.[63] One could argue that it is the bifold quality of
Freud's work that has led psychoanalytic thought in its two quite divergent
directions – broadly speaking, towards what is known as the school of
'ego-psychology', which embraces a homogenization of the self and the
efficacy of 'normal' development of the ego through adaptation to reality,
and those forms of psychoanalysis that see the ego as ex-centric to the
subject and that focus on the unconscious and the inherently irreconcilable, stubbornly non-adaptive aspects of the always divided self.[64] Freud's
rationalism tends to push him towards character-analysis, diagnosis, the
finding of origins and aetiologies; Kenneth Burke calls this Freud's 'essen-
tializing mode of interpretation' which 'is linked with a normal ideal of
science'.[65] The 'post-Freudian Freud' moves towards the vertigo of the
endless play of language and the limitless possibilities of open-ended
interpretation. And it is worth pointing out that these directions correlate
loosely with the axis upon which so much twentieth-century Shakespeare
criticism has turned (and returned): on the one hand, from A. C. Bradley
onwards, the attention to character and dramatic action; on the other, the
focus on language, metaphor and semiotic patterning.

                                        ***

I want to suggest – by way of an extended digression – that one of Freud's
best-known descriptions can give us an insight into his ambidextrousness.
In *Beyond the Pleasure Principle*, while attempting to explain the tendency
of certain patients and certain dreams to reproduce unpleasant experiences, Freud famously relates his witnessing of a little boy (Freud's own
grandson) playing with a wooden reel with some string tied around it. The
boy repeatedly throws the bobbin into his cot 'so that it disappeared into
it'; with each throw, he lets out 'a loud, long-drawn-out "o-o-o-o"', which
Freud and the boy's mother agree must represent an attempt to exclaim
'*fort*' ('gone' in German); each time he pulls the bobbin back, he greets
its reappearance 'with a joyful "*da*"' ('There!').[66] This famous scene is
understood by Freud to be the child's attempt to master, through repeated

're-enactment', the pain of separation from his mother. Making the reel disappear, writes Freud, is also a way of 'reveng[ing] himself on his mother for going away from him'; it has 'a defiant meaning: "All right, then, go away! I don't need you. I'm sending you away myself."' Like Shakespeare's Coriolanus at the point of being banished from Rome – the city is explicitly identified with the maternal body throughout the play – the boy, in the first action of flinging away the reel, effectively turns around and declares: 'I banish you!' (*Coriolanus*, 3.3.123). Or perhaps an even better parallel is with Cleopatra, who, upon learning of Antony's marriage to Octavia, pronounces: 'Let him for ever go' (*Antony and Cleopatra*, 2.5.115); better, because her next words are: '– let him not': the play, like Freud's *fort–da* vignette, is shot through with ambivalence. We can place the second part of Freud's description (the retrieval of the reel) alongside Cleopatra's stated intention, earlier in this same scene, to go 'to th' river'; 'There', she says

> I will betray
> Tawny[-finn'd] fishes; my bended hook shall pierce
> Their slimy jaws; and as I draw them up,
> I'll think them every one an Antony,
> And say, 'Ah, ha! Y'are caught' (2.5.11–15).

Like Freud's grandson, Cleopatra manages her loss, wresting pleasure out of pain by partially transferring her feelings for the beloved other on to an object – reel or fish – in order to exert control over it; and moreover the multiplication of Antonys ('every one an Antony') might function in a way similar to the multiplication of snakes on the head of Medusa, which according to Freud constitutes a warding-off of the notion of (castrative) loss. But, the passage implies, the control that is part of the pleasure of recapture is also a 'betray[al]' of something – say, of the other's autonomy or separateness. That such mastery ends up killing the object is an implication of the immediately following reminiscence about the trick Cleopatra once played on Antony, whereby she had one of her divers 'hang a salt-fish on his hook, which he / With fervency drew up' (2.5.17–18); Antony thought he was catching a living creature when in fact he was drawing up a dead one; and the trick was a source of pleasure ("'Twas merry...' – l.15). Is this a glimpse of the 'death instinct' as prank? What the joke leads to, in the next lines of Cleopatra's reminiscence, is the lovers tumbling into bed: here as everywhere in this play, the erotic and the death-bound are entwined. Indeed, once one begins to think of *Antony and Cleopatra* side-by-side with *Beyond the Pleasure Principle* as a whole (and the little vignette with Freud's grandson in particular) certain patterns of the play begin to emerge. Consider the moment, a little earlier, when Antony learns of his wife's death:

> There's a great spirit gone! Thus did I desire it.
> What our contempts doth often hurl from us,
> We wish it ours again. The present pleasure,
> By revolution low'ring, does become
> The opposite of itself. She's good, being gone;
> The hand could pluck her back that shov'd her on.
>
> (*Antony and Cleopatra*, 1.2.122–7)

A Freudian reading of the last line of this passage might see in that 'could' (which at first reading means 'would like to') a fantasy of mastery over loss akin to that described in the '*fort–da*' game, where the (hallucinated) pleasure of control usurps the pain of (real) relinquishment. But the passage taken as a whole suggests something much more complicated. We can ask in the wake of Freud's late work: which came first, the loss or the desire? Thanatos or eros? And does 'She's good, being gone' mean 'her absence is what makes her now (appear) good', or rather 'it is good that she is gone'? Both? *Beyond the Pleasure Principle* would suggest this last option; it offers what can quite accurately be summarized as a view that 'the present pleasure' ('present' here in contrast to both 'absent' and 'what's past and what's to come') 'does become / The opposite of itself': that pleasure and the death instinct are at some level inextricable, a 'knot intrinsicate' (5.2.304) (and 'become', a key word in *Antony and Cleopatra*, means throughout the play both 'turn into' and 'suit' – so that pleasure here not only changes into pain, but it also befits or is appropriate to its opposite). In his conclusion to *Beyond the Pleasure Principle*, Freud suggests that 'the pleasure principle seems actually to serve the death instincts';[67] but *Antony and Cleopatra* implies that the opposite is also the case.

The dark logic of Freud's book suggests that repetition as such – 'the compulsion to repeat' – lies at the heart of both the desire for mastery and the 'death drive'; *Antony and Cleopatra* everywhere fuses love and death in structures of repetition. We might notice here, for example, the odd repetitiveness internal to Antony's response to his wife's death, where the last line-and-a-half reiterate almost exactly the pattern of the first two-and-a-half lines; and we might also take note of the echoes of the scenes described above in the latter stages of the play: Antony's 'There's a great spirit gone' and 'She's good being gone' repeated nearly verbatim in his response to Cleopatra's late flight from his wrath with ''Tis well th'art gone' (4.12.39); Cleopatra's 'draw[ing]...up' the (Antonied) fishes recapitulated in a different key in her 'draw[ing] ... up' (4.15.13, 30) the dying Antony into her monument.

In the hide-and-seek game described by Freud, the boy's repetitive control over the reel transforms his passive helplessness in the face of his mother's independence into 'an *active* part'. So we could perhaps say that Freud, faced with the unmasterable depths of the human mind, came up with a set of theories that allowed him to say (albeit rather more tentatively than his grandson), '*da*' – 'There!' The '*fort–da*' game has been inter-rogated by a very large number of critics; here I merely want to note two aspects of it particularly relevant to Shakespearean drama. First, Freud repeatedly refers to the game in theatrical terms: he ends this section of his book with the reminder that

> the artistic play and artistic imitation carried out by adults, which, unlike children's, are aimed at an audience, do not spare the spectators (for instance, in tragedy) the most painful experiences and can yet be felt by them as highly enjoyable. This is convincing proof that, even under the dominance of the pleasure principle, there are ways and means enough of making what is in itself unpleasurable into a subject to be recollected and worked over in the mind.[68]

In the vignette itself, the boy compensates himself for his mother's departure 'by himself staging the disappearance and return'; 'the first act, that of departure, was staged as a game in itself and far more frequently than the episode in its entirety, with its pleasurable ending'. Second, as this last sentence suggests (and as Shakespeare's Antony seems to sense) there is pleasure to be gained from loss and abandon just as there is in mastery; indeed, *Antony and Cleopatra* suggests that the two are interdependent. In describing his grandson's repetitive actions (as has often enough been noted), Freud himself repeats that this 'first act' [throwing the reel into the cot] 'was repeated untiringly as a game in itself, though there is no doubt that the greater pleasure was attached to the second act'; here again, Freud's 'no doubt' incites the reader to re-evaluate the claim: it is in fact not at all clear, from Freud's description, whether the main pleasure of the boy's game consisted in the retrieval of the spool or in making it disappear (with 'an expression of interest and satisfaction'). So it may be that Freud recognized something of himself in his grandson's game, or projected something of himself on to that game; that – to stretch the analogy or

'crush this a little' – he gained at least as much satisfaction from his speculative flights as from his efforts to be 'exact and sober'. After all, he ends this
most 'far-fetched' endeavour, *Beyond the Pleasure Principle*, with a meditation
on his own uncertain conviction in the central hypotheses proposed in the
work, accompanied by the defence that 'it is surely possible *to throw oneself
into a line of thought* and to follow it wherever it leads'.[69]

***

'The poets and philosophers before me discovered the unconscious', Freud
famously declared.[70] It is by now commonplace to note how much Freud
took in, directly and indirectly, from his literary predecessors – drawing
upon literary works for inspiration, deftly deploying literary techniques
in ostensibly scientific writing, using literary characters' and writers'
names for central psychoanalytic nomenclature (the Oedipus complex,
narcissism, sadism and masochism – though notably *not* from Shakespeare:
there is no 'Hamlet Complex', no 'Learism' or 'Lady Macbeth Disorder').
Freud, argues Lacan, 'derived his inspiration, his ways of thinking and
his technical weapons' from imaginative literature; and perhaps Freud's
constant return to literature was precisely an implicit acknowledgement of,
and desire for, what Derrida has called 'literary fiction's eternally renewed
resistance to the general law of psychoanalytic knowledge'.[71] For literature,
as Shoshana Felman has argued, 'is the language which psychoanalysis
uses in order to *speak of itself*; it 'is the unconscious of psychoanalysis ...
literature in psychoanalysis functions precisely as its "unthought"; as the
condition of possibility and the self-subversive blind spot of psychoana-
lytical thought'.[72] Lionel Trilling put the question of Freud's literariness
in maximal terms when he wrote that 'the Freudian psychology makes
poetry indigenous to the very constitution of the mind', so that the latter
becomes, in Freud, 'in the greater part of its tendency exactly a poetry-
making organ'.[73]

    Freud himself acknowledged much of this – the 'particular fascination'
which the mind of the artist held for him,[74] the stimulation to his thinking
drawn from creative writers, the way 'the case histories I write ... read
like short stories'[75] or like a 'psychoanalytic novel'.[76] But Freud is, by his
own lights, irreducibly different from these creative artists, for they are
in his view almost entirely bound to the pleasure principle (*Lustprinzip*):
'Meaning is but little with these men; all they care about is line, shape,
agreement of contours. They are given up to the *Lustprinzip*. I prefer to be
cautious'.[77] Thus:

The creative writer does the same as the child at play. ... Language has preserved this relationship between children's play and poetic creation. It gives [in German] the name of '*Spiel*' ['play'] to those forms of imaginative writing which require to be linked to tangible objects and which are capable of representation. It speaks of a '*Lustspiel*' or '*Trauerspiel*' ['comedy' or 'tragedy': literally, 'pleasure play' or 'mourning play'] and describes those who carry out the representation as '*Schauspieler*' ['players': literally 'show-players'].[78]

By 'those forms of imaginative writing which require to be linked to tangible objects and which are capable of representation', Freud means dramatic works, and it is to drama that he turns most tellingly for insight into the human mind. As the psychoanalyst André Green has argued, theatre, with its dramatization of misrecognitions and enigmas, is an 'embodiment of that "other scene", the unconscious', and therefore had

a special significance for Freud—a significance that outweighed his interest in the plastic arts (despite Michelangelo's 'Moses' or Leonardo's 'St Anne'), in poetry (despite Goethe, Schiller or Heine), in the tale (despite Hoffmann), in the novel (despite Dostoievsky and Jensen). Sophocles and Shakespeare are in a class of their own, especially Shakespeare; Freud recognized in him a master whose texts he analyzes as if they were the discoveries of some illustrious precursor.[79]

One could argue that significant parts of Freud's model for the understanding of character are indebted to the work of the Renaissance playwright: 'By showing that all character develops not in a straight line but through a series of crises by which certain attitudes or roles are exchanged', writes Philip Rieff, 'Freud exhibits at once the commonplace element in tragic character and the tragic element in everyday character'.[80] And one can go further and argue that the complexity, the layering and the inconsistency, the crises and reversals and the struggle for self-knowledge, all of which permeate Freud's understanding of human nature, are all already there in Shakespeare's plays.

More than anything else, it is drama – and that of Shakespeare above all – that represents for Freud a paramount form of the theatre of the psyche. But it is not just the characters and plots that Freud took from the playwright's works – it is the very form of the theatre that influenced his understanding of the human mind. We can note, in passing, the fact that '*Lust*', '*Trauer*' and '*Spiel*' (in the passage above) are all terms which are central to Freud's thinking about the constitution and workings of the psyche (everything we do can be described as playing with – telling ourselves and others stories about – pleasure or desire and mourning or loss).[81] We might also here recall that 'catharsis' – Aristotle's term for the effects of tragedy on its spectators – was Freud and Breuer's early term for the hoped-for therapeutic effect of psychoanalysis;[82] that '*szene*' (as in the 'primal scene' or 'scenes of seduction') is one of the most frequently used terms in Freud's early papers (and in the formative correspondence with Fliess); and that – decades later – Freud was (as we have seen) still using the analogy of watching a tragic play in his explanation of the 'compulsion to repeat'.[83] Though he confessed at one point that 'I have often observed that the subject-matter of works of art has a stronger attraction for me than their formal and technical qualities',[84] there is something about drama's dialectic of presence and absence, of divided and alienated forms of seeing and being seen, and of hiding and revealing inner spaces that has led Freud – and a number of important psychoanalytic writers after him – implicitly or explicitly to turn to the 'formal and technical properties' of theatre to interrogate the very constitution of subjectivity.[85] As Barbara Freedman suggests, 'theatricality depends ... upon a constitutive displacement' based on 'a disparity between representer and represented'; it tends to subvert any claim to an objective or stable point of view, to present us with 'a fractured gaze' – one we could compare with the 'shiver[ed] mirror' (*Richard II*, 4.1.289) looking back at (the highly theatrical) Richard II in the deposition scene.[86]

Theatre multiplies and complicates identifications. It thus brings out the way the internal world of the human subject can be described as being peopled with a cast of characters (as Richard II depicts it, 'a generation of still-breeding thoughts ... [that] people this little world' – 5.5.9), and the work of the playwright is in significant ways analogous to that of every individual when he or she plays, dreams or fantasizes ('Thus play I in one person many people' – 1.31). At one point in *The Interpretation of Dreams*, Freud approvingly quotes 'the sagacious Delbœuf' (Joseph Delbœuf, a nineteenth-century French philosopher), who wrote that 'a dreamer is an actor who at his own will plays the parts of madmen and philosophers, of executioners and their victims, of dwarfs and giants, of demons and angels'.[87] As Ellmann writes: 'if dreams resemble drama, drama also owes its form to dreams; rather than mirroring the outer world, the theatre gives external form to the internal dramaturgy of the mind'.[88] Indeed, it is worth remembering that Freud writes repeatedly of 'the dramatic form in which [dreams] are couched': at one point, Freud writes that 'the transformation of thoughts into situations ("dramatisation" [*Dramatisierung*]) is the most important and peculiar characteristic of the dream-work'.[89] Additionally, 'condensation' and 'displacement' – the primary techniques of dreaming – are forms of disguise; Freud himself pointed out the parallel between these various forms of substitution in dreams and drama.[90]

So that if dreams, as Freud famously put it, lie upon 'the royal road to a knowledge of the unconscious activities of the mind',[91] that road was nothing if not dramatic, in every sense of the word. (And it is worth recalling that the analogy of dreaming and drama is one that Shakespeare draws on repeatedly in his plays – particularly, of course, in *A Midsummer Night's Dream*.) In setting out the theory of the Oedipus complex, Freud emphasizes that the 'riveting power'[92] of Sophocles' play derives from the *theatricality* of the events described: from 'the process of revealing, with cunning delays and ever-mounting excitement' the facts of Oedipus's past.[93] It is not merely the structure of the Oedipus complex itself which Freud claims holds such power; it is equally the *dramatization* of the process of revelation of the truth and the effect of this on the audience. And, just like the dream, drama – certainly the drama of the Renaissance – is obliged to work within the constraints of censorship, to represent only those things that will not be too severely punished:

> In the state of sleep this probably occurs owing to a relaxation of the censorship; when this happens it becomes possible for what has hitherto been repressed to make a path for itself to consciousness. Since, however, the censorship is never completely eliminated but merely reduced, the repressed material must submit to certain alterations which mitigate its offensive features.[94]

We could add that, in his explanation of why there is, in dreaming, a 'relaxation of the censorship', Freud argues that it is essential that in sleep our motor systems are disabled; it is this which allows us to have our dream-thoughts, since there is no danger of our physically acting on them (this is one of the main reasons for the use of the couch in psychoanalytic practice); 'like a neutral to [our] will and matter' we *do* 'nothing' (*Hamlet*, 2.2.477–8). And one could say something similar about the audience in a theatre: our 'paralysis' – our position as spectators, without the power to affect what is happening onstage – means that we can more safely experience the powerful emotions enacted before us, allowing the id 'what is now a harmless amount of liberty':[95] 'Between the acting of a dreadful thing / And the first motion, all the interim is / Like a phantasma or a hideous dream'.[96]

'The dramatist can indeed, during the representation, overwhelm us by his art and paralyse our powers of reflection; but he cannot prevent us from attempting subsequently to grasp its effect by studying its psychological mechanism'.[97] Freud's metaphors here are reminiscent of the story of Perseus and Medusa, a story usually interpreted in the Renaissance as an allegory of the triumph of reason over the senses (Freud devoted a short piece to the symbolism of Medusa's head).[98] The metaphors and the submerged myth bring out the perception of the (dramatic) agon between dramatist and psychologist in Freud's mind: here, the former is given the role of Medusa, the terrifying (female) figure Freud sees as representing the (male) horror of castration. It is sometimes the case that Freud more or less admits that Perseus' sword is not up to the task: 'Before the problem of the creative artist analysis must, alas, lay down its arms'.[99] But, at other times, he writes as if it is possible for the scientific 'powers of reflection' to overcome the taboo against looking represented by the Medusa and to attempt to tame the 'overwhelming'[100] and 'paralys[ing]' power of the theatrical spectacle: 'psycho-analysis is in a position to speak the decisive word in all questions that touch upon the imaginative life of man'.[101]

In this sense, the writer is the precise opposite of the analyst – the former more or less deliberately obscures and aestheticiszs, the latter aims to undo these processes. It is Shakespeare's genius, writes Freud, not to reveal too much about the 'secret motives' of his protagonists, thus avoiding being 'confronted by our cool, untrammelled intelligence, which would preclude any deepening of the illusion'.[102] The creative writer can 'transport us into another and imaginary world, in which spirits and ghosts are given reality. As we know from the examples of *Hamlet* and *Macbeth*, we are prepared to follow him there without hesitation'.[103] In the theatre, we are seduced, our reflection is paralyzed: the playwright, while 'engag[ing] our intellectual activity, diverts it from critical reflection and keeps us firmly identified with his hero'.[104] Again and again in his work, the seductive power of art is something to be both enviously admired and sternly resisted. On the one hand, artists are childlike in their obsession with sensual gratification ('all they care about is line, shape, agreement of contours'); on the other hand, this ostensible abandon reveals essential truths about the human psyche – they are 'the deepest observers of the human mind'.[105] So that even when Freud portrays writers and artists as 'allies', and offers praise for the insights offered by them, it is never pure, never untinged with envy and a struggle for emulation: 'Creative writers are valuable allies and their evidence is to be prized highly, for they are apt to know a whole host of things between heaven and earth of which our philosophy has not yet let us dream' – Freud is again here quoting (or misquoting) from *Hamlet,* and in the process implicitly aligning literature and dreams.[106] But note that '*not yet*' – it is entirely characteristic: a few pages later in the same work, Freud writes that the artist 'can draw from sources that have *not yet* been made accessible to science'.[107] There is always, mixed in with his admiration, the competitive impulse – a kind of will-to-power over literature: hence his lament, in an aside added in 1919 to *The Psychopathology of Everyday Life*: 'how hard it is for a psycho-analyst to discover anything new that has not been known before by some creative writer'.[108]

So a respectful distance and a rivalry characterize Freud's relations with the Old Masters. He often seems to want to have it both ways: to stand on their shoulders and also to shoulder them aside. Like the occult, literature constituted a threat to the claims of Freud's new science; he 'prefer[s] to be cautious' – he will not be paralyzed or overwhelmed. But he can hardly help but be seduced. Like Theseus, the rationalist Freud 'never may believe' the 'strong imagination' of the poets; his 'cool reason' keeps their 'shaping fantasies' at arm's length, lumping together the 'frantic ... tricks' and 'antic fables' of 'The lunatic, the lover, and the poet' (*A Midsummer Night's Dream,* 5.1.3–10). In a letter to his confidante Wilhelm Fliess, Freud writes that 'Shakespeare was right in juxtaposing fiction and madness (fine frenzy)':[109] the reference is, of course, to Theseus's

> The poet's eye, in a fine frenzy rolling,
> Doth glance from heaven to earth, from earth to heaven;
> And as imagination bodies forth
> The forms of things unknown, the poet's pen
> Turns them to shapes, and gives to aery nothing
> A local habitation and a name (ll.12–17).

But like Hippolyta, Freud also knows that this is not the whole story. He senses that literature contains deep truths; that 'all the story of the night told over /... grows to something of great constancy' (ll.23–6): like 'the fierce vexation of a dream' (4.1.69), these 'things unknown' are not (merely) irrational, not (ultimately) dismissable, but rather as true as – perhaps truer than – waking reality. The 'shaping fantasies' (1.5) of our imaginations and of our works of art are, for Freud, *both* (as Theseus says) 'More strange than true' (1.3) *and* (as Hippolyta says) 'strange and admirable' (1.27); and it is largely in and through his engagement with Shakespeare that Freud came to this ambivalent recognition.

Of his own attempts 'to assess the artist in a rational way', Freud is
at times appropriately sceptical: one cannot treat him, he writes, 'as
though he were a scholar or technician'; 'he is actually a being of a
special kind, exalted, autocratic, villainous, and at times rather incom-
prehensible'.[110] It is as if the artist were a kind of Richard III figure
(as described by Freud in the essay on 'The Exceptions'): immoral and
irresponsibly resistant to the kinds of renunciation (of the pleasure
principle) demanded by the psychoanalyst, allowing himself 'to disregard
the scruples by which others let themselves be held back';[111] the artist
has a freedom from the shackles of the reality principle that Freud
envies and at the same time wants to master: 'Poets are irresponsible
people and enjoy the privilege of poetic licence'.[112] In Freud's writing,
the conundrums of the human psyche are problems to be solved; jokes,
errors, dreams, love, sex, death – all are serious business. No wonder he
is envious of creative artists! It is not just their intuitive grasp of matters
he labours to understand, but also, surely, the ability to turn everything
into material for play.

There is a driven quality to Freud's researches into literature, a compulsive
urge to 'track down' the key that will unlock its 'tormenting' secrets: 'The
opening scene in *Lear*, the judgement of Paris, and the choice of caskets in
The Merchant of Venice are really based on the same motif which I must now
track down';[113] or: 'Today I am tormented by the secret of tragic guilt, which
will certainly not resist ΨA [psychoanalysis]'.[114] Elsewhere, Freud complains
that poets and painters 'possess in their art a master key to open with ease
all the female hearts, whereas we stand helpless at the strange designs of
the lock and have first to torment ourselves to discover a suitable key to
it'.[115] At this point, it is as if Freud himself – rather than the creative artist –
has become identified with Richard III: after quoting at length Crookback's
disquisition on the way his deformity has disqualified him from amorous
and sportive tricks, Freud argues that

> What the soliloquy thus means is: 'Nature has done me a grievous wrong
> in denying me the beauty of form which wins human love. Life owes
> me reparation for this, and I will see that I get it. I have a right to be an
> exception, to disregard the scruples by which others let themselves be
> held back. I may do wrong myself, since wrong has been done to me.'
> And now we feel that we ourselves might become like Richard, that on
> a small scale, indeed, we are already like him. Richard is an enormous
> magnification of something we find in ourselves as well. We all think
> we have reason to reproach Nature and our destiny for congenital and

infantile disadvantages; we all demand reparation for early wounds to our narcissism, our self-love.[116]

The shifting, inexplicit identifications in the few brief pages on 'The Exceptions' can thus offer an insight into Freud's ambivalence vis-à-vis 'imaginative writers': the latter are Richard-like in their untrammelled, autocratic and irresponsible natures, but Freud himself is Richard-like in his 'tormenting' sense of being disadvantaged in his innate, intuitive gifts, lesser than these same writers in the natural ability to unlock 'female hearts'. Nature has given them the 'master key'; Freud (apparently forgetting, as he periodically does, that 'we are not even master in our own house') tries to turn the tables and become the master interpreter.

***

Where Freud is closest to literature (and furthest from 'exact' science) is in his understanding of the 'plenitude' (and slipperiness) of language: where science tends to think of language as a transparent medium, literature conceives of it as constitutively and densely overdetermined and opaque; and as John Forrester writes, 'language is the central concern of psychoanalysis'.[117] This is certainly the case with Lacan, with his well-known formulation, 'the unconscious is structured like a language'; the subject, according to Lacan, is unconsciously inducted into a pre-existing lexicon; thus we are formatively 'traversed [by] a speech which comes from elsewhere'.[118] But it is already the case in Freud that the self is formed through what Laplanche and Pontalis describe as 'the family *sounds* or *sayings*, the spoken or secret discourses, going on prior to the subject's arrival, within which he must make his way'.[119] '*Sounds* or *sayings*': it is not merely the stories and meanings of the world into which we are born, but also its very signifiers and phonemes that form us. 'We learn to *speak* by associating a "sound-image of a word" with a "sense of the innervation of a word"', writes Freud; he knows that, as he puts it in *Jokes and their Relation to the Unconscious*, 'words are a plastic material with which one can do all kinds of things'.[120] In attending to his patients, Freud listens not just to what is said but to 'what is heard in the sounds of what is said' – to what Wallace Stevens called 'the less legible meanings of sounds … the inner men / Behind the outer shields'.[121] Here again, whether consciously or not, Freud must have learnt a great deal from his literary predecessors, and especially from Shakespeare, always so keenly attuned to what Joel Fineman nicely terms 'the languageness of language'.[122] Freud calls this

attunement 'a feeling for language', a crucial component of any psychoanalytic form of listening or reading. Freud is ever alert not simply to the
meanings but to the very rhythms of speech: in his well-known '*non vixit*'
dream, for instance, he recounts the way his powerfully ambivalent feelings
towards a friend (and, more broadly, towards the empiricism of science)
are traceable in the very cadence of his thoughts:

> As he had deserved well of science I built him a memorial; but as he
> was guilty of an evil wish (which was expressed at the end of the dream)
> I annihilated him. I noticed that this last sentence had a quite special
> cadence, and I must have had some model in my mind. Where was
> an antithesis of this sort to be found, a juxtaposition like this of two
> opposite reactions towards a single person, both of them claiming to
> be completely justified and yet not incompatible? Only in one passage
> in literature—but a passage which makes a profound impression on the
> reader: in Brutus's speech of self-justification in Shakespeare's *Julius
> Caesar* [iii, 2], 'As Caesar loved me, I weep for him; as he was fortunate,
> I rejoice at it; as he was valiant, I honour him; but, as he was ambitious,
> I slew him.' Were not the formal structure of these sentences and their
> antithetical meaning precisely the same as in the dream-thought I had
> uncovered? Thus I had been playing the part of Brutus in the dream.[123]

Freud knows that the very rhythms of speech can be profoundly revealing
in and of themselves; and he learnt this from Shakespeare.

Freud dubbed his therapy, following the formulation of one of his
patients, a 'talking cure', but it might just as accurately be described as a
listening cure.[124] In the psychoanalytic setting, it is through language that
we reveal our desire, and through language that we can be helped towards
a different relation to the world. Either way, it is a cure by words:

> Words are the essential tool of mental treatment. A layman will no doubt
> find it hard to understand how pathological disorders of the body and
> mind can be eliminated by 'mere' words. He will feel that he is being
> asked to believe in magic. And he will not be so very wrong, for the words
> which we use in our everyday speech are nothing other than watered-
> down magic. But we shall have to follow a roundabout path in order to
> explain how science sets about restoring to words a part at least of their
> former magical power.[125]

Magical thinking, for Freud, is rooted in the omnipotence of thoughts that belongs to infancy; and while development in the direction of reality and rationality may gradually disillusion the child, the tendency of the unconscious to equate word with deed, wish with satisfaction, is never completely eradicated ('Actually', he writes, strikingly, in a different context, 'we never give anything up: we only exchange one thing for another').[126] In 'The Question of Lay Analysis', a semi-dramatized dialogue with an imaginary, sceptical interlocutor (whom Freud wryly dubs 'The Impartial Person'), Freud's alter ego explains the working of psychoanalytic treatment: 'Nothing takes place between them [analyst and patient] except that they talk to each other'; Freud continues:

> The Impartial Person's features now show signs of unmistakable relief and relaxation, but they also clearly betray some contempt. It is as though he were thinking: 'Nothing more than that? Words, words, words, as Prince Hamlet says.' ... 'So it is a kind of magic,' he comments: 'you talk, and blow away his ailments.'
> Quite true [responds the analyst] ... Words can do unspeakable good and cause terrible wounds. No doubt 'in the beginning was the deed' and the word came later; in some circumstances it meant an advance in civilization when deeds were softened into words. But originally the word was magic—a magical act; and it has retained much of its ancient power.[127]

'Unspeakable' (translating *unsagbar*, 'unsayable')[128] may be Freud's deadpan sense of humour; but manifestly, for him, there is a life-and-death-wielding power to words, which can 'cause terrible wounds': here again, we can see Freud's interest in the way language and the body are inextricably linked. And – hardly irrelevantly, since *Hamlet* is nothing if not interested in the relation between words and deeds[129] – yet again we see the way that, even when writing about the clinical situation, Shakespeare's words keep popping up in Freud's prose.

The 'ancient power' of the word is central to Freud's interrogation of the relations between body and mind, desire and language. Language refuses to stick to the rules of rationality and chronology; and words, for Freud, are magical in the way they always exceed our intentions and fall short of our expectations; they seem to come only partly from our conscious selves, and partly from elsewhere; to quote Freud's gnomic comment from 'The Uncanny': 'we ourselves speak a language that is foreign'.[130] The sense that words and names have a power to *do* things beyond the apparently reasonable, that signifiers cannot be fully separated from their meanings, and that the '*sound-associations* and *word-associations* evoked by the spoken sounds'[131] of language are meaningful is one that Freud shares with Shakespeare. To illustrate our persistent belief in the omnipotence of language, Freud at one point quotes Claudius's 'My words fly up, my thoughts remain below' (*Hamlet*, 3.3.96), adding that 'the magical power of prayer fails … unless it is accompanied by faith'.[132] Again we can see here evidence of Freud's Medieval-Renaissance – and hardly empirical or 'scientific' – habits of mind.

Freud knows, with Feste, that 'They that dally nicely with words may quickly make them wanton' (*Twelfth Night*, 3.1.14–15), and he often draws attention to this wantonness: his early works (in particular *The Interpretation of Dreams* and *Jokes and their Relation to the Unconscious*) constitute a linguistic almost as much as a psychological investigation, and they are peppered with examples from Shakespeare. Indeed, Freud's joke-book is as obsessed with quibbles, bawdy and just plain bad puns, and homonymic and homophonic play as any of the playwright's works. The jokes Freud analyses in *Jokes and their Relation to the Unconscious* as a whole can remind one of Mark Twain's definition of a German joke as 'no laughing matter'; they often threaten to reverse the effect that Freud ascribes to Falstaff – of turning 'indignation' into 'comic pleasure'.[133] At times in the joke-book, Freud seems to forget that 'A jest's prosperity lies in the ear / Of him that hears it, never in the tongue / Of him that makes it' (even though he himself quotes the comment, explaining that 'jokes are confronted by subjective determinants in the case of the third person too, and these may make their aim of producing pleasurable excitation unattainable').[134] Freud argues that the Falstaffian transformation epitomizes humour's 'economized expenditure of affect',[135] and indeed his general theory of jokes is 'economic', which is to say that there is in humour a saving of expenditure of psychic energy. Paradigmatic of this is 'the multiple use of the same words' for different ends:

> play upon words is nothing other than a condensation *without* substitute-formation; condensation remains the wider category. All these techniques are dominated by a tendency to compression, or rather to saving. It all seems to be a question of economy. In Hamlet's words: 'thrift, thrift Horatio!'[136]

Freud sums up the topic of the pithiness of jokes by citing Shakespeare's poking fun at 'the old chatterbox Polonius': 'Therefore, [since] brevity is the soul of wit, / And tediousness the limbs and outward flourishes, / I will be brief' (*Hamlet*, 2.2.90–2).[137] (Not that any of this prevented Freud from extending his joke book with each succeeding edition.)

Words, according to Freud, are 'predestined to ambiguity'.[138] In discussing the use of ambiguity in jokes, his first illustration of 'cases of the double meaning of a name and of a *thing* denoted by it' is Falstaff's implicitly obscene 'Discharge thyself of our company, Pistol!' (*2 Henry IV*, 2.4.137); a couple of lines later Freud quotes Heine's joke about the power of capitalism: 'Vile Macbeth does not rule here in Hamburg: the ruler here is *Banko* [bank-money]'.[139] The incident in *Julius Caesar* (3.3) when the poet Cinna is murdered because his name is the same as that of Cinna the conspirator is adduced as an instance of the way hostile feelings can be hidden or revealed by displacement of a person by a name.[140] One form jokes can take is a simple reversal or 'representation through the opposite' – an instance Freud gives is Antony's 'Brutus is an *honourable* man' (*Julius Caesar*, 3.2.82).[141] As an example of jokes using 'slight verbal modification', Freud gives the allusion to 'a fat lady' as '"Every fathom a queen", a modification of Shakespeare's familiar "every inch a king"' (*King Lear*, 4.6.107).[142]

Freud thus finds in Shakespeare a wealth of examples of the way signifiers hold us in their grip (turning us all into poets and conspirators). Freudian psychoanalysis promotes nothing so much as an alertness to the ambiguities, nooks and crannies in the labyrinth of language; it knows that we are all, always, 'imperfect speakers' (*Macbeth*, 1.3.70). The misuse of a pronoun can reveal a whole world: Freud mentions, for example, the Duke of York's address to the Queen in *Richard II*, 'Come, sister – cousin, I would say – pray pardon me' (2.2.105),[143] as well as Portia's slip of the tongue in the casket scene of *The Merchant of Venice*:

One half of me is yours, the other half yours —
Mine own, I would say; but if mine, then yours,
And so all yours (3.2.16–18).

Freud quotes his colleague Otto Rank, from whom he borrowed this example on two occasions:

the poet, with a wonderful psychological sensitivity, causes [Portia's secret] to break through openly in her slip of the tongue; and by this artistic device he succeeds in relieving both the lover's unbearable uncertainty and the suspense of the sympathetic audience over the outcome of his choice.[144]

And Freud adds: 'Observe, too, how skillfully Portia in the end reconciles the two statements contained in her slip of the tongue, how she solves the contradiction between them and yet finally shows that it was the slip that was in the right'.[145] Perhaps we should be calling such moments 'Shakespearean slips'.

***

Our *lapsi linguae* are always 'right', in that they 'Lay open to [our] earthy-gross conceit …/ The folded meaning of [our] words' deceit' (*The Comedy of Errors*, 3.2.34–6): our language always, in the end, expresses (and hence decrypts) our 'folded' intents. This is why at the foundation of any psycho-analytic – as of any literary – reading lies a practice of tremendously attentive reading; the devil is in the details. Things may appear to be inadvertent or chaotic, but, says Freud, there is nothing random about the manifestations of our unconscious selves; and, he adds, a great author 'never introduces a single idle or unintentional feature into his story'.[146] This may put us in mind again of Shakespeare's astounding craft, of which Thomas de Quincey remarked: 'The further we press in our discoveries, the more we shall see proof of design and self-supporting arrangement where the careless eye had seen nothing but accident'.[147] (de Quincey, not altogether coincidentally, is credited by the *Oxford English Dictionary* with bringing the term 'subconscious' into the English language.) Freud finds order in places we had been taught only to see irrationality, madness or randomness – in the slippages of language, in forgetting all manner of things, in day-dreams, in delusions – as well as in what he calls 'symptomatic acts':

> I give the name of symptomatic acts to those acts which people perform, as we say, automatically, unconsciously, without attending to them, or as if in a moment of distraction. They are actions to which people would like to deny any significance, and which, if questioned about them, they would explain as being indifferent and accidental. Closer observation, however, will show that these actions, about which consciousness knows nothing or wishes to know nothing, in fact give expression to unconscious thoughts and impulses, and are therefore most valuable and instructive as being manifestations of the unconscious which have been able to come to the surface.[148]

Like Ulysses reading Cressida's body, Freud finds 'language in her eye, her cheek, her lip, / Nay, her foot speaks' (*Troilus and Cressida*, 4.5.55–6):

When I set myself the task of bringing to light what human beings keep hidden within them, not by the compelling power of hypnosis, but by observing what they say and what they show, I thought the task was a harder one than it really is. He that has eyes to see and ears to hear may convince himself that no mortal can keep a secret. If his lips are silent, he chatters with his finger-tips; betrayal oozes out of him at every pore.[149]

We might pause for a moment to consider this well-known passage, which gives a nice sense of the literariness of Freud's writing. The resonance here owes something to the muted reference to Ezekiel (12.2: 'Sonne of man, thou dwellest in the middest of a rebellious house, which have eyes, and see not: they have eares to heare, and heare not: for they are a rebellious house');[150] Freud's inversion of the biblical subtext could be taken as emphasizing that much of the time it is only a kind of rebelliousness or willful ignorance – a *refusal* to see and hear – that prevents us from grasping 'what human beings keep hidden within them'. But there might also be a half-buried memory here of Shakespeare's Bottom, whose description of his 'bottomless' dream deploys similar language (which, like Freud's language here, owes much to biblical echoes):[151] 'The eye of man hath not heard, the ear of man hath not seen, man's hand is not able to taste, his tongue to conceive, nor his heart to report, what my dream was' (*A Midsummer Night's Dream*, 4.1.211–14).

However much he felt able to bring to light the concealed depths of the psyche, Freud also has a keen sense of the self's constitutive blindness and deafness to itself. If 'betrayal oozes out of [us] at every pore', it is, Freud seems to suggest, also implicitly a betrayal not to see and hear the truth about ourselves and about others. Hence we can follow *Macbeth*'s Ross in saying that 'We are traitors, / And do not know our selves' (4.2.20–1): we are traitors in part because we reveal ourselves all the time in spite of our best efforts to repress our hidden desires; but we are traitors, too, *because* we do not know ourselves – indeed, in large measure do not *want* to know ourselves: as Macbeth admits, 'To know my deed, 'twere best not know myself' (2.2.70). In a phrase that has become widely used, Freud's sceptical (but rarely cynical) position has been termed by Ricoeur a 'hermeneutics of suspicion':[152] there is always the sense of an unknown intent, a hidden meaning. But since these ulterior motives are often unconscious, we need to be mistrustful of ourselves no less than of others, for, as Freud says, 'who can tell all that is stirring in your mind of which you know nothing or are falsely informed?'[153] Freud's is thus, equally, a hermeneutics of self-suspicion, 'a mistrust [as Thomas Mann wrote] that unmasks all the schemes and subterfuges of our own souls'.[154] And his work has made us all into suspicious readers: after Freud, it is hard not to read with a strong sense of the ambiguous, ambivalent meanings latent in all characters, all texts – questioning (say) Coriolanus's valour, or Othello's love, or Orsino's nobility, or *Henry V*'s celebration of royalty; and in retrospect, one begins to trace both the self-deceptions and the seeds of self-doubt in many of these characters' own words and actions. Or should I have said, 'after Shakespeare...'? – for it is equally true to say that Shakespeare's texts *taught* Freud to see the hermeneutics of suspicion as a form of self-suspicion.

***

Both these writers are nothing if not aware of the deeply problematical nature of the self's unity. Just as Shakespeare's characters are never single, never at one with themselves, Freud's subjects are multiple and ex-centric: 'it is as though the self is no longer the unity [one] has always taken it to be,' writes Freud, 'as though there were something else in him, which can set himself up in opposition to the self'.[155] 'O, how comes it, / That thou art then estranged from thyself?' (*The Comedy of Errors*, 2.2.119–20): throughout Shakespeare's works, one feels this self-estrangement or self-opposition. Lacan, extrapolating from Freud's work to argue for the essential and inescapable division of the subject, quotes Rimbaud's famous dictum: 'Je est un autre':[156] he might just as well have quoted Viola's – or Iago's – 'I am not what I am' (*Twelfth Night*, 3.1.141; *Othello*, 1.1.65). We can again note in passing the way Shakespeare (like Freud) takes up a biblical register – these statements glance at God's gnomic words to Moses in Exodus (3.14), 'I am that I am' – to address his own (humanistic) concerns: the mysteriousness of God's statement is here transposed to the human realm; with the insertion of 'not', it evokes a no less unsettling enigma. Editors usually gloss these sentences (we could gloss 'gloss' here (as so often) to mean 'tame') as something along the lines of 'I am not what I seem', or 'I am not what (you think) I am'. A Freudian view of the constitutive role of the unconscious might lead one to gloss them to mean 'I am not what *I* think I am' – not a matter of appearance-versus-reality but rather of self-knowledge-versus-self-ignorance. But there is something even more radical and troubling going on in the bare syntactic form of Iago's and Viola's resonant words.

Freud's use of the term 'negation' may help us take a step further with Iago's and Viola's self-descriptions. Freud uses the term to refer both to denial (*Verleugnung*: 'disowning' or 'disavowing') and to logical or grammatical reversal (*Verneinung*: 'negating'). In so far as he leans towards reliance on the first of these, we can discern a relatively conservative Freud, prone to read into every disowned thought a sign of the truth of the unconscious idea being denied, into every denial a 'proof positive'[157] (though Viola might have called this 'a vulgar proof' – 3.1.122) of the patient's resistance: 'there is no stronger evidence that we have been successful in uncovering the unconscious than when the patient reacts with the words "I didn't think that" or "I never thought that"' – so that when the patient says '"It was *not* my mother"', the analyst can 'emend this: so it *was* his mother.'[158] We could call this rather chilling 'emending' a form of taming or glossing – though we should also note that Freud is often far more circumspect about the heads-I-win-tails-you-lose aspect of the procedure.[159] In this scenario, the character claims not to be what he or she is, and 'in our interpretation, we take the liberty of disregarding the negation'.[160] Jean Hyppolite's concise explication of Freud's essay on negation is of relevance here: '"I am going to tell you what I am not; pay attention, that is exactly what I am." This is how Freud engages with the function of negation'.[161] What Iago or Viola claims not to be may be precisely what they are.

A second possible reading of Viola's or Iago's 'I am not what I am' presents an even more radical possibility: the possibility that there *is* no 'exactly what I am'. In a late admission (in his 1937 essay 'Constructions in Analysis'), Freud admits that 'the only safe interpretation of [the patient's] "No" is that it points to incompleteness'[162] – the fundamental incompleteness that characterizes any attempt to come to terms with the unconscious. 'I, no; no, I; for I must nothing be' (*Richard II*, 4.1.201):[163] Richard's punning disclaimer epitomizes the complex relations between selfhood, knowledge and negation in both Shakespeare and Freud, encompassing the range of possibilities from 'I have no knowledge of my self' to 'there is no such thing as "I"'. 'With the help of the symbol of negation', writes Freud, 'thinking frees itself from the restrictions of repression and enriches itself with material that is indispensable for its proper functioning';[164] as Cynthia Marshall has argued in showing the relevance of this claim to the doubling of the name 'Jaques' in *As You Like It*: 'Freud stakes no less than the proper functioning of thought itself on the "symbol of negation." Without the ability to have things two ways at once, to confirm through denial, thinking would remain brittle, univalent, impoverished, gripped by repression'.[165]

From this point of view, we must entertain the possibility that Iago's and Viola's statements (and Juliet's, in similarly saying that 'I am not I' (*Romeo and Juliet*, 3.2.48) – or indeed Freud's, in declaring that 'Je ne suis pas un Freudiste') are quite accurate – that *Verneinung* (logical or grammatical reversal) is integral to being, and that therefore indeterminacy and multiplicity lie at the heart of 'what I am'; that selfhood, in short, is not self-identical, or to put it another way, that identity always falls short of, or lies at an oblique angle to, any imagined fullness or stability. If so, then the speaker's claim, in Sonnet 121, that 'I am that I am' (line 9), or Richard III's statement that 'I am myself alone' (*3 Henry VI*, 5.6.83) – let alone Descartes' claim, 'I think therefore I am' – are no more reliable, no more final, than the claim that 'I am not what I am'; indeed, Crookback's assertion that 'I [am] I' (*Richard III*, 5.3.183), like Parolles' statement that 'Simply the thing I am / Shall make me live' (*All's Well that Ends Well*, 4.3.333–4), come across as desperate attempts to uphold the idea of singular (or 'simple') identity (approaching objecthood) in the face of the inevitability of self-division and self-loss. One might as well try to tame Troilus's 'This is, and is not, Cressid!' (*Troilus and Cressida*, 5.2.146), or Orsino's 'A natural perspective, that is and is not!' (*Twelfth Night*, 5.1.216–17), or Macbeth's 'nothing is / But what is not' (*Macbeth*, 1.3.141–2). For the 'single state of man' (*Macbeth*, 1.3.140) is a chimera; in Shakespeare, as in Freud, there is no oneness of identity. Selves, like words, are always overdetermined. Within this non-logical or supra-rational framework, we might even question the efficacy of trying to uphold the most famous opposition in Shakespeare, that between 'to be' and 'not to be': whether we think of these options as 'being alive' and 'being dead' or, say, as something like 'being oneself' and 'refusing to be(come) oneself', it is one implication of Freud's work (and, following him, of Derrida's deconstructive thinking) that the opposed positions will always, at some level, haunt each other.

So that regarding the authorship controversy, one might imagine Shakespeare's response as being: 'I am not what I am'. Indeed, it is particularly odd that Freud should have engaged in this debate, given the structural similarities between the role of the psychoanalyst and Shakespeare's position: for the analyst knows that, at least in the consulting room, he is never himself, being always the object of the most intense transference; as Thomas Ogden writes, the analyst lets himself be 'everyone in the patient's life (transferentially) and no-one (a person who is content not to be noticed)'; in a good analysis, 'we find not the signature of the analyst (i.e. his presence) nor his absence (which marks his presence in his absence), but traces of him'.[166] Something very similar could be said of Shakespeare. The dramatist and the analyst share a kind of Keatsian 'negative capability'; Keats famously described the 'poetical character' (which 'has as much delight in conceiving an Iago as an Imogen') thus: 'it is not itself – it has no self – it is everything and nothing – It has no character ... no Identity'.[167]

'Everything and Nothing' is the title of Jorge Luis Borges's short piece on the playwright, which ends with these words:

> History adds that before or after dying he found himself in the presence of God and told Him: 'I who have been so many men in vain want to be one and myself.' The voice of the Lord answered in a whirlwind: 'Neither am I anyone: I have dreamt the world as you dreamt your work, my Shakespeare, and among the forms in my dream are you, who like myself are many and no one.'[168]

***

In Shakespeare's plays and poems, as in Freud's work, there is a constant sense of the nothingness at the heart of what we call the self. That two such different characters as Iago and Viola (and in two such different plays as *Othello* and *Twelfth Night*) can both be taken to claim such fundamental alterity indicates, I think, the complex, self-alienated, perhaps paradoxical nature of identity in Shakespeare as a whole; even a relatively straightforward character like Mistress Page can declare: 'I'll entertain myself like one that I am not acquainted withal' (*The Merry Wives of Windsor*, 2.1.86–7). 'All the acts and manifestations which I notice in myself and do not know how to link up with the rest of my mental life must be judged *as if* they belonged to someone else' – but for Freud, although they may once have 'belonged to someone else', they no longer do; they have become 'myself', or at least my unconscious.[169] There is always, for Freud, 'a shadowy intimation of something like an opposition between one's self and one's mental life in a broader sense'.[170] In Freudian terms, it is because the unconscious is radically other that alien-ness is inescapable, internal to who we are.[171] Nothing is stranger, we learn from Freud's essay 'The Uncanny', than what is most familiar. And it is one of the central aims of analysis to come to terms with this otherness within – with the bizarreness and foreignness of one's own unconscious being: to treat it as, say, interesting rather than threatening – to realize that, in the words of Sophocles' Oedipus, 'That stranger is I'.[172] If the unconscious is 'wondrous strange', it is up to us as its hosts to 'as a stranger give it welcome' (*Hamlet*, 1.5.164–5): the injunction is one which (as we have seen)[173] Freud embraced, and one which could be taken as a motto for any patient coming into an analysis. 'For Freud', writes Adam Phillips, 'to be a person is to be a stranger to oneself, to be continually meeting oneself as though one was somebody else … The repressed unconscious may be an uninvited guest, but the patient can learn inner hospitality'.[174] The psychoanalyst, writes Freud, 'plays the part of this effective outsider'; in talking to him, one is in a sense conversing with one's own unconscious.[175] At one point Freud avers that those who promote the alternative method to this – letting the sleeping dogs of our unconscious lie – are making a 'fatal' error:

> Wise men like these [physicians] are being no more than consistent when they implore us for heaven's sake not to meddle with the evil things that lurk behind a neurosis. ... their words bear a fatal resemblance to Dogberry's, when he advised the Watch to avoid all contact with any thieves they might happen to meet: 'for such kind of men, the less you meddle or make with them, why, the more is for your honesty' (*Much Ado About Nothing*, 3.3.52–3).[176]

Trying to suppress the irrepressible, transgressive unconscious is a mug's game. And it is only by recognizing and making contact with the foreignness inside us, Freud's work suggests, that one can find ways of living with others.

For Shakespeare's characters, as for Freud's subjects, alterity is always already within; here again, we could argue, what Freud offers as a theory of the mind, Shakespeare gives us in dramatized form, as theatre: Freud names this alterity 'the unconscious' and refers to it as 'the other scene'; Shakespeare shows its (dramatic) effects, giving 'A local habitation and a name' (*A Midsummer Night's Dream*, 5.1.17) to the ways in which we are always, inevitably, 'creatures of another place' (*All's Well That Ends Well*, 1.2.42). We could say that Shakespeare gives an 'outward strangeness' (*Venus and Adonis*, l. 310) to parts of the self, so that often in the plays the categories of (spatial, geographic, anatomical, imaginary) otherness (Moors, Jews, Goths, barbarians, men, women, the underprivileged, kings) end up embodying a self-alienation akin to that of Freud's subjects: they give tangible dramatic 'form[s] of strangeness' (*Troilus and Cressida*, 3.3.51) to the internal otherness of identity. Over and over, what is revealed in Shakespeare's as in Freud's writing is both the uncanny otherness of the supposedly self-same and the sameness of the ostensibly other – though it may be the case that the analyst's clinical work tends to bring out the former, while Shakespeare's plays give clearer instances of the latter.

Perhaps this is one reason why Freud seems to be more interested in what we could call Shakespeare's 'psychological outsiders' – rather than in the various concretely alien figures in the plays: 'Delicately, analytically, Freud does not speak of foreigners,' writes Julia Kristeva; 'he teaches us how to detect foreignness in ourselves'.[177] Shakespeare's plays include numerous alien figures, and in almost every case the perceived binaries (Christian and Jew, Venetian and Moor or Turk, Roman and Goth or barbarian, and so on) 'lose distinction' (*Troilus and Cressida*, 3.2.27), keep collapsing into each other in ways that reveal their powerful internal identity. We could say that, broadly speaking, in the comedies this self-alienation evokes an openness to and eventual acceptance of previously-unacknowledged parts of the self, while in the tragedies, such receptiveness is far more problematic; on the contrary, it is the fate of these 'other selves' – and therefore of the self – to be disavowed and violently rejected. Hence, for instance, Othello's self-figuration at the point of suicide as, in quick succession, a loyal Venetian, a 'base Indian' (or, in the Folio, 'Iudean'), a 'turban'd Turk' and a 'circumcised dog' (5.2.338–55).

In thinking about the prevalence of war in the history of the world, Freud bemoans the fact that the human race has still not overcome the propensity to treat otherness as threatening: 'it might have been supposed', he writes sadly, 'that "foreigner" and "enemy" could no longer be merged' (compare Helena's lament to the unwilling Bertram in *All's Well That Ends Well*, that only 'Strangers and foes do sunder, and not kiss' – 2.5.86).[178] Yet again enlisting Hamlet's egalitarianism, Freud expressed the (rather forlorn) hope that psychoanalysis could teach us greater forbearance towards alienated – or perhaps better, 'strangered' – parts of ourselves, thereby enabling greater tolerance towards others: 'It would also be too sad if psychoanalysis could not exert an improving influence on our own characters and move us to mutual tolerance. Let us remember the line from our Prince: "use every man after his desert, and who should [shall] 'scape whipping?"'.[179] As he points out, though, in *Group Psychology and the Analysis of the Ego*, the stranger has always been regarded with intense suspicion, especially by groups.[180] The intolerance of the 'stranger' – that which is more strange than we can bear, as well as the gendered, sexual, ethnic, religious or cultural other – is, in the end, according to Freud, an intolerance of the internal alien residing in the unconscious; so that the acknowledgement of this self-alienation becomes, for him, an ethical and political act. 'According to Freud', writes Roland Barthes – echoing Ulysses's 'one touch of nature makes the whole world kin' (*Troilus and Cressida*, 3.3.175) – 'one touch of difference leads to racism. But a great deal of difference leads away from it, irremediably'.[181]

It is because our 'selves' are so constitutively intertwined with our 'others' that, for Freud, the disentanglement is necessarily a dialogic process; for Freud, as Rieff puts it, to "know thyself" is to be known by another. This was Freud's powerful revision of the Delphic injunction, and by which he intended to make psychoanalysis the most disenchanting of sciences'.[182] It is as if Freud were doing for self-knowledge or the confessionary tradition what Sophocles and the Greek tragedians did for the development of drama – adding (as he himself puts it, in a different context) 'a second and third actor … to play as counterpart to the Hero and as characters split off from him'.[183] Like a character in a play (even the many soliloquies in Shakespeare's plays almost always seem closer to self-dialogues than monologues), Freud is always in conversation – with himself, his patients, his followers and correspondents, prior authorities, creative artists and writers; even his supposed 'self-analysis' was conducted in large part in epistolary conversation with his close friend and confidante Wilhelm Fliess, to whom he wrote: 'I can analyze myself only with the help of knowledge obtained objectively (like an outsider). True self-analysis is impossible'.[184]

Freud knew, as Shakespeare did, that it was out of the question to live 'As if a man were author of himself' (*Coriolanus*, 5.3.36), and what he rapidly discovered was that the unconscious motivations and desires of the analyst (his or her counter-transference) are a crucial part of the analytic process and must be taken as fully as possible into account; that taking Dogberry's view in relation to the analyst's own unconscious is also a 'fatal' mistake. He could have learnt this from reading Shakespeare; for one could say that the analyst tries to behave rather like Cassius in offering his services to Brutus: 'I, your glass, / Will modestly discover to yourself / That of yourself which you yet know not of' (*Julius Caesar*, 1.2.68–70); or like Hamlet, who, in haranguing Gertrude, similarly offers to 'set you up a glass / Where you may see the [inmost] part of you' (*Hamlet*, 3.4.19–20). The notion that we need an external perspective in order to see ourselves aright was already philosophically well-worn by Shakespeare's day – as Achilles says in response to Ulysses' similar suggestion, it 'is not strange … [that] speculation turns not to itself / Till it hath travell'd and is [mirror'd] there / Where it may see itself. This is not strange at all' (*Troilus and Cressida*, 3.3.109–11). But neither Ulysses nor Achilles, nor indeed Cassius or Hamlet, is of course anything like an objective, dispassionate or innocent mirror or sounding-board. Similarly, we could think of Iago as a kind of malignant psychoanalyst, doing no more – he could claim – than excavating the darker recesses of Othello's mind. In this regard, we could argue that Iago is actually quite as 'honest' as Othello keeps insisting – 'honest' in the sense of 'embodying a deep truth'; in which case Dogberry's advice ('for such kind of men, the less you meddle or make with them, why, the more is for your honesty') is altogether apt. Better, surely, no analyst than a malevolent one! What Shakespeare's plays can help us to see, and what Freud eventually learnt, is that no mirror is, as it were, completely flat or 'on the level'. The analyst's unconscious plays a crucial role, and the analytic conversation is always, inviolably, two-way – in Peter Brooks's description, 'a perpetually reversing counterpoint of self and other'.[185]

What Freud might also fruitfully have borne in mind is the propensity of Shakespeare's fools and incompetent speakers inadvertently to disclose important truths in their doggerel; for Dogberry's counsel, absurd though it may be, is by no means entirely without merit (and it is indeed the case that, in *Much Ado About Nothing*, it is precisely the ineptitude of Dogberry and his companions that eventually elicits the truth: in this play, as so often in Shakespeare, 'What your wisdoms could not discover, these shallow fools have brought to light' – 5.1.232–4). For however necessary it may be from a certain (say, a socially responsible) point of view to police or censor transgression – to 'meddle or make' with dishonesty – it is usually the case that, as Dogberry says, 'they that touch pitch will be defil'd' (3.3.57). (Indeed, the expression 'meddle or make' had strong sexual connotations in Elizabethan English, so that the risk of (as it were) infection is highlighted through the malapropism.) Perhaps what many people find most intolerable about Freud – or 'most tolerable, and not to be endur'd' (ll. 36), to use Dogberry's own famously mangled phrase – is his relentless urge to 'track down', in the face of all resistance, our 'black and deep desires' (*Macbeth*, 1.4.62). Here again, Dogberry's muddled instructions to his watch can be suggestive:

> If you meet the prince in the night, you may stay him … marry, not without the Prince be willing, for indeed the watch ought to offend no man, and it is an offence to stay a man against his will.
>
> (*Much Ado About Nothing*, 3.3.75–82)

Necessary though it may be, it can indeed be described as a kind of offence to impose something (an interpretation or a label) upon a patient in the face of his or her resistance. Unlike the 'merciful' (1.61) Dogberry ('Truly, I would not hang a dog by my will, much more a man who hath any honesty in him' – ll. 63–4), Freud rarely takes 'The most peaceable way' (ll. 57–8); he is unwavering in his commitment to finding the truth at any cost, in his insistence on facing up to 'reality', in his presumption to move the powers below. Shakespeare's plays deliberately refuse to close off the questions they raise; they never enjoin us to take the side of a single point of view and treat it as definitive. And perhaps it is in this area that we can begin to understand something about the gap between the positive and negative responses to the writings of Shakespeare and Freud. 'Between what Shakespeare presents to our senses and what he allows the unconscious to say there stands the difference that Freud aims to decipher', writes André Green.[186] Shakespeare accommodates our will-to-ignorance; Freud besieges it. (Here it is worth pointing out that Freud shares with Marx a sense of the strength of the human will-to-ignorance – though for Marx this unconsciousness is of the social present rather than the individual past. In both cases the resistance they evoke is partly to be attributed to their respective insistence upon 'just deserts'.) Freud turns us all into sceptics and detectives, hardly able to escape the work of decipherment.

These differences are of course crucial, but we should not let them obscure the many ways in which what we think of as 'Shakespeare' would hardly be recognisable without the huge influence of Freud's work, as well as the profound ways in which the latter is nothing if not Shakespearean. *Wo Shakespeare war soll Freud werden.*

Notes

Introduction

[1] Diana Trilling, quoted by Mark Krupnick, *Lionel Trilling and the Fate of Cultural Criticism* (Evanston, IL: Northwestern University Press, 1986), 38.

[2] For the former, see the letter of Friedrich Engels to Eduard Bernstein, 2–3 November, 1882: 'Now what is known as "Marxism" in France is, indeed, an altogether peculiar product – so much so that Marx once said to Lafargue: "*Ce qu'il y a de certain c'est que moi, je ne suis pas Marxiste.*" ' Available online – http://www.marxists.org/archive/marx/works/1882/letters/82_11_02.htm (accessed 6 September 2011). For the latter, see Meredith Anne Skura, *The Literary Use of the Psychoanalytic Process* (New Haven and London: Yale University Press, 1981), 17; cited by Hillman, 149.

[3] *Das Unbehagen in der Kultur* (1930); it can also be rendered as 'The Uneasiness in Culture'.

Chapter 1

The contributors appreciatively acknowledge Emily Shortslef's expert labor in preparing the index. Crystal Bartolovich is grateful in addition to Peter Holland and Adrian Poole for their epic patience; to Jean Howard for being a delightful collaborator; and to Margreta de Grazia, whose generous and timely reading not only led to many improvements, but helped me to let this book go.

[1] I begin with this point because heretofore critics attracted to the project of Marx's use of Shakespeare (as opposed to Marxist criticism of Shakespeare's plays) have not yet got the balance between them quite right in my view. By concentrating their attention disproportionately on the literary – or, as Richard Halpern has brilliantly shown in the case of Derrida – otherwise wrenching the Marxian archive out of all recognition, they have often misrepresented what is actually going on in the political and philosophical texts in which the Shakespeare citations appear. See Halpern's 'An Impure History of Ghosts' in Jean Howard and Scott Cutler Shershow (eds), *Marxist Shakespeares* (London: Routledge, 2001). This is perhaps most problematically the case with Peter Demetz's *Marx, Engels and the Poets* (Chicago: University of Chicago Press, 1967), which tendentiously contrasts what it presents as a dogmatic and

inflexible Marx with a moderate, accommodating – and even gentlemanly – Engels, but it is even the case with R. S. White's 'Marx and Shakespeare' (*Shakespeare Survey*, 45, 1993) in which the author feels compelled to reassure us that his essay 'is not in itself guided by Marxist ideology' and that he is coming at the subject primarily as a literary scholar (89). Gabriel Egan's *Marx and Shakespeare* (Oxford: Oxford University Press, 2004) moves to the opposite extreme. It certainly cannot be accused of indifference or antipathy to Marxist ideology, since after unfolding a set of key Marxian concepts, Egan uses readings of Shakespeare plays to elaborate them. What it sacrifices, however, as Douglas Bruster's review of Egan's book for *Shakespeare Quarterly*, 57, 1 (2006) points out, is any exploration of 'the role of Shakespeare's works in the writings of Marx' – as is typical in Marxist literary criticism of Shakespeare (105). For a thorough and balanced survey of Marx's use of literature, then, one must consult S. S. Prawer's *Karl Marx and World Literature* (Oxford: Clarendon, 1976), a truly stunning work of scholarship. Prawer does not, however, offer focused attention to Marx's Shakespeare in particular as I will be doing in this chapter, since he is examining the role of literary allusion and quotation more generally in Marx's work.

2 'The Task of the Translator', *Walter Benjamin, Selected Writings, Volume 1*, ed. Marcus Bullock and Michael W. Jennings (Cambridge, MA: Harvard University Press, 1996), 255.

3 *A Contribution to the Critique of Political Economy*, trans. S. W. Ryazanskaya (New York: International Publishers, 1970), 21.

4 *Search for a Method*, trans. Hazel Barnes (New York: Vintage, 1968), 7.

5 Karl Marx and Friedrich Engels, *Communist Manifesto*, trans. Samuel Moore (Oxford: Oxford University Press, 1998), 26.

6 'Species being' receives extended treatment by Marx in the 'Economic and Philosophical Manuscripts', *Early Writings*, trans. Rodney Livingstone and Gregor Benton (New York: Vintage Books, 1975), 279–400. I cite from this edition in the body of the text.

7 'King Lear: A Retrospect', *Shakespeare Survey*, 55 (2002): 5.

8 See Marx's chapters in 'The Holy Family', *Marx-Engels Collected Works*, vol. 4 (New York: International Publishers, 1975).

9 Susan Buck-Morss's indispensable *Origin of Negative Dialectics* (New York: Free Press, 1977) makes this point especially clearly and convincingly throughout. See especially 57–62.

10 Karl Marx, 'Theses on Feuerbach', collected in Karl Marx and Fredrick Engels, *German Ideology* (Moscow: Progress Publishers, 1968), 667.

11 'Why Does Puck Sweep?' *Shakespeare Quarterly*, 52, 1 (2001): 67.

12 On the history – and future – of the *Manifesto*, see Ellen Wood's excellent 'The Communist Manifesto After 150 Years', *Monthly Review*, 50, 1 (1998).

13 '[L]ike every generation that has preceded us, we have been endowed with a weak messianic power, a power on which the past has a claim', from 'On the Concept of History', *Selected Writings*, vol. 4 (Cambridge, MA: Harvard University Press, 2003), 390.

14 See for example, White, 'Marx and Shakespeare', 90.

15 See, for example, Roger Paulin, *The Critical Reception of Shakespeare in Germany*

1682–1914 (Hildesheim, Zurich and New York: Georg Olms Verlag, 2003). Also, the essays on Goethe by Stephen Fennell, and on A. W. Schlegel by Christine Roger and Roger Paulin, in *Great Shakespeareans*, vol. III, ed. Roger Paulin (London: Continuum, 2010).

16 'Traveling Theory', *The World, the Text and the Critic* (Cambridge, MA: Harvard University Press, 1983).

17 For a discussion of the early interchange of drama between England and the Continent, see Anston Bosman, 'Renaissance Intertheater and the Staging of Nobody', *ELH*, 71, 3 (2004): 559–85. Also useful on the early German context: Simon Williams, *Shakespeare on the German Stage, volume 1, 1586–1914* (Cambridge: Cambridge University Press, 1990).

18 *Shakespeare*, trans. Gregory Moore (Princeton: Princeton University Press, 2008), 32.

19 On the remarkable effort put into securing German translations of the entire Shakespearean canon in the early nineteenth century, see Kenneth E. Larson, 'The Origins of the "Schlegel-Tieck" Shakespeare in the 1820s', *German Quarterly*, 60, 1 (1987).

20 *Manifesto*, 6–7. On Goethe, see David Damrosch's compelling and balanced portrait in *What is World Literature?* (Princeton and Oxford: Princeton University Press, 2003), which, however, necessarily notes that 'the world literature [Goethe] prefers is the production of a guiding elite whose international brotherhood compensates for their small numbers and neglect by the masses' (13). Surely, it is to misconstrue Marx's passage in the *Manifesto* to assume he intends to designate literature as the preserve of a 'guiding elite', since he consistently works to put literature into the hands of the very 'masses' Goethe dismisses, for use as a revolutionary medium, and also forcefully argues for 'common property' of economic, not merely cultural, capital, in a far more expansive and egalitarian sense than Goethe has in mind.

21 'Conjectures on World Literature', *New Left Review*, 1 (Jan–Feb 2000): 54–5.

22 *Hamlet in Purgatory* (Princeton and Oxford: Princeton University Press, 2001), 229.

23 Johann Wolfgang von Goethe, *Wilhelm Meister's Apprenticeship*, trans. Eric A. Blackall (New York: Suhrkamp Publishers, 1989), 146.

24 Ibid., 128.

25 Ibid., 301.

26 *Human Rights, Inc.: The World Novel, Narrative Form and International Law* (New York: Fordham University Press, 2007), 109.

27 *Genesis and Structure of Hegel's Phenomenology of Spirit*, trans. Samuel Cherniak and John Heckman (Evanston: Northwestern University Press, 1974), 12.

28 Ibid., 42.

29 Ibid., 45. Hyppolite goes on here to try to defend Hegel from the charge that this passage implies his system marks the end of time; conceding that this (common) reading is not unjust, he (Hyppolite) goes on to insist that he is interested in the implications of Hegel's system for subjective relations to the 'past' not the 'future' so he can lay the problem of the future aside. Obviously, Marx could not.

30 Ibid., 49.

31 *The Holy Family*, 82.

32 *Capital*, vol. 1, trans. Ben Fowkes (London: Penguin, 1976), 102–3. All citations to *Capital* are from this edition, and will appear parenthetically in the body of the text.

33 *The Way of the World*, trans. Albert Sbragia (London and New York: Verso, 2000), 10.

34 *Manifesto*, 21–2.

35 *Holy Family*, 131.

36 To compare and contrast *Capital* with a novel in this way is not to suggest it is primarily a 'work of art', itself a novel instead of an 'economic treatise', the position that Francis Wheen has championed recently – one that tames the book too much, it seems to me: *Marx's Das Kapital: A Biography* (New York: Atlantic Monthly Press, 2006). To the contrary, I am drawing attention to Marx's *Capital* as an unBildungsroman to indicate why Marx might particularly appreciate the role that literature plays as a site of struggle, among others, and yet see that the classic Bildungsroman was a form he had to write against. While I appreciate, then, Anna Kornbluh's attempt to describe *Capital* as a novel affirmatively – to show, in fact, that it is like a Victorian Bildungsroman in some respects – I cannot agree. As I show in this section, in *Capital* Marx was writing in dialectical opposition to classic Bildungsroman, which is why it incorporates some aspects of Bildungsroman into its fabric – but it does so to transform them. See 'On Marx's Victorian Novel', *Mediations*, 25, 1 (2010).

37 *Way of the World*, 10.

38 'Can the Subaltern Speak', *Marxism and the Interpretation of Culture*, ed. C. Nelson and L. Grossberg (Urbana and Chicago: University of Illinois Press, 1988), 291.

39 Marx brings in Dogberry twice more in *Capital*, once in a similar way to make fun of capital's organic intellectuals as 'English Dogberries' (750), and, in another place, to highlight the absurdity of a court in prosecuting a worker twice for the same 'crime' of abandoning a two-year contract in a steel factory. This judgement was not, Marx emphasizes, handed down by one of the 'Provincial Dogberries' but 'one of the highest courts of justice in London' (551). In all cases, Dogberry exposes a world in which justice, sense and social relations have been turned upside down.

40 Melissa Hull Geil also reads this particular section of *Capital* as a prelude to producing a reading of *Much Ado About Nothing*. Her conclusions and emphases are very different from my own, in part because she puts the emphasis on 'drama' whereas I am examining the anti-Bildungsroman function of *Capital*, but also theoretically in that she lacks a concept of 'real abstraction' and so argues that there is ultimately 'nothing' to be revealed about capitalism, which she presents as sheer performance. But history and, of course, social relations of production are material for Marx, even when they generate illusions. 'Shakespeare and the Drama of Capital', *Cultural Logic* (2008). Available at: http://clogic.eserver.org/2008/2008.html (accessed 5 January 2012).

41 'Against Human Rights', *New Left Review*, 34 (2005): 117.

42 David Campbell, 'Friday Closing Market: Heroic bank gains fail to shift FTSE', June 13, 2008. Available at: http://citywire.co.uk/money/friday-closing-market-heroic-bank-gains-fail-to-shift-ftse/a305732 (accessed 5 January 2012).

43 I will not single out anyone in this citation (you know who you are!), except to note the astonishing fact that this claim is still being made, not only in playnotes, blogs and journalism, where one might expect errors of this kind, but even in scholarly books and articles, and as recently as 2006 (that I have seen). It is often hard to trace the origin of such myths, but it might derive from Demetz, who, writing at a time when fewer texts by Marx were available, claims that *Timon* was the play that 'young Marx admired above all', presumably because of its relatively extended treatment in the *1844 Manuscripts*, though he gives no rationale for his assertion. See *Marx, Engels and the Poets*, 154. Certainly it is true that *Timon* comes up more than once in key locations in Marx's writing, but in the totality of Shakespeare citations, they are comparatively few. There are many more citations to other individual plays – especially the two *Henry IV*s. Furthermore, while Marx does claim Shakespeare to be his 'favourite writer', he never singled out a particular play as his favourite that I know of, nor do the authors that claim *Timon* was his favourite provide any such evidence.

44 I am using 'thinking with Shakespeare' here in a more precise and therefore limited sense than Julia Lupton, *Thinking with Shakespeare* (Chicago: University of Chicago Press, 2011). Marx's instances of 'thinking with Shakespeare' are, in this conceptual sense, quite rare, since he appreciated the very different modes in which philosophy and literature work.

45 *Class, Critics and Shakespeare: Bottom Lines on the Culture Wars* (Ann Arbor: University of Michigan Press, 2000), 59.

46 See, for example, *Manifesto*, 5, 29.

47 *Class*, 65.

48 I do not dispute that an attempt to protect 'status' is rife in academia. Where I differ, absolutely, with O'Dair, is that this has anything to do with Marx(ism). Even if it were possible to show that some individual 'Marxist' errs along the lines she proposes, I would adamantly counter that this was in spite of the Marxism, not because of it. Certainly Marxism is not, in any of its main or influential strands, sentimental about Feudalism. Raymond Williams, among others, has vehemently denounced such views, and exposed the frank contempt for the working class bound up with them, but not in terms that coincide with O'Dair's defense of Capitalism, nor with her association of the aristocratic view with Marxism as such. See, for example, 'Culture is Ordinary', *Resources of Hope* (London and New York: Verso, 1989). Furthermore, Marxists have been deeply attuned to the ways that class is a complex category, and that individuals and groups are inflected by multiple social forces – Marx notes this himself in 'historical' works, such as the *Eighteenth Brumaire*, which I examine in section 3.

49 *Class*, 60.

50 C. L. Barber, *Shakespeare's Festive Comedy*, 2nd edn (Princeton: Princeton University Press, 1972). Harry Berger, *Second World and Green World* (Berkeley and Los Angeles: University of California Press, 1990). This is not to suggest that there are no other sorts of readings of the play – there are: many. My point, rather, is that there is a long tradition (still going strong) in which the comedies in particular have been read in terms of (ideological) resolution of conflict, however temporary or illusory, and that this is the sort of experience of both the plays and of life that Marx is attempting to undermine through *Capital*.

⁵¹ Henry Sussman, 'The Metaphor in Hegel's Phenomenology of Mind', *Hegel's Dialectic of Desire and Recognition,* ed. John O'Neill (Albany: State University of New York Press, 1996), 307. This 'monologue' is interrupted from time to time by a transcendent voice that comments on it. Sussman further distinguishes these two voices as 'a character recently undergoing an experience' and an 'omniscient narrator', with the latter finally enveloping the former. In any case, the effect is very different from the cacophony of voices collected in *Capital.*

⁵² *Dialogic Imagination,* trans. Caryl Emerson and Michael Holquist (Austin: University of Texas Press, 1981), 259–422.

⁵³ *A Companion to Marx's Capital* (London and New York: Verso, 2010), 5.

⁵⁴ *Way of the World,* 48–60. Moretti also makes the point that 'conversation' is nothing like heteroglossia, since it seeks to merge various social languages into neutrality, 253, n. 44.

⁵⁵ Andrew Murphy, *Shakespeare for the People* (Cambridge: Cambridge University Press, 2008), 3.

⁵⁶ In the Introduction to the *Political Unconscious* (Ithaca: Cornell University Press, 1981), Fredric Jameson was already lamenting the tiresomeness of having to continually confront these same charges – 30 years ago.

⁵⁷ Richard Halpern deals with this problem nicely in the Introduction to *Poetics of Primitive Accumulation* (Ithaca and London: Cornell University Press, 1991), 10–11.

⁵⁸ 'Traveling', 239.

⁵⁹ *Political Unconscious,* 9.

⁶⁰ This brief letter appears in its entirety in *Marx-Engels Collected Works* vol. 40, 418.

⁶¹ Engels, *Peasant War in Germany,* International Publishers, 1926 (2006), 82–3.

⁶² Marx, *Grundrisse,* trans. Martin Nicolaus (New York: Vintage, 1973). The entire brief note on uneven development can be found on 109–11.

⁶³ Though it gets only fragmentary and brief attention in Marx, the concept of 'uneven' development has received extensive treatment in twentieth-century Marxism, precisely to critique 'linear' and simple 'stages' theories of history. A sampling: Ernst Bloch, 'Nonsynchronism and the Obligation to its Dialectics', trans. Mark Ritter, *New German Critique* 11 (1977): 22–38; Michael Lowy, *The Politics of Combined and Uneven Development* (New York and London: Verso, 1981); Neil Smith, *Uneven Development: Nature, Capital, and Geography,* now in its third edition (Athens: University of Georgia Press, 2008).

⁶⁴ 'Eighteenth Brumaire' is collected in *Surveys from Exile,* trans. Ben Fowkes (Harmondsworth: Penguin, 1973), 143–249. I will cite from this edition parenthetically in the body of the text.

⁶⁵ These ties and limits are being interestingly explored in Eco-Marxist theory and activism by figures such as John Bellamy Foster, *Marx's Ecology: Materialism and Nature* (Monthly Review Press, 2000).

⁶⁶ Especially important previous discussions of Marx's mole by Shakespeareans include: Margreta de Grazia's 'Teleology, Delay and the "Old Mole" ', *Shakespeare Quarterly,* 50, 3 (1999): 251–67; Peter Stallybrass's, ' "Well grubbed, old mole": Marx, *Hamlet* and the (un)fixing of Representation' in *Marxist Shakespeares,* ed. Jean Howard and Scott Cutler Shershow (London and New York: Routledge,

2001), and Martin Harries's *Scare Quotes from Shakespeare: Marx, Keynes and the Language of Reenchantment* (Stanford: Stanford University Press, 2000).

[67] *Empire* (Cambridge and London: Harvard University Press, 2000), 57.

[68] *Specters of Marx*, trans. Peggy Kamuf (New York and London: Routledge, 1994), 93.

[69] *The Country and the City* (New York: Oxford University Press, 1973), 50.

[70] For a discussion of a Shakespeare sensitive to the common folk, see Annabel Patterson, *Shakespeare and the Popular Voice* (Cambridge: Basel Blackwell, 1989). Marx's own views of how art works do not depend on intentionality in this way, however.

[71] Albert B. Friedman, ' "When Adam Delved …" Contexts of a Historic Proverb', *The Learned and the Lewed*, ed. Larry D. Benson (Cambridge, MA: Harvard University Press, 1974). The Sexton does not state the proverb as such outright, but it permeates his speech and character, as I discuss in this section.

[72] Robert Weimann in *Shakespeare and the Popular Tradition in the Theater* (Baltimore: Johns Hopkins University Press, 1978) argues that the generic mixing and especially the clowning tradition as integrated into Shakespeare's plays are necessary to the 'richness, the complexity of the play's vision of reality' and thus cannot be considered mere 'safety valves' or 'foils' for the 'serious' part of the plays, and certainly not mere pandering to the pit. They are, instead, essential – and this is so even if not every word in the playscripts handed down to us were written by Shakespeare, 242.

[73] Friedman, 213–14.

[74] This is one of his favourite themes, and so is scattered throughout the writings, but see, for example, 'The New Law of Righteousness', *The Works of Gerrard Winstanley*, ed. George Sabine (Ithaca and New York: Cornell University Press, 1941), 158.

[75] *Saint Paul: the Foundation of Universalism*, trans. Ray Brassier (Stanford: Stanford University Press, 2003).

[76] The question would then arise why I would argue for preserving the 'mole' as a figure for Revolution (in contrast to many recent theorists) and yet applaud the shift from 'spectre' to 'mole' between the *Manifesto* and the *Brumaire* in Marx's own work. The short answer would be that the dismissal of the 'mole' stands in too often for what is, in effect, a dismissal of Marx(ism) altogether, overtly or covertly. Halpern makes a similar point in his review essay on Derrida's *Specters* (which I bring up in note 1 above) – though by way of contrast with the *Hamlet*ian 'skull' rather than the 'mole.'

[77] *Manifesto*, 16.

[78] For a fascinating discussion of the politics of translation around this phrase, see Harries, *Scare Quotes from Shakespeare*, 79–89.

[79] I very much admire Harries's reading of *Brumaire/Hamlet,* but I part ways with his emphasis on the ghost (the mole has more to do with the 'gravedigger' than the ghost in my view, as I have been arguing), and also on Marx's putative quest for revolutionary 'language' (85). What Marx was seeking, surely, was 'revolution' as an act – content – that finally got beyond the mere phrase.

[80] *Lectures on the History of Philosophy*, trans. E. S. Haldane and Frances H. Simpson, 3 vols (Lincoln: University of Nebraska Press, 1995), III: 547.

[81] The full text of the speech is collected in *Surveys from Exile*, 299–300.

[82] Egan, too, makes a case for an unacknowledged Marxist presence in Shakespeare Studies in *Shakespeare and Marx*, though with different emphases than mine here. As he puts it: 'a central theme of my argument is that Marx's ideas have pervaded all aspects of Shakespeare criticism, theory and performance, in ways not fully appreciated', 46.

[83] *Hamlet Without Hamlet* (Cambridge: Cambridge University Press, 2007), 25.

[84] Ibid., 43.

[85] Ibid., 43.

[86] United Nations Department of Economic and Social Affairs, *World Urbanization Prospects, 2009 Revision* (New York: United Nations, 2010), 1.

[87] See, for example, David Harvey's influential discussion of 'accumulation by dispossession' in *The New Imperialism* (Oxford: Oxford University Press, 2003).

[88] John Taylor, *Part of this Summers Travels, Or News from Hell* (London: 1639), 11.

[89] The Peasant Revolts are enormous sites of struggle among historians on the right and the left. Norman Cohn's *Pursuit of the Millennium* (Oxford: Oxford University Press, 1970), for example, is a major work of scholarship, but it is at the same time a polemic against what he sees as Marxist distortions of the Millenarians to suit their own agenda, a typical claim of historians on the right. And it is certainly the case that Guy Debord, Christopher Hill, Eric Hobsbawn, James Holstun and numerous other left and Marxist historians have eagerly adapted Millenarianism to the Long Revolution in a variety of ways. I am attempting in this chapter to show how it would be possible for the Peasants' Revolts (and other early rebellions) to be part of a 'revolutionary' tradition – understood as an incomplete project – while retaining their historical specificity.

[90] *The Order of Things* (New York: Vintage Books, 1973), 262.

[91] I allude, obviously, to Stephen Greenblatt's famous first line of Chapter 1 of *Shakespearean Negotiations* (Berkeley and Los Angeles: University of California Press, 1988).

[92] Raymond Williams, *The Long Revolution* (London: Chatto and Windus, 1961).

Chapter 2

[1] For one version of this argument, see both the introduction to and the essays collected in *Marxist Shakespeares*, ed. Jean E. Howard and Scott Cutler Shershow (London: Routledge, 2001).

[2] L. C. Knights, *Drama and Society in the Age of Shakespeare* (London: Chatto and Windus, 1937).

[3] For representative work by each of these critics, see Crystal Bartolovich, 'Putting Tamburlaine on a Cognitive Map', *Renaissance Drama* n.s. XXVIII (1997): 29–72, '"Baseless Fabric": London as a World City' in *'The Tempest' and Its Travels*, ed. Peter Hulme and William H. Sherman (London: Reaktion Press, 2000), 13–26, 'Shakespeare's Globe?' in *Marxist Shakespeares*, ed. Jean E. Howard and Scott Shershow, 178–205, 'London's the Thing: Alienation, the Market, and *Englishmen for My Money*', *Huntington Library Quarterly*, 71, 1 (2008): 137–56,

and 'Travailing Theory: Global Flows of Labor and the Enclosures of the Subject' in Jyotsna Singh ed., *Companion to the Global Renaissance* (London: Blackwell, 2009), 50–66; David Hawkes, *Idols of the Marketplace: Idolatry and Commodity Fetishism in English Literature, 1580-1680* (New York: Palgrave, 2001), *Faust Myth: Religion and the Rise of Representation* (New York: Palgrave, 2007) and *John Milton: A Hero of Our Time* (Berkeley: Counterpoint, 2009); James Holstun, *Rational Millennium: Puritan Utopias of Seventeenth-Century England and America* (New York: Oxford University Press, 1987) and *Ehud's Dagger: Class Struggle in the English Revolution* (New York: Verso, 2000); and Christopher Kendrick, *Milton: A Study in Ideology and Form* (New York: Methuen, 1986) and *Utopia, Carnival, and Commonwealth in Renaissance England* (Toronto: University of Toronto Press, 2004).

4   This much quoted and much discussed line begins Stephen Greenblatt's *Shakespearean Negotiations: The Circulation of Social Energy in Renaissance England* (Berkeley: University of California Press, 1988), 1. Greenblatt, of course, is quite careful to say that one never can find the 'untranslatable essence' of past texts (5), and that such texts are only approached through a series of mediations and negotiations. Nonetheless, the impossible desire for the presence of the past remains a feature of much of Greenblatt's critical writing.

5   Robert Weimann, *Shakespeare and the Popular Tradition in the Theater: Studies in the Social Dimension of Dramatic Form and Function*, ed. Robert Schwartz (Baltimore: The Johns Hopkins University Press, 1978).

6   Weimann's views on the tension between an actor-centered and an author-centered theatre are most fully developed in his later book, *Author's Pen and Actor's Voice: Playing and Writing in Shakespeare's Theatre*, ed. Helen Higbee and William West (Cambridge: Cambridge University Press, 2000).

7   See in particular Chapter 6, 'Shakespeare's Theater: Tradition and Experiment' in *Shakespeare and the Popular Tradition*, 208–52.

8   *Authority and Representation in Early Modern Discourse*, ed. David Hillman (Baltimore: Johns Hopkins University Press, 1996) and *Author's Pen and Actor's Voice*, ed. Helen Higbee and William West.

9   For Taylor's discussion of the 'nonarchival system of transfer I call the repertoire' see her *Archive and the Repertoire: Performing Cultural Memory in the Americas* (Durham: Duke University Press, 2003), xvii. Taylor focuses on the performance practices of the illiterate and the oppressed, arguing that their embodied behaviours are a source of cultural continuity and memory. I would argue that the non-textualized performance traditions of the early Elizabethan stage had much the same purpose and political effect.

10 Phyllis Rackin, *Stages of History: Shakespeare's English Chronicles* (Ithaca: Cornell University Press, 1990), esp. 206–208.

11 *Rematerializing Shakespeare: Authority and Representation on the Early Modern English Stage*, ed. Bryan Reynolds and William N. West (New York: Palgrave Macmillan, 2005).

12 See, in particular, Bakhtin's *Rabelais and His World*, trans. Helene Iswolsky (Cambridge, MA: MIT Press, 1968).

13 Michael Bristol, *Carnival and Theater: Plebeian Culture and the Structure of Authority in Renaissance England* (New York: Methuen, 1985).

14 Peter Stallybrass and Allon White, *The Politics and Poetics of Transgression* (Ithaca: Cornell University Press, 1986), 14.

15 This is particularly true of many American new historicists who, influenced by Foucault's disciplinary theories, began to stress the inescapability of power and the impossibility of individual agency. For an early critique that cogently made this point, see Walter Cohen's 'Political Criticism of Shakespeare' in *Shakespeare Reproduced: The Text in History and Ideology*, ed. Jean E. Howard and Marion F. O'Connor (London: Methuen, 1987), 18–46.

16 The focus on Shakespeare as a writer rather than a playmaker reached its apogee with Lucas Erne's *Shakespeare as Literary Dramatist* (Cambridge: Cambridge University Press, 2003).

17 Walter Cohen, *Drama of a Nation: Public Theater in Renaissance England and Spain* (Ithaca: Cornell University Press, 1985).

18 Perry Anderson, *Lineages of the Absolutist State* (London: Verso, 1974).

19 Franco Moretti, ' "A Huge Eclipse": Tragic Form and the Deconsecration of Sovereignty' in *The Forms of Power and the Power of Forms in the Renaissance, Genre* XV (1982), 7–40.

20 For an analysis of this movement, in both its Marxist and non-Marxist forms, see Stephen Cohen ed., *Shakespeare and Historical Formalism* (Aldershot: Ashgate, 2007), particularly Cohen's 'Introduction', 1–27.

21 For an interesting examination of the fraught and complex relationship between Marxism, American New Left thought and practice and new historicism, see Catherine Gallagher's 'Marxism and The New Historicism' in *The New Historicism*, ed. H. Aram Veeser (London: Routledge, 1989), 37–48.

22 Ellen Schrecker, *No Ivory Tower: McCarthyism and the Universities* (Oxford: Oxford University Press, 1986).

23 In the pages that follow I draw on my earlier assessment of new historicism in 'The New historicism in Renaissance Studies', *English Literary Renaissance* 16 (1986): 13–42. Obviously, 25 years later, I see some things differently, including the unique ways American new historicism and British cultural materialism engage with Marxism. These divergences were not so apparent to me when I wrote my earlier essay, but I stand by the general claims of that piece.

24 Stephen Greenblatt, *Renaissance Self-Fashioning from More to Shakespeare* (Chicago: University of Chicago Press, 1980).

25 Stephen Greenblatt, 'Murdering Peasants: Status, Genre, and the Representation of Rebellion', *Representations*, 1 (1983): 1–29.

26 James Holstun, 'Ranting at the New Historicism', *English Literary Renaissance*, 19 (1989): 189–225, at 203.

27 'Towards a Poetics of Culture' in *The New Historicism*, ed. H. Aram Veeser, 2. Elsewhere in this essay, Greenblatt recounts with characteristic humour the casual, almost inadvertent, way in which he invented the term 'new historicism' when editing a collection of essays for *Genre* in the early 1980s. Consistently refusing to define the new historicism, he calls it a 'practice rather than a doctrine' ('Towards a Poetics of Culture', [1]), a position he elaborates in *Practicing New Historicism*, co-written with Catherine Gallagher (Chicago: University of Chicago Press, 2001), esp. 1–19.

28 At one point, Walter Cohen called new historicism a form of 'left disillusionment'.

See his 'Political Criticism of Shakespeare' in *Shakespeare Reproduced*, ed. Jean E. Howard and Marion O'Connor, 36.

[29] See Greenblatt's '*King Lear* and the Exorcists' in *Shakespearean Negotiations*, 94–128.

[30] Stephen Greenblatt, *Hamlet in Purgatory* (Princeton: Princeton University Press, 2001).

[31] Louis Montrose, 'Professing the Renaissance: The Poetics and Politics of Culture' in *The New Historicism*, ed. H. Aram Veeser, 15–36, esp. 20.

[32] For his debt to Williams, see Louis Montrose, 'Of Gentlemen and Shepherds: The Politics of Elizabethan Pastoral Form', *English Literary History* 50 (1983): 415–59, esp. 419. In his provocative 'Against Materialism in Literary Theory' (*The Return of Theory in Early Modern English Studies: Tarrying with the Subjunctive*, ed. Paul Cefalu and Bryan Reynolds [New York: Palgrave Macmillan, 2011], 237–59, at 244), David Hawkes argues that it was Gramsci in *Prison Notebooks* who first applied cultural materialism to literary studies and asserted the relative autonomy of the cultural realm. For a fuller account of Montrose's work in relationship to Stephen Greenblatt's as alternative versions of new historical practice, see my 'The New Historicism in Renaissance Studies', 13–42.

[33] Louis Montrose, 'The Purpose of Playing: Reflections on a Shakespearean Anthropology', *Helios*, 7 (1980): 51–74.

[34] Among others, see his 'Of Gentlemen and Shepherds; "Eliza, Queene of Shepheards" and the Pastoral of Power', *English Literary Renaissance*, 10 (1980): 153–82, and ' "Shaping Fantasies": Figurations of Gender and Power in Elizabethan Culture', *Representations*, 2 (1983): 61–94.

[35] Louis Montrose, ' "The Place of a Brother" in *As You Like It*: Social Process and Comic Form', *Shakespeare Quarterly*, 32 (1981): 28–54.

[36] Ivo Kamps ed., *Material Shakespeare: A History* (London: Verso, 1995). The contributors to the Kamps volume included Walter Cohen and Robert Weimann, notable Marxists, for example, but also Katharine Maus and Claire McEachern, neither of whom makes any direct use of Marxist categories, and Alan Sinfield and John Drakakis, prominently associated with British cultural materialism. Kamps was far from alone in this eclecticism. The essays in *Shakespeare Reproduced*, ed. Jean E. Howard and Marion F. O'Connor, include many American and European Marxists, but also non-Marxist feminists and deconstructive critics. It has often been in hindsight that the real differences in method and in political vision among the political critics of the 1980s have become apparent.

[37] For early accounts of the difference between new historicism and cultural materialism see Walter Cohen, 'Political Criticism of Shakespeare' and Don Wayne, 'Power, Politics and the Shakespearean Text: Recent Criticism in England and the United States', both in *Shakespeare Reproduced: The Text in History and Ideology*, 18–46 and 47–67; Jonathan Dollimore's 'Shakespeare, Cultural Materialism, and the New Historicism' in *Political Shakespeare: New Essays in Cultural Materialism*, ed. Jonathan Dollimore and Alan Sinfield (Ithaca: Cornell University Press, 1985), 2–17; and Steven Mullaney's 'After the New Historicism' in *Alternative Shakespeares* 2, ed. Terence Hawkes (London: Routledge, 1996), 17–37.

[38] Jonathan Dollimore, *Radical Tragedy: Religion, Ideology and Power in The Drama of Shakespeare and His Contemporaries* (Chicago: University of Chicago Press, 1984).

[39] See, for example, the complex review of Dollimore's book written by Jonathan Goldberg in *Modern Philology*, 84 (1986): 71–5.

[40] See, in particular, Louis Althusser, 'Ideology and Ideological State Apparatuses' in *Lenin and Philosophy and Other Essays* (New York: Monthly Review Press, 1971), 127–86.

[41] See, in particular, Terence Hawkes, *That Shakespeherian Rag: Essays on a Critical Process* (London: Methuen, 1986) and *Meaning by Shakespeare* (London: Routledge, 1992).

[42] Richard Halpern, *The Poetics of Primitive Accumulation: English Renaissance Culture and the Genealogy of Capital* (Ithaca: Cornell University Press, 1991). Scott Shershow and I briefly discuss the importance of Halpern's work in our introduction to *Marxist Shakespeares*, esp. 9.

[43] Walter Cohen in 'Political Criticism of Shakespeare' in *Shakespeare Reproduced*, ed. Jean E. Howard and Marion O'Connor, 18–46, esp. at 32–8, makes a related point about the 'arbitrary connectedness' that infuses (and disables the political coherence) of much new historicist work.

[44] Friedrich Engels, *The Origin of the Family, Private Property and the State* (1884, Middlesex, England: Penguin, 1985).

[45] Alice Clark, *Working Life of Women in the Seventeenth Century* (1919; 3rd edn, London: Routledge, 1992).

[46] For a discussion of this issue see Walter Cohen's 'Political Criticism of Shakespeare', 18–46.

[47] Two influential critiques from the 1980s were lodged by Lynda Boose in 'The Family in Shakespeare Studies; or – Studies in the Family of Shakespeareans; or – The Politics of Politics', *Renaissance Quarterly*, 40 (1987): 707–42 and by Carol Neely in 'Constructing the Subject: Feminist Practice and New Renaissance Discourses', *English Literary Renaissance*, 18 (1988): 5–18. A slightly different account of what she sees as the pernicious effects of new historicism on feminism is offered by Phyllis Rackin in *Shakespeare and Women* (Oxford: Oxford University Press, 2005) in which she argues that rather than ignoring women, new historicists have created narratives emphasizing female disempowerment and the pervasiveness of Renaissance misogyny, in the process obscuring the many kinds of authority and autonomy early modern women exercised (see esp. 1–25).

[48] Among the books that have contributed to a feminist transformation of the Marxist project I would include Michele Barrett's *Women's Oppression Today: Problems in Marxist Feminist Analyses* (London: Verso, 1980); Christine Delphy's *Close to Home: A Materialist Analysis of Women Oppression* (Amherst: University of Masschusetts Press, 1984); Teresa Ebert, *Ludic Feminism and After: Postmodernism, Desire and Labor in Late Capitalism* (Ann Arbor: University of Michigan Press, 1996); Rosemary Hennessy, *Materialist Feminism and the Politics of Desire* (New York: Routledge, 1993) and *Profit and Pleasure: Sexual Identities in Late Capitalism* (New York: Routledge, 2000); Annette Kuhn and AnnMarie Wolpe (eds), *Feminism and Materialism: Women and Modes of Production* (London: Routledge and Kegan Paul, 1978); Donna Landry and

Gerald MacLean's *Materialist Feminisms* (Oxford: Blackwell, 1993); and Zillah Eisenstein, *Capitalist Patriarchy and the Case for Socialist Feminism* (New York: Monthly Review Press, 1979).

[49] Valerie Wayne, *The Matter of Difference: Materialist Feminist Criticism of Shakespeare* (New York: Harvester Wheatsheaf, 1991). The term was popularized by Judith Newton and Deborah Rosenfelt in their essay, 'Introduction: Toward a Materialist-feminist Criticism' in the collection they edited entitled *Feminist Criticism and Social Change* (New York: Methuen, 1985).

[50] Natasha Korda and Jonathan Gil Harris, 'Introduction: Towards a Materialist Account of Stage Properties' in *Staged Properties in Early Modern* Drama, ed. Natasha Korda and Jonathan Gil Harris (Cambridge: Cambridge University Press, 2002), 1–31, at 17. For a more extended critique of the antiquarian and empiricist cast of some 'material' criticism see Jean E. Howard, 'Material Shakespeare/Materialist Shakespeare' in *Shakespeare Matters: History, Teaching, Performance*, ed. Lloyd David (Newark: University of Delaware Press, 2003), 29–45.

[51] Jean E. Howard, *The Stage and Social Struggle in Early Modern England* (London: Routledge, 1994).

[52] A recent book by Natasha Korda, *Labors Lost: Women's Work and the Early Modern English Stage* (Philadelphia: University of Pennsylvania Press, 2011), reveals new ways in which women, while not allowed to act, were nonetheless integral to the institution of the theatre as seamstresses, pawnbrokers, laundresses and in other roles.

[53] Natasha Korda, *Shakespeare's Domestic Economies: Gender and Property in Early Modern England* (Philadelphia: University of Pennsylvania, 2002).

[54] Rosemary Kegl, *The Rhetoric of Concealment: Figuring Gender and Class in Renaissance Literature* (Ithaca: Cornell University Press, 1994); Dympna Callaghan, esp. *Woman and Gender in Renaissance Tragedy: A Study of 'King Lear', 'Othello', 'The Duchess of Malfi', and 'The White Devil'* (Atlantic Highlands, New Jersey: Humanities Press International, 1989) and *Shakespeare Without Women: Representing Gender and Race on the Renaissance Stage* (London: Routledge, 2000).

[55] Ania Loomba, *Shakespeare, Race, and Colonialism* (Oxford: Oxford University Press, 2002), 4.

[56] Hugh Grady, *The Modernist Shakespeare* (Oxford: Clarendon Press, 1991); *Shakespeare's Universal Wolf: Studies in Early Modern Reification* (Oxford: Clarendon Press, 1996); *Shakespeare, Machiavelli, and Montaigne: Power and Subjectivity from 'Richard II' to 'Hamlet'* (Oxford: Oxford University Press, 2002); and *Shakespeare and Impure Aesthetics* (Cambridge: Cambridge University Press, 2009).

[57] As Ewan Fernie, among others, has emphasized in 'Shakespeare and the Prospect of Presentism', *Shakespeare Survey 58* (Cambridge: Cambridge University Press, 2006): 169–84, new historicists often expressed the same views about the relationship of past to present and about the structural relationship between the beginning and the end of modernity (173), but agrees with Grady that these views are then suppressed or neglected in much of their criticism, especially that produced by second and third generation practitioners.

[58] Kiernan Ryan shares with Grady commitments to a Frankfurt School Marxism

and to revealing the utopian dimensions of Shakespeare's works. In *Shakespeare* (Atlantic Highlands, NJ: Humanities Press International, 1989), he says that he reads Shakespeare 'to activate the revolutionary imaginative vision which invites discovery in his plays today' (1) and argues that even the tragedies can be read as opening to a more utopian future. Ryan repeats his call to renew attention to the utopian writings of thinkers such as Bloch, Benjamin and Marcuse in an imaginative reading of *Measure for Measure* in '*Measure for Measure*: Marxism Before Marx', *Marxist Shakespeares*, ed. Jean E. Howard and Scott Shershow, 227–44.

59 Terence Hawkes, *That Shakespeherian Rag: Essays on a Critical Process*, 124.

60 As Grady and Hawkes say in the introduction to their jointly-edited collection, *Presentist Shakespeares* (London: Routledge, 2007), '... the critic's own "situatedness" does not—cannot—contaminate the past. In effect, it constitutes the only means by which it's possible to see the past and perhaps comprehend it' (3).

61 *Ibid.*, 3–4.

62 Terence Hawkes, *Shakespeare in the Present* (London: Routledge, 2002), esp. chapters 2, 3, and 4.

63 Richard Halpern, *Shakespeare Among the Moderns* (Ithaca: Cornell University Press, 1997), 10.

64 Denise Albanese, *Extramural Shakespeare* (New York: Palgrave Macmillan, 2010), 4.

Chapter 4

I would like to express my gratitude to Adrian Poole and Peter Holland for inviting me to write this essay, and my very warm thanks to Adrian for all his help, advice and encouragement throughout the process of writing. I am also extremely grateful to John Forrester, Julian Leff, Adam Phillips, Joan Raphael-Leff, Anita Sokolsky and Steve Tifft for reading all or parts of this essay and commenting in detail. My deepest thanks, as always, go to Jessa Leff and Noa Hillman, who have been encouraging and distracting in equally helpful measures.

1 W. H. Auden, 'In Memory of Sigmund Freud', in *Collected Poems* (London: Faber and Faber, 1976), 275.

2 Paul Ricoeur, *Freud and Philosophy: An Essay on Interpretation* (New Haven: Yale University Press, 1977), 60; George Steiner, *Voices: Psychoanalysis*, ed. Bill Bourne, Udi Eichler, and David Herman (Nottingham: Spokesman/Hobo Press, 1987), 11.

3 Jacques Derrida, *The Post Card: from Socrates to Freud and Beyond*, trans. Alan Bass (Chicago: University of Chicago Press, 1987), 262.

4 David Willbern, 'Phantasmagoric *Macbeth*', *ELR*, 16 (1986), 520–49, 544.

5 Harold Bloom, *The Western Canon* (London: Macmillan, 1994), 371.

6 *Ibid.*, 371–2; Meredith Anne Skura, *The Literary Use of the Psychoanalytic Process* (New Haven and London: Yale University Press, 1981), 37; Philip Armstrong, *Shakespeare in Psychoanalysis* (London and New York: Routledge, 2001), 42.

Norman N. Holland's *Psychoanalysis and Shakespeare* (New York: McGraw-Hill, 1964) is the classic (and, though somewhat dated, invaluable) work on the topic.

7   Joel Fineman, *Shakespeare's Perjured Eye: The Invention of Poetic Subjectivity in the Sonnets* (Berkeley and Los Angeles: University of California Press, 1985), 46.

8   I quote from the 'Prospectus for Contributors' to the Great Shakespeareans series.

9   Compare Lynn Enterline, 'Psychoanalytic Criticisms', in *Shakespeare: An Oxford Guide,* ed. Stanley Wells and Lena Cowen Orlin (Oxford: Oxford University Press, 2003), 451–71, esp. 451.

10   Auden, 'In Memory of Sigmund Freud', 275.

11   All quotations from Shakespeare (unless otherwise indicated) throughout this essay are from *The Riverside Shakespeare*, 2nd edn, ed. G. Blakemore Evans and J. J. M. Tobin (Boston: Houghton Mifflin Company, 1997)

12   Cynthia Chase, 'Oedipal Textuality: Reading Freud's Reading of *Oedipus*', in Maud Ellmann, ed., *Psychoanalytic Literary Criticism* (London and New York: Longman, 1994), 56–75, 70.

13   See Sigmund Freud, 'The Unconscious' (1915), SE, 14: 186–90. All quotations from Freud throughout this essay are from *The Standard Edition of the Complete Psychological Works of Sigmund Freud*, trans. and ed. James Strachey (London: The Hogarth Press and the Institute of Psychoanalysis, 1953–74), abbreviated as 'SE', followed by volume and page number. I occasionally refer, where these have struck me as apropos, to the more recent Penguin translations, under the general editorship of Adam Phillips. When referring to the German original, I am using: Freud, *Gesammelte Werke: Chronologisch Geordnet* (London: Imago Publishing Co., 1991), available through the Psychoanalytic Electronic Publishing website: http://www.pep-web.org/static.php?page=gesammeltewerke, and hereafter abbreviated as 'GW'.

14   Freud, *An Outline of Psycho-Analysis* (1938), SE, 23: 168–9.

15   Freud, 'Creative Writers and Day-dreaming' (1908), SE, 9: 144.

16   Jacques Lacan, *The Four Fundamental Concepts of Psycho-Analysis*, ed. Jacques-Alain Miller, trans. Alan Sheridan (New York: Norton & Company, 1981), 124. For more on this topic vis-à-vis Freud and Shakespeare, see my essay 'Transference, Love and *Antony and Cleopatra*' (forthcoming in *Shakespeare Quarterly*).

Chapter 5

1   *The Letters of Sigmund Freud and Arnold Zweig*, ed. Ernst L. Freud, trans. Elaine and William Robson-Scott (New York: Harcourt Brace Jovanovich, 1970), 139–40.

2   C. L. Barber, transcript of a lecture, 'Piety and Outrage in Kyd's *Spanish Tragedy* and in *Hamlet*', SUNY/Buffalo, Spring 1969, as cited in C. L. Barber and Richard P. Wheeler, *The Whole Journey: Shakespeare's Power of Development* (Berkeley: University of California Press, 1986), xxii.

3   See Peter Gay, *Freud: A Life for our Times* (New York and London: Norton, 1988), 166.

4   Hans Sachs, *Freud: Master and Friend* (Cambridge, MA: Harvard University Press, 1944), 108n.7, cited in Norman N. Holland, *Psychoanalysis and Shakespeare* (New York: McGraw-Hill, 1964), 56.

5   Freud, *Introductory Lectures on Psycho-Analysis* (1917), SE, 16: 441.

6   Harold Bloom, *The Western Canon* (London: Macmillan, 1994), 391. The argument about Freud's anxiety of influence is made throughout the chapter on Freud in this work: 'Freud: A Shakespearean Reading', 371–94.

7   Freud's interest in these topics is spelled out most notably in 'Some Neurotic Mechanisms in Jealousy, Paranoia and Homosexuality' (1922), SE, 18: 221–32.

8   Freud, ' "Civilised" Sexual Morality and Modern Nervous Illness' (1908), SE, 9: 198.

9   Freud, *Civilization and Its Discontents* (1930), SE, 21: 128.

10 Leo Bersani's words summarising a central thread of *Civilization and Its Discontents*: Bersani, Introduction to *Civilization and Its Discontents*, trans. David McLintock (London: Penguin, 2002), xvi.

11 Freud, 'The Goethe Prize Lecture' (1930), SE, 21: 211.

12 Freud, Letter to Eduard Silberstein, 4 September 1872, in *The Letters of Sigmund Freud to Eduard Silberstein*, ed. Walter Boehlich, trans. Arnold J. Pomerans (Cambridge, MA.: Harvard University Press, 1990), as cited in James Shapiro, *Contested Will: Who Wrote Shakespeare?* (London: Faber and Faber, 2010), 339.

13 Freud, Letter to [his brother] Alexander Freud, 19 April 1938, in *Selected Letters*, 442 (cited in Holland, *Psychoanalysis and Shakespeare*, 63).

14 Freud, Letter to Fliess, 15 October 1897, in *The Complete Letters of Sigmund Freud to Wilhelm Fliess, 1887–1904*, trans. and ed. Jeffrey Moussaieff Masson (Cambridge, MA.: Harvard University Press, 1985), 270–3, 272.

15 Ibid.

16 See, e.g., Freud, *Five Lectures on Psycho-analysis* (1910), SE, 11: 47.

17 Freud, *On the History of the Psycho-Analytic Movement* (1914), SE, 14: 16.

18 Freud, *An Outline of Psycho-Analysis* (1940 [1938]), SE, 23: 174.

19 Freud, Letter to Arnold Zweig, 7 Febuary 1931, in *Letters of Freud and Zweig*, 403.

20 The painful renunciation of the 'seduction theory' is announced in a letter to Fliess on 21 September 1897 (the so-called 'letter of the equinox'); here Freud vividly describes his disappointment in having to give up his cherished theory regarding the aetiology of the neuroses, adding that 'in spite of all this, I am in very good spirits': 'I vary Hamlet's saying, "To be in readiness": to be cheerful is everything'. The reference is of course to Hamlet's 'the readiness is all' (5.2.222). *Letters of Freud to Fliess*, 265–6.

21 On which, see especially Freud, *From the History of an Infantile Neurosis* ('The Wolf-Man') (1918), SE, 17: 38–42; as well as Peter Brooks, 'Fictions of the Wolf Man: Freud and Narrative Understanding', in Steven Vine, *Literature in Psychoanalysis: A Reader* (Houndmills: Palgrave Macmillan, 2005), 122–35, 129–30, and the entry for 'Primal Scene' in Jean Laplanche and Jean-Bertrand Pontalis, *The Language of Psychoanalysis*, trans. Donald Nicholson-Smith (London: The Hogarth Press, 1973).

22 Wallace Stevens, 'An Ordinary Evening in New Haven', x, in *The Palm at the End of the Mind*, ed. Holly Stevens (New York: Vintage Books, 1990), 337.

23 Paul Ricoeur, *Freud and Philosophy: An Essay on Interpretation* (New Haven: Yale University Press, 1977), 6–7.

24 On these dreams, and more generally on the understanding of dreams in the Renaissance, see especially Marjorie B. Garber, *Dream in Shakespeare: from metaphor to metamorphosis* (New Haven: Yale University Press, 1974); Frankie Rubinstein, 'Shakespeare's Dream-Stuff: A forerunner of Freud's "Dream-Material"', *American Imago*, 43 (1986), 335–55; Peter Holland, '"The Interpretation of Dreams" in the Renaissance', in *Reading Dreams: The Interpretation of Dreams from Chaucer to Shakespeare*, ed. Peter Brown (Oxford: Oxford University Press, 1999), 125–46; and Kathleen McLuskie, 'The "Candy-Colored Clown": Reading Early Modern Dreams', in Brown, ed., 147–67.

25 Freud, Letter to Arnold Zweig, 25 February 1934, *The International Psycho-Analytical Library*, 84: 65, and Freud, Letter to Ernst Freud, 20 February 1934, *Letters of Sigmund Freud 1873–1939*, 420.

26 Freud, 'Some Dreams of Descartes' (1929), SE, 21: 199–204; see Holland, '"The Interpretation of Dreams"', 125–31.

27 Freud, *The Interpretation of Dreams*, SE, 4: 212.

28 Ibid., SE, 5: 442. (Riverside has 'caviary'.)

29 Ibid., SE, 5: 484 (*Julius Caesar*, 3.2.26–7).

30 Ibid., SE, 4: 175.

31 Ibid., SE, 5: 444.

32 Freud, *Jokes and their Relation to the Unconscious* (1905), SE, 8: 44; cf. p. 42, where the same passage is used in relation to the 'economy' or 'saving' of double-meanings.

33 Freud, *The Interpretation of Dreams*, SE, 4: 177.

34 Freud, Ibid., SE 4:60 (referring to *Hamlet*, 2.2.205–06); cf. Letter to Ernest Jones, 16 April 1909, in *The Complete Correspondence of Sigmund Freud and Ernest Jones 1908–1939*, ed. R. Andrew Paskauskas (Cambridge, MA.: Harvard University Press, 1993), 219.

35 Freud, 'Constructions in Analysis' (1937), SE, 23: 267 (Freud's italics).

36 Ernest Jones, 'The Oedipus-Complex as an Explanation of Hamlet's Mystery: A Study in Motive', *American Journal of Psychology*, 22: 72–113; later expanded and published as a book-length study: *Hamlet and Oedipus* (New York: Doubleday Anchor, 1949).

37 Freud, *The Interpretation of Dreams*, SE, 4: 264–6.

38 Cynthia Chase, 'Oedipal Textuality: Reading Freud's Reading of *Oedipus*', in Ellmann, *Psychoanalytic Literary Criticism*, 56–75, 62 (originally published in *Diacritics: A Review of Contemporary Criticism*, 9: 1 (Spring 1979), 53–68).

39 See especially 'The Moses of Michelangelo' (1914), SE, 13: 211–12, and the (weak) paragraph on *Hamlet* in Freud's posthumously-published essay 'Psychopathic Characters on the Stage' (1942 [written in 1905 or 1906]), SE, 7: 309–10.

40 Freud, 'The Moses of Michelangelo' (1914), SE, 13: 212.

41 Freud, *The Interpretation of Dreams*, Preface to the Second Edition [1908], xxvi.

42 Freud, 'The Moses of Michelangelo', SE, 13: 211

43 Freud, 'Mourning and Melancholia' (1917), SE, 14: 237–58; 245.

44 Ibid., SE, 14: 246.

45 In, respectively, Freud, 'On Psychotherapy', SE, 7: 261–2; *The Interpretation of Dreams*, SE, 4: 266; Letter to Fliess, 15 October 1897 (cited above).

46 Freud, 'On Psychotherapy', SE, 7: 261–2.

47 Cf. Freud's use of the phrase ('Use every man...') in the letter to Fliess (15 October 1897, cited above), 273. Freud uses the quotation several times; see, e.g., 'Dostoevsky and Parricide' (1928), SE, 21: 189; Letter to Ernest Jones, 11 January 1910: *The Freud/Jones Correspondence*, 41.

48 Freud, Letter to Arnold Zweig, 31 May 1936, *Letters of Freud and Zweig*, 127.

49 Strong correctives to Freud's paternocentric vision, beginning with the work of Melanie Klein, have been legion over the years since Freud's death; and numerous psychoanalytically-influenced critics have powerfully shown how the figure of the mother is central to Shakespeare's plays. See for example Janet Adelman, *Suffocating Mothers: Fantasies of Maternal Origin in Shakespeare's Plays, Hamlet to The Tempest* (New York and London: Routledge, 1992); Coppélia Kahn, 'The Absent Mother in *King Lear*', in *Rewriting the Renaissance: The Discourse of Sexual Difference in Early Modern Europe*, ed. Margaret Ferguson, Maureen Quilligan and Nancy Vickers (Chicago: University of Chicago Press, 1986), 33–49; and Julia Reinhard Lupton and Kenneth Reinhard, *After Oedipus: Shakespeare in Psychoanalysis* (Ithaca and London: Cornell University Press, 1993).

50 Lupton and Reinhard, *After Oedipus*, 153.

51 Freud, 'The Theme of the Three Caskets' (1913), SE, 12: 292; further references are in parentheses in the main text.

52 E.g., 'I loved her most, and thought to set my rest / On her kind nursery' – 1.1.117–18. On this confusion, see Adelman, *Suffocating Mothers*, especially 116–17. Adelman's influential interpretation of Shakespeare is more indebted to Klein (and her ideas of pre-Oedipal issues) than to Freud directly.

53 Nicholas Royle, *The Uncanny* (Manchester and New York: Manchester University Press, 2003), 143.

54 Elizabeth Bronfen, 'The death drive (Freud)', in *Feminism and Psychoanalysis: A Critical Dictionary*, ed. Elizabeth Wright (Oxford: Blackwell, 1992), 52.

55 Shakespeare seems to allow Freud to access not only a sense of his own murderous wishes (as in the dreams of Brutus and Hal at his father's bedside, mentioned above and below), but also thoughts about death as such: he uses the phrase 'that undiscover'd country, from whose bourn no traveller returns', for instance, as a euphemism for death (*The Interpretation of Dreams*, SE, 4: 255); quotes Antony's 'My heart is in the coffin here' (*Julius Caesar*, 3.2.104) (Freud, Letter to Fliess, 27 April 1895, in *Letters of Freud to Fliess*, 128); and repeatedly misquotes Prince Hal's comment to Falstaff, 'Thou owest God a death' (*1 Henry IV*, 5.1.127), rendering it as 'Thou owest Nature a death' (see Freud, Letter to Fliess, 6 February 1899, in *The Complete Letters of Sigmund Freud to Wilhelm Fliess, 1887-1904*, 343–4; *The Interpretation of Dreams*, SE, 4: 205; and 'Thoughts For The Times On War And Death' (1915), SE, 14: 289).

56 Freud, *Letters of Freud and Zweig*, 2 May 1935, 106.

57 Freud, Letter of 13 July 1883, in *Letters of Sigmund Freud*, selected and edited by Ernst L. Freud, trans. Tania and James Stern (New York: Basic Books, 1960), 65.

58 See Lupton and Reinhard, *After Oedipus*, 145–62.

59 Freud, Letter to Fliess, October 15, 1897. *Letters of Freud to Fliess*, 270–3, 271. See Lupton and Reinhard, *After Oedipus*, 17–19.

60 Holland, *Psychoanalysis and Shakespeare*, 72.

61 Freud, 'The Resistances to Psycho-Analysis' (1925), SE, 19: 222.

62 Freud, *Moses and Monotheism* (1939), SE, 23: 52.

63 Freud, 'Some Character-Types Met with in Psycho-Analytic Work' (1916), SE, 14: 309–33. Further references to this essay will appear in parentheses in the text.

64 See, e.g., Freud, 'Charcot' (1893), SE, 3: 13; Freud, Preface and Footnotes to the Translation of Charcot's *Tuesday Lectures* (1892), SE, 1: 139. This can be translated loosely as: 'Theory is all well and good, but that does not prevent things from existing [or: being as they are]'.

65 Freud, 'Libidinal Types', SE, 21: 217.

66 As Rieff writes, 'Freud's self-exposure becomes exemplary only as it becomes impersonal' (*Freud*, 66).

67 Freud, 'Some Character-Types Met with in Psycho-Analytic Work', SE, 14: 312.

68 Freud, *Three Essays on the Theory of Sexuality* (1905), SE, 7: 171.

69 Rieff, *Freud*, 354.

70 Freud, *The Interpretation of Dreams*, SE, 5: 474 (quoting the Austrian poet Peter Rosegger).

71 Samuel Johnson, *Johnson on Shakespeare*, in *The Yale Edition of the Works of Samuel Johnson*, ed. Arthur Sherbo (New Haven and London: Yale University Press, 1968), VII: 523. This is the case (as we have already seen) even when the identification is as close as possible to the surface – as in Freud's eventual confession of the importance of the death of his own father in the writing of *The Interpretation of Dreams*.

72 The quotations in this sentence are from p. 317 (Freud's italics).

73 Freud apparently got this notion from James Darmesteter's edition of *Macbeth* (Paris, 1881), 322.

74 As in Macbeth's 'no son of mine succeeding' (3.1.63). In this regard, Strachey's translation trumps the original '*Erfolge*', which does not have the same double meaning.

75 Ned Lukacher, 'Chiasmatic Reading, Aporetic History: Freud's *Macbeth*', in *Reading Freud's Reading*, ed. Sander L. Gilman et al. (New York and London: New York University Press, 1994), 152–79, 159.

76 Freud, interestingly, uses the term '*Der Stoff*' to refer to the plot or raw material of the play: GW, 10: 375; Strachey translates this, not quite exactly, as 'plot': SE, 14: 320.

77 Freud, Letter to Oskar Pfister, 6 March 1910. *International Psycho-Analytic Library*, 59: 35.

78 Freud, Letter to C. G. Jung, 1 September 1911, *The Freud/Jung Letters*, 442.

79 Freud, Letter to Wilhelm Knöpfmacher, 6 August 1878. *Letters of Sigmund Freud 1873–1939*, 6.

80 Freud, 'The Moses of Michelangelo' (1914), SE, 13: 211.

81 Freud, *Introductory Lectures on Psycho-Analysis* (1916), SE, 15: 96.

82 See note 76.

83 Freud, *The Interpretation of Dreams*, SE, 4: 525.

[84] Ibid., SE, 4: 143n.; 4: 266.

[85] The story of Freud's attitude to the authorship issue has been well told, most recently by James Shapiro in *Contested Will: Who Wrote Shakespeare?* (London: Faber and Faber, 2010), 173–86 and 206–14. See also Holland, *Psychoanalysis and Shakespeare*, 55–8; Garber, *Shakespeare's Ghost Writers*, chapter one; and Nicholas Royle, 'The Distraction of "Freud": Literature, Psychoanalysis, and the Bacon-Shakespeare Controversy', *Oxford Literary Review*, 12, nos. 1–2 (1990): 101–38.

[86] Freud, Letter to Martha Bernays, June 1883, cited in Shapiro, *Contested Will*, 176.

[87] Freud, *Totem and Taboo* (1913), SE, 13: 154.

[88] Freud, Ibid., 155; *The Tempest*, 1.2.397–402 (Riverside has 'fadom' for 'father').

[89] Georg Brandes, *William Shakespeare* (Munich, 1895–6).

[90] Freud, Letter to Ernest Jones, 31 October 1909, in *Freud/Jones Correspondence*, 32.

[91] J. Thomas Looney, *Shakespeare Identified* (London: C. Palmer, 1921).

[92] Freud, Letter to Theodore Reik, 23 March 1930, in Theodore Reik, *The Search Within* (New York: Grove Press, 1956), cited in Holland, *Psychoanalysis and Shakespeare*, 57.

[93] Freud, *An Autobiographical Study* (1925; revised 1935), SE, 20: 63–4.

[94] Freud, Letter to Arnold Zweig, 2 April 1937, in *The Letters of Freud and Zweig*, 140.

[95] Freud, Letter to Arnold Zweig, 31 May 1936, in Ibid., 127 (cf. p. 77: 'Where there is an unbridgeable gap in history and biography, the writer can step in and try to guess how it all happened. In an uninhabited country he may be allowed to establish the creatures of his imagination ... it cannot be held against Shakespeare that in about the year 1000 Macbeth was a just and benevolent king of Scotland').

[96] Freud, *Civilization and its Discontents* (1930), SE, 21: 93.

[97] Freud uses the phrase repeatedly; e.g: *New Introductory Lectures On Psycho-Analysis* (1933), SE, 22: 11.

[98] Freud, *On Dreams* (1901), SE 5: 636 (GW 2: 648: '*wertloser Abfall beseitigten*').

[99] Freud, 'The Moses of Michelangelo' (1914), SE 13: 222 (GW 10: 185: '*dem Abhub – dem "refuse"*').

[100] Freud, *The Interpretation of Dreams*, SE 5: 589.

[101] Freud's footnote in *An Outline of Psycho-analysis* (1938), SE, 23: 192n.1, translating '*Der Name William Shakespeare ist sehr wahrscheinlich ein Pseudonym, hinter dem sich ein grosser Unbekannter verbirgt*': GW, 17: 119n.2.

Chapter 6

[1] *The Letters of Sigmund Freud and Arnold Zweig*, ed. Ernst L. Freud, trans. Elaine and William Robson-Scott (New York: Harcourt Brace Jovanovich, 1970), 106, adapting Hamlet's 'The time is out of joint – O cursed spite, / That ever I was born to set it right!' (1.5.188–9).

[2] I use the term 'Enlightenment' as shorthand (for a heightened belief in the centrality of rationality, empiricism, science); it is, of course, something of a

caricature of the multiplicity and complexity of the so-called 'Age of Reason'. (See, e.g., Philip Rieff, *Freud: The Mind of the Moralist* (Chicago: University of Chicago Press, 1959), 146.)

3   Most prominent amongst these is Joel Fineman, who has shown how the sonnets in particular introduce a suspicion of vision that prefigures the psychoanalytic (especially Lacanian) interrogation of optical epistemologies and the gaze. See Joel Fineman, *Shakespeare's Perjured Eye: The Invention of Poetic Subjectivity in the Sonnets* (Berkeley: University of California Press, 1986); Fineman, *The Subjectivity Effect in Western Literary Tradition: Essays Towards the Release of Shakespeare's Will* (Cambridge, MA: MIT Press, 1991); Barbara Freedman, *Staging the Gaze: Post-modernism, Psychoanalysis, and Shakespearean Comedy* (Ithaca and London: Cornell University Press, 1991); and Christopher Pye, *The Vanishing: Shakespeare, the Subject, and Early Modern Culture* (Durham and London: Duke University Press, 2000).

4   See Rieff, *Freud*, 66.

5   Freud, 'A Seventeenth Century Demonological Neurosis' (1923), SE, 19: 73.

6   See *The Complete Letters of Sigmund Freud to Wilhelm Fliess, 1887–1904*, ed. Jeffrey Moussaieff Masson (Cambridge, MA: Harvard University Press, 1985), 395n.5; Freud refers to him as 'our old Jacob' (Letter of January 8, 1900), 394.

7   The question of what criteria we might use to assess the validity of Freudian modes of analysis in addressing early modern texts continues to exercise literary critics. It is largely because Freud and psychoanalysis more generally seem so enmeshed in the structures of thought that emerged in early modernity that critics like Stephen Greenblatt have argued against the appropriateness of using psychoanalytic theory to interpret the earlier period: if 'psychoanalysis is, in more than one sense, the end of the Renaissance', Greenblatt has written, then it can only be shown to follow rather than explain the earlier period ('Psychoanalysis and Renaissance Culture', in *Literary Theory/Renaissance Texts*, ed. Patricia Parker and David Quint (Baltimore, MD: Johns Hopkins University Press, 1986), 210–24; 221). But this participation of psychoanalysis in early modernity can also be taken dialectically – as it has been by several of the best recent psychoanalytically-influenced critics – as offering a way back to the earlier age; the fact that the former has its roots in the latter means that juxtaposing the two is not necessarily an ahistorical procedure. As David Willbern argues, 'Greenblatt's essay offers substantial evidence to enrich [psychoanalytic] theory' (*Poetic Will: Shakespeare and the Play of Language*, (Philadelphia: University of Pennsylvania Press, 1997), 73); and as Fineman has suggested, 'either Shakespeare was very theoretically acute' or theory is 'itself very Shakespearean' (*The Subjectivity Effect*, 112). Moreover, current psychoanalytic literary criticism uses the work of Freud and his followers not as a set of keys to unlock the Renaissance and its texts but as a self-reflexive set of questions to pose in relation to both. On this topic, see especially Elizabeth J. Bellamy, *Translations of Power: Narcissism and the Unconscious in Epic History* (Ithaca, NY: Cornell University Press, 1992), 1–13; Carla Mazzio and Douglas Trevor, (eds), *Historicism, Psychoanalysis and Early Modern Culture* (New York and London: Routledge, 2000), Introduction; and Cynthia Marshall, 'Psychoanalyzing the Prepsychoanalytic Subject', *PMLA*, 117: 5 (October 2002), 1207–16.

8   Freud, *Civilization and Its Discontents* (1930), SE, 21: 65–6.

9   Ibid., SE, 21: 68.

10 See Peter Stallybrass, 'Shakespeare, the Individual, and the Text', in *Cultural Studies*, ed. Lawrence Greenberg et al. (New York and London: Routledge, 1992), 593–612.

11 Pye, *The Vanishing*, 1.

12 Jacques Lacan, *The Four Fundamental Concepts of Psychoanalysis (The Seminar, Book XI)*, trans. Alan Sheridan (London: Hogarth Press, 1977), 76.

13 Freud, 'A Seventeenth Century Demonological Neurosis', SE, 19: 72.

14 Freud, *Introductory Lectures on Psychoanalysis* (1916), SE, 15: 20.

15 To a large extent, Freudian notions of subjectivity may be indebted to the increasingly disembodied and fractured interiority of early modernity. See David Hillman, *Shakespeare's Entrails: Belief, Scepticism and the Interior of the Body* (Houndmills: Palgrave Macmillan, 2007), 1–57.

16 Freud and Breuer, *Studies on Hysteria* (1893), SE, 2: 6.

17 Freud, *The Interpretation of Dreams* (1900), SE, 4: 314.

18 Freud, 'Some Character-Types Met with in Psycho-Analytic Work' (1916), SE, 14: 323.

19 Freud, *Civilization and Its Discontents* (1930), SE, 21: 69, 71.

20 Freud, 'Instincts and their Vicissitudes' (1915), SE, 14: 123.

21 Theodore Reik, from *Thirty Years with Freud*, trans. Richard Winston (New York: Farrar and Rinehart, 1940), 12–13; cited in Holland, *Psychoanalysis and Shakespeare*, 62.

22 Freud, 'Analysis of a Phobia in a Five-Year-Old Boy' ['Little Hans'] (1909), SE, 10: 122.

23 Freud, 'Constructions in Analysis' (1937), SE, 23: 262.

24 Freud, *Inhibitions, Symptoms and Anxiety* (1926), SE, 20: 121.

25 Ibid., SE, 20: 119; GW, 14: 149.

26 Freud misquotes this line as 'undo the deed which cannot be undone [*die Tat ungeschehen zu machen, die nicht mehr ungeschehen werden*]': 'Some Character-Types', SE, 14: 319; GW, 10: 374.

27 Freud, quoting Goethe (*Faust*, Part I, scene 4) in *New Introductory Lectures on Psychoanalysis* (1933), SE, 22: 33.

28 Ibid., SE, 22: 31.

29 Freud, *Contributions to the Neue Freie Presse* (1904), SE, 9: 255. On Freud's struggle to distance himself from 'supposedly discredited things like religion, glamour, mysticism, radical politics, the paranormal', see Adam Phillips, *Terrors and Experts* (Cambridge, MA.: Harvard University Press, 1996), 18–32: 'sexuality and the unconscious were the new, scientifically prestigious words for the occult, for that which is beyond our capacity for knowledge ... In psychoanalysis the supernatural returns as the erotic' (19).

30 '*Nun ist die Luft von solchem Spuk so voll, / Dass niemand weiss, wie er ihn meiden soll*'. (*Faust*, Part II, Act V, scene 5), quoted in SE, 6: vii.

31 '*Flectere si nequeo Superos, Acheronta movebo*': Virgil, *Aeneid*, VII, 312; quoted in *The Interpretation of Dreams*, SE, 4: ix

32 Freud, 'Fragment of an Analysis of a Case of Hysteria' (1905), SE, 7: 109.

[33] Freud, 'Observations on Transference-Love (Further Recommendations on the Technique of Psycho-Analysis III)' (1915), SE, 12: 164.

[34] Freud, *Introductory Lectures on Psycho-Analysis*, SE, 16: 284.

[35] See Ann Rosalind Jones and Peter Stallybrass, 'Fetishisms and Renaissances', in Mazzio and Trevor, (eds), *Historicism, Psychoanalysis and Early Modern Culture*, 20–35, 20.

[36] Freud, *Beyond the Pleasure Principle* (1920), SE, 18: 59.

[37] Ibid., SE, 18: 36; cf. 44 and 65.

[38] Freud, *New Introductory Lectures On Psycho-Analysis*, SE, 22: 31.

[39] Ernest Jones, *Freud*, 3: 408. *Hamlet*, 1.5.166–7. See also chapter 14 of this third vol. of Jones's biography, on Freud and occultism.

[40] In addition to the above citations, Freud cites this remark as 'our philosophy' in 'Delusions and Dreams in Jensen's *Gradiva*' (1907), SE, 9: 8, and in 'From the History of an Infantile Neurosis' (1918), SE, 17: 12; and as 'your philosophy' in *Jokes and their Relation to the Unconscious* (1901), SE, 8: 72, and in 'Leonardo da Vinci and a Memory of his Childhood' (1910), SE, 11: 137.

[41] Freud, *The Future of an Illusion* (1927), SE, 21: 29.

[42] C. L. Barber, *Creating Elizabethan Tragedy: The Theater of Marlowe and Kyd*, ed. Richard P. Wheeler (Chicago: University of Chicago Press, 1988), 19.

[43] Freud, Letter to Martha Bernays, 23 July 1882, *Letters of Sigmund Freud 1873–1939*, 19; *Hamlet*, 2.2.559: 'What's Hecuba to him?' On Shakespeare as a 'post-Christian' writer, see especially C. L. Barber, 'The Family in Shakespeare's Development: Tragedy and Sacredness' in *Representing Shakespeare: New Psychoanalytic Essays*, ed. Murray M. Schwartz and Coppélia Kahn, 188–202, 200. On Freud's relation to religious belief, see especially Adam Phillips, 'The Soul of Man Under Psychoanalysis', in *Equals* (London: Faber and Faber, 2002), 89–114.

[44] Freud, *Introductory Lectures on Psycho-Analysis*, SE,16: 285; cf. 'The Resistances to Psychoanalysis' (1925), SE, 17: 140. It is worth pointing out that when Freud was once asked to list 'the ten most important books from a scientific point of view', he selected just three: Copernicus's *De revolutionibus*, Darwin's *Descent*, and *De Praestigiis Daemonum* by 'old Doctor Johann Weier'– a sixteenth-century physician and occultist whose debunking of belief in witches, published in 1563, prepared the ground for Reginald Scot's *Discoverie of Witchcraft* (1584).

[45] Freud, 'The Theme of the Three Caskets' (1913), SE, 12: 298.

[46] Indeed, near the end of *Beyond the Pleasure Principle*, Freud claimed that the hypothesis of a death drive was 'the third step in the theory of the instincts' following 'the two earlier ones – the extension of the concept of sexuality and the hypothesis of narcissism'. Freud, *Beyond the Pleasure Principle*, SE, 18: 59.

[47] Freud, 'The Economic Problem of Masochism' (1924), SE, 19: 163.

[48] Freud, 'Leonardo da Vinci and a Memory of his Childhood', SE, 11: 134.

[49] On this topic, see especially Harry Berger, Jr., *Making Trifles of Terrors: Redistributing Complicities in Shakespeare* (Stanford: Stanford University Press, 1997)

[50] Freud, 'The History of the Psychoanalytic Movement', *Psychoanalytic Review*,

3 (1916), 406–54, 419; the third use of Falstaff's phrase is in Freud, 'On the History of the Psychoanalytic Movement' (1914), SE, 14: 24.

[51] Freud, 'Thoughts for the Times on War and Death' (1915), SE, 14: 287.

[52] 'brain' is the Folio reading; the Quarto has 'balance', and most modern editors accept Theobald's emendation to 'beam'.

[53] Freud, 'An Outline of Psycho-Analysis' (1940), *International Journal of Psycho-Analysis*, 21: 27–84; 72.

[54] Freud, *The Future of an Illusion*, SE, 21: 28.

[55] Although it is in some of the other *Seminars* that Lacan most consistently 'returns to Freud', his thinking is perhaps most accessibly set out in *The Four Fundamental Concepts of Psycho-Analysis*, ed. Jacques-Alain Miller, trans. Alan Sheridan (New York: Norton & Company, 1981) and in *Écrits*, trans. Alan Sheridan (London: Tavistock, 1977); it is superbly summarized in Malcolm Bowie's *Lacan* (Cambridge, MA.: Harvard University Press, 1993); for the specific matter of Lacan's revision of Freud, see Samuel Weber's *Return to Freud: Jacques Lacan's Dislocation of Psychoanalysis*, trans. Michael Levine (Cambridge: Cambridge University Press, 1991). Laplanche's main works on the topic – apart from the indispensable *The Language of Psychoanalysis*, co-authored with Jean-Bertrand Pontalis, trans. Donald Nicholson-Smith (London: The Hogarth Press, 1973) – are *Life and Death in Psychoanalysis*, trans. Jeffrey Mehlman (Baltimore and London: Johns Hopkins University Press, 1976) and *Essays on Otherness*, trans. Luke Thurston and others (London and New York: Routledge, 1999).

[56] Mark Edmundson, *Towards Reading Freud: Self-Creation in Milton, Wordsworth, Emerson, and Sigmund Freud* (Chicago: University of Chicago Press, 1990), 24 and ix–xii; Phillips, *Terrors and Experts*, 6–7; Leo Bersani, *The Freudian Body: Psychoanalysis and Art* (New York: Columbia University Press, 1986), 12; Shoshana Felman, *Jacques Lacan and the Adventure of Insight: Psychoanalysis in Contemporary Culture* (Cambridge, MA: Harvard University Press, 1987), 90.

[57] Freud, *New Introductory Lectures on Psycho-Analysis*, SE, 22: 80 and Freud, 'Analysis Terminable and Interminable' (1937), SE, 23: 214. Lacan, *Écrits*, 129.

[58] The pleasure principle and the reality principle are the names Freud gave the 'two principles of mental functioning' in his metapsychology (SE, 12: 219). The former aims to avoid unpleasurable sensations of all kinds mainly by an immediate (hallucinatory) discharge of tension. The latter is a subsequent development of the psyche; it takes into account external circumstances that force one to take more circuitous routes to satisfaction, thus introducing into the psyche concepts of delayed gratification, compromise and practicality.

[59] Freud, *Beyond the Pleasure Principle*, SE, 18: 24.

[60] Freud, 'Analysis Terminable and Interminable', SE, 23: 245.

[61] Ibid.

[62] Cited (without source) in Skura, *The Literary Use of the Psychoanalytic Process*, 17.

[63] Freud, *Beyond the Pleasure Principle*, SE, 18: 53; Freud's italics.

[64] The former can be said to derive, broadly speaking, from the strand of Freud's thinking elaborated upon most prominently in Anna Freud's *The Ego and the Mechanisms of Defense* (1936); its significant proponents include Jacob Arlow, Charles Brenner, Heinz Hartmann, Ernst Kris and Rudolph Loewenstein. The

latter derives – even more broadly speaking – from the work of Melanie Klein and Jacques Lacan, and includes such figures as Jean Laplanche and André Green.

65 Burke, 'Freud – and the Analysis of Poetry', in *Psychoanalysis and Literature*, ed. Hendrick M. Ruitenbeek (London: Dutton, 1964), 117.

66 The quotations in this section, except where indicated, are all from *Beyond the Pleasure Principle* (1920), SE, 18: 14–16. It may be pure coincidence that, in the first Quarto of *Hamlet*, the protagonist's final sound is reproduced as 'o, o, o, o—'. Seminal interpretations of the 'fort-da' scene appear in Lacan's *Freud's Papers on Technique, 1953–54*, trans. John Forrester (New York: Norton, 1991) [vol. I of *The Seminar of Jacques Lacan*, ed. Jacques-Alain Miller], and in Derrida's *The Post Card: From Socrates to Freud and Beyond*, trans. Alan Bass (Chicago: University of Chicago Press, 1987), 292–37.

67 Freud, *Beyond the Pleasure Principle*, SE, 18: 63.

68 Ibid., SE, 18: 17.

69 Ibid., SE, 18: 59; my emphasis.

70 Cited (without reference) in Lionel Trilling, 'Freud and Literature' (1940; revised 1947), rept. in (and here citing) *Freud: A Collection of Critical Essays*, ed. Perry Meisel (Englewood Cliffs, NJ: Prentice-Hall, 1981), 95–111, 98.

71 Derrida, *The Post Card*, 426–7. Freud, as Edmundson writes, 'is in his major dimension a literary writer, and not the scientist that he claimed to be': Edmundson, *Towards Reading Freud*, 168.

72 Shoshana Felman, 'Introduction: To Open the Question', in *Literature and Psychoanalysis: The Question of Reading: Otherwise*, ed. Felman (Baltimore and London: Johns Hopkins University Press, 1982), 9–10.

73 Trilling, 'Freud and Literature', 107–8.

74 Freud, Preface to Marie Bonaparte's *The Life and Works of Edgar Allan Poe: A Psycho-Analytic Interpretation* (1933), SE, 22: 254.

75 Freud and Breuer, *Studies on Hysteria*, SE, 2: 160.

76 Freud, 'Leonardo da Vinci and a Memory of his Childhood', SE, 11: 134.

77 Letter from Freud to Jones, 8 February 1914. *The Complete Correspondence of Sigmund Freud and Ernest Jones 1908–1939*, ed. R. Andrew Paskauskas (Cambridge, MA: Harvard University Press, 1993), 260–61; 261.

78 Freud, 'Creative Writers and Day-Dreaming', SE, 9: 144.

79 André Green, *The Tragic Effect: The Oedipus Complex in Tragedy*, trans. Alan Sheridan (Cambridge: Cambridge University Press, 1979), 1.

80 Rieff, *Freud*, 131.

81 Ellmann points to other key Freudian terms – 'acting out', 'projection', 'screen memories' – that correspond to those of the theatre (or cinema): Ellmann, *Psychoanalytic Literary Criticism*, 6.

82 Freud and Breuer, 'Frau Emmy von N,' in *Studies on Hysteria*, SE, 2: 93.

83 See above, p. 153.

84 Freud, 'The Moses of Michelangelo' (1914), SE, 13: 211.

85 See, e.g., André Green's *The Tragic Effect*, and Philippe Lacoue-Labarthe, 'Theatrum Analyticum', trans. Robert Vollrath and Samuel Weber, *Glyph*, 2: 122–43.

[86] Freedman, *Staging the Gaze*, 74; 47. See also Lacan, *The Four Fundamental Concepts*, 67–78.

[87] Freud, *The Interpretation of Dreams*, SE, 4: 60, citing Delbœuf, J. R. L., *Le sommeil et les rêves* (Paris, 1885)

[88] Ellmann, *Psychoanalytic Literary Criticism*, 6.

[89] Freud, *The Interpretation of Dreams*, SE, 4: 69. For 'dramatisation' see SE, 5: 653 ('On Dreams' [1901]); '*der "Dramatisierung"*': *Über den Traum*, GW, 2/3: 666.

[90] Freud's comment to this effect is recalled by Ludwig Binswanger (*Sigmund Freud: Reminiscences of a Friendship* (New York and London: Grune and Stratton, 1947), 5, cited in Holland, *Psychoanalysis and Shakespeare*, 56.

[91] Freud, *The Interpretation of Dreams*, SE, 4: 609.

[92] Freud, Letter to Wilhelm Fliess (Letter 71 in *Extracts from the Fliess Papers*), SE, 1: 265.

[93] Freud, *The Interpretation of Dreams*, SE, 4: 261–2. Cf. Ellmann, *Psychoanalytic Literary Criticism*, 8–9.

[94] Freud, 'On Dreams', SE, 5: 676. Freud himself draws the analogy between censorship in dreams and in creative writing: 'A writer must beware of the censorship...' (*The Interpretation of Dreams*, SE, 4: 142). On censorship and drama, see especially Annabel Patterson, *Censorship and Interpretation: The Conditions of Writing and Reading in Early Modern England* (Madison: University of Wisconsin Press, 1984), and Freedman, *Staging the Gaze*, chapter 5.

[95] Freud, *An Outline of Psycho-Analysis*, SE, 23: 166.

[96] *Julius Caesar*, 2.1.63–5; 'motion' here means something like 'impulse'.

[97] Freud, 'Some Character-Types Met with in Psycho-Analytic Work', SE, 14: 323.

[98] Freud, 'Medusa's Head' (1922), SE, 18: 273–4.

[99] Freud, 'Dostoevsky and Parricide' (1928), SE, 21: 177.

[100] Freud refers again to 'the overwhelming effect of' *Oedipus Tyrranus* in *An Autobiographical Study* (1925), SE, 20: 63.

[101] Freud, 'A Short Account of Psycho-Analysis' (1924), SE, 19: 208.

[102] Freud, 'Some Character-Types Met with in Psycho-Analytic Work', SE, 14: 315.

[103] Freud, 'Delusions and Dreams in Jensen's *Gradiva*', SE, 9: 17.

[104] Ibid.

[105] Ibid., SE, 9: 9.

[106] Ibid., SE, 9: 8.

[107] Ibid., SE, 9: 27; my emphasis.

[108] Edmundson, *Towards Reading Freud*, 54; Freud, *The Psychopathology of Everyday Life: Forgetting, Slips of the Tongue, Bungled Actions, Superstitions and Errors* (1901), SE, 6: 205.

[109] *Letters of Freud to Fliess*, 'Draft N' (May 31, 1897), 251.

[110] Freud, Letter to Hermann Struck, 7 November 1914. *The Letters of Sigmund Freud 1873–1939*, 305–7; 305.

[111] 'The Exceptions', in 'Some Character-Types Met with in Psycho-Analytic Work', SE, 14: 314–15.

[112] Freud, *New Introductory Lectures On Psycho-Analysis*, SE, 22: 106.

[113] I quote from Peter Gay's translation, in *Freud: A Life for our Times* (New York and London: Norton, 1988), 313. See Freud, Letter to Karl Abraham, 14 June 1912, *The Complete Correspondence of Sigmund Freud and Karl Abraham 1907–1925*, 156–7.

[114] Freud, Letter to Sándor Ferenczi, 21 May 1911. *The Correspondence of Sigmund Freud and Sándor Ferenczi Volume 1, 1908–1914*, 281 ('ΨA' is Freud's habitual shorthand for 'psychoanalysis').

[115] Cited in Gay, *Freud*, 317–18; Gay gives no source, but the contextual implication is that this is from a letter to Arthur Schnitzler; I have been unable to trace the original quotation.

[116] Freud, 'Some Character-Types Met with in Psycho-Analytic Work', SE, 14: 314–15.

[117] John Forrester, *Language and the Origins of Psychoanalysis* (New York: Columbia University Press, 1980), x. See also Marshall Edelson, *Language and Interpretation in Psychoanalysis* (Chicago: University of Chicago Press, 1975). 'Overdetermined' is Freud's word for the way a single element in the manifest content (of a dream) will express several latent thoughts, and conversely a single wish or thought will find multiple expressions in the manifest content.

[118] Lacan, *The Four Fundamental Concepts,* 20; Lacan, *The Ego in Freud's Theory and in the Technique of Psychoanalysis* (*The Seminar, Book II*), trans. Sylvana Tomaselli (Cambridge: Cambridge University Press, 1988), 272, cit. Ellmann, *Psychoanalytic Literary Criticism,* 89; see Vine 11–12.

[119] The quotation is from Laplanche and Pontalis, *The Language of Psycho-Analysis,* cited without reference in Cavell, *Disowning Knowledge,* 189.

[120] Freud, 'The Unconscious', SE, 14: 210; Freud, *Jokes and their Relation to the Unconscious* (1905), SE, 8: 34. (Laplanche and Pontalis explain 'innervation' (s.v.) thus: 'Term used by Freud in his earliest works to denote the fact that a certain energy is transported to a particular part of the body where it brings about motor or sensory phenomena'.)

[121] Mutlu Konuk Blasing, *Lyric Poetry: The Pain and the Pleasure of Words* (Princeton, NJ: Princeton University Press, 2006), 136. Wallace Stevens, 'An Ordinary Evening in New Haven', x, in *The Collected Poems of Wallace Stevens* (New York: Vintage Books, 1982), xxxi.

[122] Fineman, *Perjured Eye,* 44. Cf. Fineman, *The Subjectivity Effect,* 112.

[123] Freud, *The Interpretation of Dreams*, SE, 4: 423–4. The reference is to *Julius Caesar*, 3.2.24–7. Freud goes on: 'Strange to say, I really did once play the part of Brutus. I once acted in the scene between Brutus and Caesar from Schiller [*Die Räuber*]'.

[124] Freud, *Five Lectures on Psycho-analysis* (1910), SE, 11: 13. On psychoanalysis as a listening cure, see Adam Phillips, *Equals* (London: Faber and Faber, 2002), xii.

[125] Freud, 'Psychical (or Mental) Treatment' (1890/1905), SE, 7: 283.

[126] Freud, 'Creative Writers and Day-dreaming', SE, 9: 145.

[127] Freud, 'The Question of Lay Analysis' (1926), SE, 20: 187–8, citing *Hamlet*, 2.2.192. 'In the beginning was the deed' is from Goethe, *Faust*, I, 3.

[128] Freud, 'Die Frage Der Laieanalyse' (1926), in *Gesammelte Werke* (Imago Publishing Co., Ltd., London, 1991), XIV: 214.

[129] See, e.g., Hillman, *Shakespeare's Entrails*, chapter 3.

[130] Freud, 'The Uncanny', SE, 17: 221.

[131] Freud, *The Psychopathology of Everyday Life*, SE, 6: 60.

[132] Freud, *Totem and Taboo*, SE, 13: 84n.

[133] 'The grandiose humorous effect of a figure like that of the fat knight Sir John

Falstaff rests on an economy in contempt and indignation. We recognize him as an undeserving gormandizer and swindler, but our condemnation is disarmed by a whole number of factors. We can see that he knows himself as well as we do; he impresses us by his wit, and, besides this, his physical misproportion has the effect of encouraging us to take a comic view of him instead of a serious one, as though the demands of morality and honour must rebound from so fat a stomach. His doings are on the whole harmless, and are almost excused by the comic baseness of the people he cheats. We admit that the poor fellow has a right to try to live and enjoy himself like anyone else, and we almost pity him because in the chief situations we find him a plaything in the hands of someone far his superior. So we cannot feel angry with him and we add all that we economize in indignation with him to the comic pleasure which he affords us apart from this. Sir John's own humour arises in fact from the superiority of an ego which neither his physical nor his moral defects can rob of its cheerfulness and assurance': Freud, *Jokes and their Relation to the Unconscious*, SE, 8: 231n.1.

[134] Freud, *Jokes*, SE, 8: 144, quoting Rosaline in *Love's Labour's Lost*, 5.2.861–3.

[135] Ibid.

[136] Ibid, SE, 8: 42.

[137] Ibid., SE, 8: 13.

[138] Freud, *The Interpretation of Dreams*, SE, 5: 340.

[139] Freud, *Jokes*, SE 8:36 (citing in the latter case Heine, *Schnabelewopski*, Chap. III).

[140] Freud, *The Psychopathology of Everyday Life*, SE, 6: 117n.3.

[141] Freud, *Jokes*, SE, 8: 73.

[142] Freud, *Jokes*, SE, 8: 76–7.

[143] Freud, *Psychopathology*, SE, 6: 100.

[144] Ibid., SE 6:97–8, quoting Otto Rank, 'Ein Beispiel von poetischer Verwertung des Versprechens', *Zbl. Psychoan.*, 1, 109 (37–8).

[145] Freud, *Introductory Lectures on Psychoanalysis*, SE, 15: 37–8.

[146] Freud, 'Delusions and Dreams in Jensen's *Gradiva*', SE 9:68 (though he is writing here specifically about Jensen).

[147] Thomas de Quincey, 'On the Knocking at the Gate in *Macbeth*' [1823], in *Romanticism: An Anthology*, 2nd edn, ed. Duncan Wu (Oxford: Blackwell, 1998), 640.

[148] Freud, *Fragment of an Analysis of a Case of Hysteria* (1905 [1901]), SE, 7: 76.

[149] Ibid., SE, 7: 77–8.

[150] King James (1611) version.

[151] Cf. 1 Corinthians 2:9: 'The eye hath not seen, and the ear hath not heard, neither have entered into the heart of man the things which God hath prepared for them that love him'.

[152] See Paul Ricoeur, *Freud and Philosophy: An Essay on Interpretation* (New Haven: Yale University Press, 1977), 32–6.

[153] Freud, 'A Difficulty in the Path of Psycho-Analysis' (1917), SE, 17: 143.

[154] Thomas Mann, 'Freud and the Future', cited from *Freud: A Collection of Critical Essays*, ed. Meisel, 45–60, 59; rept. in Mann, *Essays of Three Decades*, trans. H. T. Lowe-Porter (New York: Knopf, 1947), 411–28.

[155] Freud, 'The Question of Lay Analysis' (1926), in *Wild Analysis*, trans. Alan Bance (London: Penguin, 2002), 100.

156 Lacan, *Écrits*, 23, referring to Arthur Rimbaud, Letter to George Izambard (1871), in *Oeuvres-Vie*, ed. Alain Borer with André Montègre (Arléa, 1991), 184.

157 Freud, 'Notes Upon a Case of Obsessional Neurosis' (1909), SE, 10: 183n.2.

158 Freud, 'Negation' (1925), SE, 19: 235; 240.

159 See 'Constructions in Analysis', where Freud urges the analyst always to seek confirmation from the wider context and development of the whole treatment: SE 23: 257, 262–5.

160 Freud, 'Negation', 233.

161 Jean Hyppolite, 'A Spoken Commentary on Freud's *Verneinung*', Appendix to Lacan, *Freud's Papers on Technique*, Book 1 of *The Seminar of Jacques Lacan*, ed. Jacques-Alain Miller, trans. John Forrester (New York: Norton, 1988), 291.

162 'Constructions in Analysis', SE, 23: 263.

163 I quote the First Folio; modern editors usually emend to 'Ay, no, no ay' (Riverside) or 'Aye—no. No—aye' (Cambridge).

164 Freud, 'Negation', 235–6.

165 Cynthia Marshall, 'The Doubled Jaques and Constructions of Negation in *As You Like It*', *Shakespeare Quarterly*, 49: 4 [Winter 1998], 375–92, 378.

166 Thomas Ogden, *The Art of Psychoanalysis: Dreaming Undreamt Dreams and Interrupted Cries* (New York and London: Routledge, 2005), 67–8.

167 Keats, Letter LXXVIII (to Richard Woodhouse, 27 October 1818), in *The Letters of John Keats*, ed. H. Buxton Forman (Cambridge: Cambridge University Press, 2011), 210.

168 Jorge Luis Borges, 'Everything and Nothing' (trans. James E. Irby) in *Labyrinths*, ed. Donald A. Yates and James E. Irby (Harmondsworth: Penguin Books, 1970), 285.

169 Freud, 'The Unconscious' (1915), SE, 14: 169; my emphasis.

170 Freud, 'The Question of Lay Analysis', in *Wild Analysis*, 100.

171 It is worth pointing out that the term 'other' can implicate several possible forms of alien-ness; Lacan differentiates between the capitalised 'Other' (that which is equated with the symbolic order, the source of all meaning) and the lower-case 'other' (which refers to another person, an (actual and fantasised) object of desire).

172 Sophocles, *Oedipus at Colonus*, in *The Theban Plays*, trans. E. F. Watling (Harmondsworth: Penguin, 1947; rept. 1965), scene 1, 84.

173 See above p. 141.

174 Phillips, *Terrors and Experts*, 15

175 Freud, 'Some Character-Types', SE, 14: 312.

176 Freud, 'Analysis of a Phobia in a Five-Year-Old Boy', SE, 10: 144.

177 Julia Kristeva, *Strangers to Ourselves*, trans. Leon S. Roudiez (New York: Columbia University Press, 1991), 191.

178 Freud, 'Thoughts for the Times on War and Death', SE, 14: 277.

179 Freud, Letter to Ernest Jones, 11 January 1910, *The Correspondence of Freud and Jones*, 41.

180 E.g., Freud, *Group Psychology and the Analysis of the Ego* (1921), SE, 18: 102.

181 Roland Barthes, *Roland Barthes*, trans Richard Howard (London: Macmillan, 1986), 69.

182 Rieff, *Freud*, 69–70.

[183] Freud, *Totem and Taboo* (1913), SE, 13: 155.

[184] Freud, Letter of 14 November 1897, in *The Letters of Freud to Fliess*, 281.

[185] Peter Brooks, 'Fictions of the Wolf Man: Freud and Narrative Understanding', in Vine, *Literature in Psychoanalysis: A Reader*, 122–35, 132–3.

[186] Green, *The Tragic Effect*, 135.

Select Bibliography

Marx

Albanese, Denise. *Extramural Shakespeare*. New York: Palgrave Macmillan, 2010.

Bristol, Michael. *Carnival and Theater: Plebeian Culture and the Structure of Authority in Renaissance England*. New York: Methuen, 1985.

Cohen, Walter. *Drama of a Nation: Theater in Renaissance England and Spain*. Ithaca: Cornell University Press, 1985.

Derrida, Jacques. *Specters of Marx*. Translated by Peggy Kamuf. New York and London: Routledge, 1994.

Dollimore, Jonathan. *Radical Tragedy: Religion, Ideology and Power in the Drama of Shakespeare and His Contemporaries*. Chicago: University of Chicago Press, 1984.

—and Alan Sinfield, (eds) *Political Shakespeare: New Essays in Cultural Materialism*. Ithaca: Cornell University Press, 1985.

Egan, Gabriel. *Shakespeare and Marx*. Oxford: Oxford University Press, 2004.

Grady, Hugh. *Shakespeare's Universal Wolf: Studies in Early Modern Reification*. Oxford: Clarendon Press, 1996.

—*Shakespeare and Impure Aesthetics*. Cambridge: Cambridge University Press, 2009.

—and Terence Hawkes, (eds) *Presentist Shakespeares*. London: Routledge, 2007.

Greenblatt, Stephen. 'Murdering Peasants: Status, Genre, and the Representation of Rebellion'. *Representations*, 1 (1983): 1–29.

—and Catherine Gallagher. *Practicing New Historicism*. Chicago: University of Chicago Press, 2000.

Halpern, Richard. *The Poetics of Primitive Accumulation: English Renaissance Culture and the Genealogy of Capital*. Ithaca: Cornell University Press, 1991.

—*Shakespeare Among the Moderns*. Ithaca: Cornell University Press, 1997.

Harries, Martin. *Scare Quotes from Shakespeare: Marx, Keynes, and the Language of Reenchantment*. Stanford: Stanford University Press, 2000.

Hawkes, Terence. *That Shakesperian Rag: Essays on a Critical Process*. London: Methuen, 1986.

—*Meaning by Shakespeare*. London: Routledge, 1992.

—*Shakespeare in the Present*. London: Routledge, 2002.

Howard, Jean E. *The Stage and Social Struggle in Early Modern England*. London: Routledge, 1994.

—and Marion F. O'Connor. *Shakespeare Reproduced: The Text in History and Ideology*. London: Methuen, 1987.

—and Scott Cutler Shershow. *Marxist Shakespeares*. London: Routledge, 2001.

Korda, Natasha. *Shakespeare's Domestic Economies: Gender and Property in Early Modern England*. Philadelphia: University of Pennsylvania Press, 2002.

Loomba, Ania. *Shakespeare, Race, and Colonialism*. Oxford: Oxford University Press, 2002.

Marx, Karl and Fredrick Engels. *On Literature and Art*. Moscow: Progress Publisher, 1976.

Montrose, Louis. 'Of Gentlemen and Shepherds: The Politics of Elizabethan Pastoral Form'. *English Literary History*, 50 (1983): 415–59.

Prawer, S. S. *Karl Marx and World Literature*. Oxford: Clarendon, 1976.

Wayne, Valerie, ed. *The Matter of Difference: Materialist Feminist Criticism of Shakespeare*. New York: Harvester Wheatsheaf, 1991.

Weimann, Robert. *Shakespeare and the Popular Tradition in the Theater: Studies in the Social Dimension of Dramatic Form and Function*. Edited by Robert Schwartz. Baltimore: The Johns Hopkins University Press, 1978.

—*Author's Pen and Actor's Voice: Playing and Writing in Shakespeare's Theatre*. Edited by Helen Higbee and William West. Cambridge: Cambridge University Press, 2000.

White, R. S. 'Marx and Shakespeare'. *Shakespeare Survey*, 45 (1993): 89–100.

Freud

Adelman, Janet. *Suffocating Mothers: Fantasies of Maternal Origin in Shakespeare's Plays, Hamlet to The Tempest*. New York and London: Routledge, 1992.

Armstrong, Philip. *Shakespeare in Psychoanalysis*. London and New York: Routledge, 2001.

Berger, Harry, Jr. *Making Trifles of Terrors: Redistributing Complicities in Shakespeare*. Stanford: Stanford University Press, 1997.

Bersani, Leo. *The Freudian Body: Psychoanalysis and Art*. New York: Columbia University Press, 1986.

Cavell, Stanley. *Disowning Knowledge: In Seven Plays of Shakespeare*. 2nd edn. Cambridge: Cambridge University Press, 2003.

Derrida, Jacques. *The Post Card: From Socrates to Freud and Beyond*. Translated by Alan Bass. Chicago: University of Chicago Press, 1987.

Ellmann, Maud, ed. *Psychoanalytic Literary Criticism*. London and New York: Longman, 1994.

Felman, Shoshana, ed. *Literature and Psychoanalysis: The Question of Reading: Otherwise*. Baltimore and London: The Johns Hopkins University Press, 1982.

Fineman, Joel. *Shakespeare's Perjured Eye: The Invention of Poetic Subjectivity in the Sonnets*. Berkeley and Los Angeles: University of California Press, 1985.

Freedman, Barbara. *Staging the Gaze: Post-modernism, Psychoanalysis, and Shakespearean Comedy*. Ithaca and London: Cornell University Press, 1991.

Freud, Sigmund. *The Standard Edition of the Complete Psychological Works of Sigmund Freud*. Translated and edited by James Strachey. London: The Hogarth Press and the Institute of Psychoanalysis, 1953–74.

—*The New Penguin Freud*. General Editor Adam Phillips, various translators. London: Penguin Books, 2002–6.

Garber, Marjorie. *Shakespeare's Ghost Writers: Literature as Uncanny Causality.* New York and London: Routledge, 1987.

Green, André. *The Tragic Effect: The Oedipus Complex in Tragedy.* Translated by Alan Sheridan. Cambridge: Cambridge University Press, 1979.

Holland, Norman N. *Psychoanalysis and Shakespeare.* New York: McGraw-Hill, 1964.

Jones, Ernest. *Hamlet and Oedipus.* New York: Doubleday Anchor, 1949.

Kahn, Coppélia. 'The Absent Mother in *King Lear*'. In *Rewriting the Renaissance: The Discourse of Sexual Difference in Early Modern Europe*, ed. Margaret Ferguson, Maureen Quilligan and Nancy Vickers. Chicago: University of Chicago Press, 1986.

Lacan, Jacques. *The Four Fundamental Concepts of Psycho-Analysis.* Edited by Jacques-Alain Miller. Translated by Alan Sheridan. New York: Norton & Company, 1981.

Laplanche, Jean and Jean-Bertrand Pontalis. *The Language of Psychoanalysis.* Translated by Donald Nicholson-Smith. London: The Hogarth Press, 1973.

Lukacher, Ned. *Daemonic Figures: Shakespeare and the Question of Conscience.* Ithaca: Cornell University Press, 1994.

Lupton, Julia Reinhard and Kenneth Reinhard. *After Oedipus: Shakespeare in Psychoanalysis.* Ithaca and London: Cornell University Press, 1993.

Marshall, Cynthia. *The Shattering of the Self: Violence, Subjectivity and Early Modern Texts.* Baltimore and London: The Johns Hopkins University Press, 2002.

Mazzio, Carla and Douglas Trevor, (eds) *Historicism, Psychoanalysis and Early Modern Culture.* New York and London: Routledge, 2000.

Phillips, Adam. *Promises, Promises: Essays on Literature and Psychoanalysis.* London: Faber and Faber, 2000.

Pye, Christopher. *The Vanishing: Shakespeare, the Subject, and Early Modern Culture.* Durham, NC, and London: Duke University Press, 2000.

Rieff, Philip. *Freud: The Mind of the Moralist.* Chicago: University of Chicago Press, 1959.

Royle, Nicholas. *The Uncanny.* Manchester and New York: Manchester University Press, 2003.

Schwartz, Murray M. and Coppélia Kahn, (eds) *Representing Shakespeare: New Psychoanalytic Essays.* Baltimore and London: The Johns Hopkins University Press, 1980.

Skura, Meredith Anne. *The Literary Use of the Psychoanalytic Process.* New Haven: Yale University Press, 1981.

Smith, Joseph. *The Literary Freud: Mechanisms of Defense and the Poetic Will.* New Haven: Yale University Press, 1980.

Traub, Valerie. *Desire and Anxiety: Circulations of Sexuality in Shakespearean Drama.* London: Routledge, 1992.

Willbern, David. *Poetic Will: Shakespeare and the Play of Language.* Philadelphia: University of Pennsylvania Press, 1997.

Wright, Elizabeth. *Psychoanalytic Criticism: Theory in Practice.* London: Methuen, 1984.

Index